Michael Chiarello's
BOTTEGA

Michael Chiarello's
BOTTEGA

Bold Italian Flavors from the
Heart of California's Wine Country

WITHDRAWN

with Ann Krueger Spivack and Claudia Sansone
photographs by Frankie Frankeny

CHRONICLE BOOKS

SAN FRANCISCO

Library of Congress
Cataloging-in-Publication
Data available.

ISBN 978-0-8118-7539-4

Manufactured in China.

Designed by Michael Mabry
Prop and food styling by
Nissa Quanstrom

The photographer wishes to
thank Anne Gaede of Pro Camera—
you are a gift to all Bay Area
photographers. Chloé and the
girls, thanks for weeks of patience!
Thanks to the entire front and
back of the house at Bottega for
your instrumental help throughout the creation of this book. To
Claudia Sansone and Ann Spivack,
many thanks for keeping us all
in good spirits on such a tight
schedule. And especially: *Grazie*,
Michael! You're an outstanding
chef, entertainer, and a most
gracious host. Bottega is an
exhilarating restaurant to capture
in motion!

10 9 8 7 6 5 4 3 2 1

Chronicle Books LLC
680 Second Street
San Francisco, California 94107
www.chroniclebooks.com

Dedication

To Nick, Joël, and the rest of our
Bottega family. You give our guests a
simple and powerful gift. You "throw
the party" and make each guest
welcome. You are Bottega!

To my life's partner, Eileen. That
you knew what Bottega should look
and feel like astounded me. You are
what love should be.

To my kids: Aidan, li'l chef/dirt
bike rider/photographer; Giana, my
little 4x4 country girl; Felicia, artist
with a Pop's-like sense of humor; and
Margaux, lover of all things Spanish.
I love sharing your dreams and watching as you achieve them.

Mom, I promise to work less, play
more, love as I cook, and smile with
my heart as I serve. I miss you each
day but you live in the fabric of my
spirit and everything I touch. The
gift of how to love and leave room
for growth is one I will share each
and every day.

To our guests: thank you for
loving what we do and for always,
always coming back.

Acknowledgments

The Italian culinary journey that began for me at Tra Vigne in 1987 led to our opening Bottega in 2008, and many, many people have helped along the way.

First, always first, thanks to my wife, Eileen; once again you surprise and delight me by knowing in your heart that I belong in a restaurant. Thank you for the gigantic leap of faith that I can balance our family with the restaurant family. To Prince Aidan for suiting up in his "whites" and sharing with me the joys of our kitchen Saturdays. (I'm hoping for many more to come.) To Giana, forever my baby girl, for insisting I take this opportunity with Bottega and finish out my culinary dream. To Felicia for being proud of her Pops for what we have created and for having the courage to work her way through school in my favorite Italian restaurant in San Francisco. To Miss Margaux for enjoying Bottega as an adult as she charts a course for her life ahead.

The Bottega Management Team: To Chef Nick Ritchie, my surrogate baby brother. I am eternally grateful to you for putting all your culinary soul into Bottega. Executive Sous Chef Ryan McIlwraith, you are truly and deeply talented and have sensitively brought your brilliance to the food, kitchen, and experience at Bottega. Pastry Chef Michael Glissman, super talent, great spirit, and best laugh in the biz. I so appreciate you applying your tremendous skillset to a cuisine that was literally foreign to you (which you now speak in dialect!). General Manager Joël Hoachuck, for taking the plunge with Nick and me, building the spirit that Bottega would become and for never, ever losing your cool. I have loved each and every day we have worked together over the last twenty years. Wine Director/Assistant General Manager Michael Iglesias, the day you walked in the door and said "I'm in!" Bottega became a better restaurant. The rest of the kitchen and front of the house management: Nick Petrilli, Arthur Coutinho Doyal, James Darden, Allan (Badger) Mochwart—wow, what a team! The entire kitchen and service staff: Your attention to the needs of our guests, and the quality of food and service makes me very proud. Bottega would not be possible without your dedication, input, and discipline. I will forever be in all of your debt and service.

Bottega partners: Without your absolute commitment to bringing the Bottega dream to life it would have stayed a dream and never become the success it is today. I am eternally grateful to all of you.

Michael Guthrie and Associates: The space you created for our food to ring true is amazing and twice what I dreamed of.

V Marketplace and Villagio Partners: Your vision and foresight is truly remarkable. I can't thank you enough for making room for us and our dream and letting it grow.

The cookbook team: Claudia Sansone, the most gracious, loving, and thoughtful book partner any chef could hope for. Your warm spirit was a guide in discovering the truth of Bottega and getting it into print. Ann Spivack, never have I met a writer that loved her topic as much as you have. Thank you for keeping my voice intact and bringing your creativity and passion to this book. Frankie Frankeny, with Molly Johnstone and Nissa Quanstrom, you did the impossible: You walked into the fray of a super-hectic restaurant, in the height of the season, and captured the Magic! What a pleasure and honor to work with you. Michael Laukert, my culinary brother of twenty years, thanks for rolling up your sleeves like you did at Tra Vigne, Consorzio, and NapaStyle. My life is much better with you in it! To super-testers Maria Bautista, Wendy Rupprecht, and Bob Schooler, *grazie tante* for making hard recipes easier for the home cook.

Many thanks to Michael Mabry, Peter Soe, and Lilyana Bone at Mabry Design. After the many projects we've done together, you still blow my mind with amazing, one-of-a-kind design as well as your calm and sureness at all the right times.

My publisher Chronicle Books for being a true partner in a world where that is hard to find. To Bill LeBlond, my editor and, more important, my friend. Thanks for your courage for letting this book be exactly what it needed to be. Thanks to Sarah Billingsley, Vanessa Dina, Doug Ogan, Tera Killip, Peter Perez, David Hawk, and Carolyn Miller for assuring it read and looked like the book we all dreamed it could be.

My NapaStyle family for knowing that if I followed my dream it would enhance the dream we built together. Much more fun to come!

My father Fortunato, my mother Antoinette, and my brothers Ron and Kevin. Forever you put up with my dreaming bigger than I could reach, working longer than I should, missing more than I wanted to, but your steady love and encouragement brought me around to what is truly important. My in-laws Denis and Judy Gordon, and my brother-in-law Tim, thanks for playing such a great supporting role in getting this off the ground. I promise I will keep my date nights with our little girl.

Mom, you are with me each day as I step into my clogs and, more important, each day as I take them off. You are forever etched into my culinary being as the person who taught me that flavor is more important than taste. That simple fact — and your love—changed my life.

Let's go "throw the party."

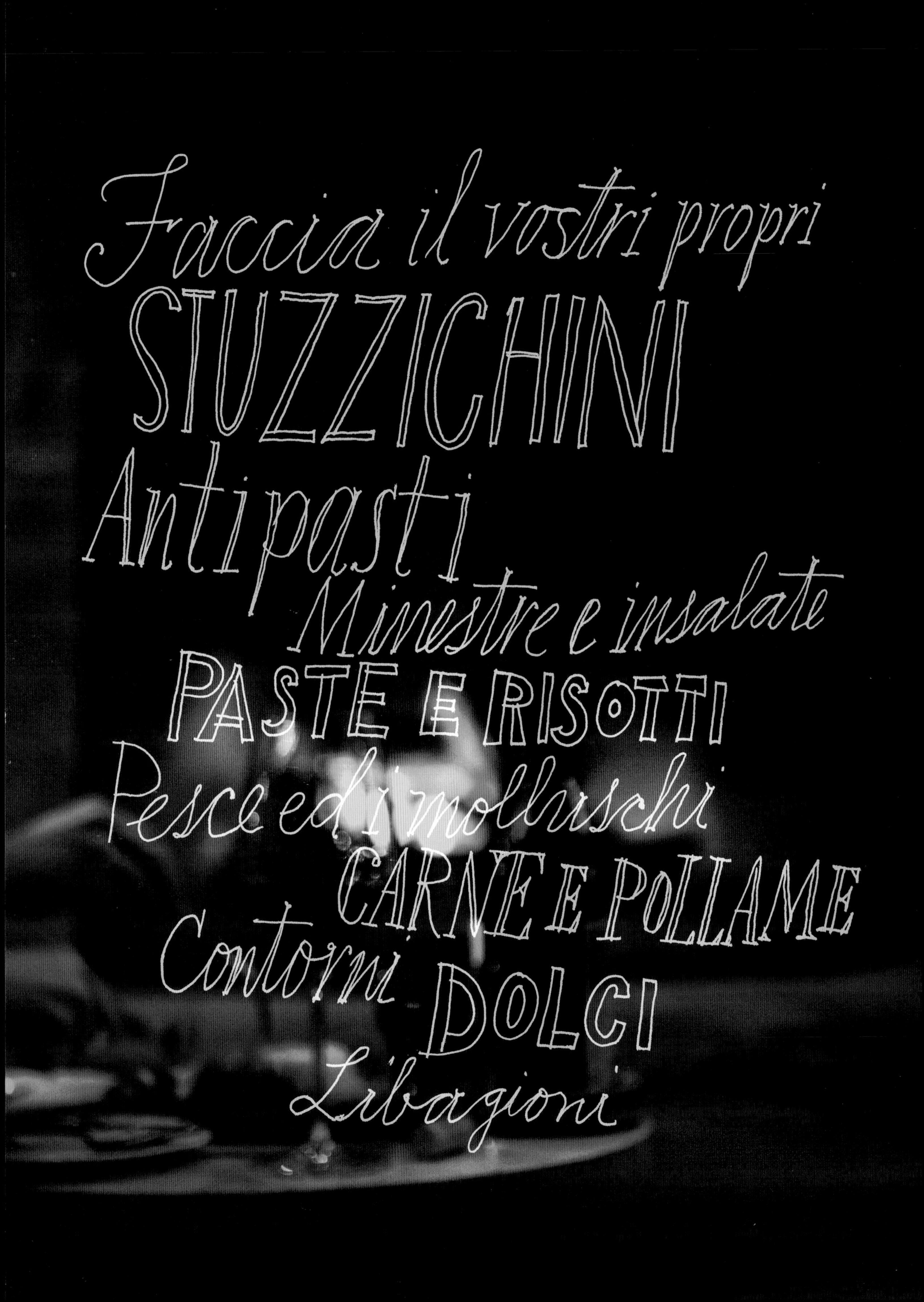

Faccia il vostri propri

STUZZICHINI

Antipasti

Minestre e insalate

PASTE E RISOTTI

Pesce ed i molluschi

CARNE E POLLAME

Contorni DOLCI

Libagioni

Contents

Introduction

With this book, I hope to share the recipes for Bottega's food and drinks but also to share our cooking philosophy: That you can make anything in your kitchen at home—anything you truly want to make—but how well you cook depends on how often you are willing to practice.

I grew up with some fantastic cooks, and none of them had expensive cooking tools or formal culinary training. Yet, night after night, they put great food on the table, food that was slow-cooked before "slow cooking" was a slogan. People ask me how they can "get up to speed" on their cooking skills, which classes they can take, which chef they should study under, which countries and regions they can visit to improve their cooking skills overnight. My answer is there is no answer—there is no credit-card path to instant cooking abilities. The good news is that the power to cook well is in your own hands, literally. The three main tools you'll need to cook good food are your hands, your mind, and your heart.

For most home cooks, about a dozen recipes account for 75 percent of the dishes they serve. That's fine. If three or four of my recipes find their way into your repertoire, then I've succeeded. With this book, I'll tell you what I tell every cook who's ever worked with me in a restaurant: "Cook these dishes my way until you have it right. Don't innovate until you've made the dish three dozen times and can do it without the recipe."

Truly, for me, there is no pleasure in making something until I can do it without glancing at the recipe at all. If the first time you make gnocchi, it's not as good as the gnocchi you had at Bottega—well, Bottega chef Nick Ritchie has been making gnocchi for years and years; he could make it with his eyes closed. You'll need to have at least a few more dozen gnocchi-making sessions under your belt before your gnocchi can even begin to compare. But don't let that discourage you. If you are determined to become good at making gnocchi, you can do it. Cooking is a craft, and with any craft it's just a matter of having the interest and devoting the time.

In Italy, the word *bottega* means "artist's workshop." I think of Bottega as more of a workout space, a gymnasium. It's where I get to flex my culinary muscles, to rediscover my own culinary path with a more mature outlook. I'm hoping the recipes in this book will inspire you to flex your culinary muscles, too.

COOKING AS EXTREME SPORT

Did you fall in love with the *garganelli* at Bottega, or maybe the Polenta "Under Glass?" Do you want to re-create the dish exactly the way it appeared on your table when you were here with us? You can. We've shown you how to make our *brodetto*, for example, with all the bells and whistles: the tomato confit, the saffron rouille, the fantastic Fisherman's Sauce, perfect croutons. This book leads you step by step through every component of each recipe for those occasions when you want to pull out all the stops.

If you want to make a dish Bottega style, get your game on. You can forget about sipping Champagne while you lean against the counter and occasionally stir. Bottega-style cooking demands that you be involved; these recipes want your head and your heart in the game. Psychically, when I'm pulled into the moment when every burner is firing on high, I feel like I'm hovering over the stove and every thought outside of the cooking fades away. It's demanding, it's exhausting, it's exhilarating. If this isn't your style, read on.

COOKING AS A GOOD WAY TO SPEND A SATURDAY

We've also suggested some shortcuts and family-friendly ways to make our food when you don't want to spend your whole weekend cooking five components but just want a great steak or a fantastic pasta on a Saturday night. My hope is that you will start simply, feel confident making a basic version of a dish, and eventually add on the bells and whistles to suit your own style. Even if you are new to the kitchen, you will find in this book recipes that are welcoming and simple. Someone who's never cooked can learn to make a great risotto, and what a fine first dish to have in your back pocket.

The Pantry

My pantry at home is a smaller version of Bottega's. Here's a list of the basics that I have on hand, always.

Anchovies

I prefer salt-packed anchovies, because oil-packed anchovies aren't always canned in the high-quality oil I'd use. Soak salt-packed anchovies for 30 minutes in cool water before using. Oil-packed anchovies don't require soaking. Remove the bones by running your thumb down the length of each anchovy.

Beans

Seek out the more unusual heirloom varieties in farmers' markets and from specialty providers such as Rancho Gordo (see Resources). Store all beans in airtight containers and date them. Don't keep beans longer than one year. I don't use canned beans often except for chickpeas, which hold up to canning and work well in soups, salads, and antipasti.

Bread and bread crumbs

I like country-style bread, which means loaves with a good sturdy crust and a dense, chewy interior. Buy breads that contain nothing but flour, water, yeast, and salt. When your bread grows stale, make bread crumbs by cutting the bread into cubes and then whirring them in your food processor to the coarseness you want (see page 35). Freeze bread crumbs for up to 1 month.

Calabrian chile paste

I go crazy for this stuff, adding it to everything from pizza, pasta, and grilled bread to aioli nero and my mom's pastina soup. It has a smoky flavor and a warm, rich spiciness that isn't ever overwhelmingly hot. Look for the words *Silafunghi, Specialità dalla Calabria* or *Peperoncino Tritato Piccante* on the jar; see Resources to order this online.

Capers

I prefer salt-packed capers for the same reason I use salt-packed anchovies. Rinse salt-packed capers, then soak them in cold water for 30 minutes before using. Oil-packed capers don't need to be soaked.

Cheese

I have Parmigiano-Reggiano, which is Italian Parmesan, in my house at all times. Whenever you see Parmesan cheese in this book, know that at Bottega we use only the real thing. Look at the rind of the cheese for the words *Parmigiano-Reggiano* to know you're buying cheese with optimal flavor.

I grew up on pecorino cheese, so this has a prominent spot in my pantry. I use pecorino fulvi to cook with (as with the warm budini on page 62). I also keep fontina on hand, and robiola, which isn't a well-known cheese but has become one of my favorites in recent years. Try it in Pasta "Bezza" with Robiola and Braised Asparagus Sauce on page 113.

Chocolate

Whether buying dark, milk, or white chocolate, buy a premium brand such as Scharffen Berger, Callebaut, Guittard, or Valrhona. (This goes for cocoa powder, too.) Keep chocolate well wrapped in a cool, dark place for up to 1 year.

Flour

For regular baking needs, we use Giusto flour or King Arthur flour. You can buy Giusto flour and their fine-ground polenta online. For pasta making, I use *doppio zero* pasta flour imported from Italy. (*Doppio zero*, or "double zero," refers to how finely the flour is ground; it's almost as fine as talcum powder.) Look for Italian manufacturers such as Caputo. See Resources.

Herbs

I use homegrown herbs whenever I can. You can't beat the flavor of leaves picked from the plant and put right into the pot. Even the urban cook can have a small windowsill garden with fresh thyme, rosemary, and basil. For bay leaves, we use true Mediterranean bay laurel leaves at Bottega. They put up well and make great gifts. Because most folks don't have fresh bay, the recipes in this book use dried bay leaves.

Mushrooms

I always have dried porcini (*Boletus edulis*) in my pantry, and I make sure they're from Italy. When soaked in warm water for 15 to 30 minutes, these give an earthy, woodsy flavor to dishes such as the Butternut Squash and Fontina Risotto with Squab Ragù (page 114). Soak them in water that feels comfortable to the touch; too-hot water can change their flavor. Store dried mushrooms in an airtight container for up to 1 year.

Mustard

I rely on French Dijon mustard to emulsify salad dressings while adding a pungent note. Mustard's flavor can fade over time, so taste it to make sure it still has some punch before whisking any into dressings. I also use coarse-grain mustards for Frutta di Mostarda (page 164).

Nuts

Marcona almonds from Spain are a godsend. I cook with them and serve them warm in bowls alongside cocktails. Pine nuts, walnuts, hazelnuts, and pistachios all have a place in my pantry. I like to buy nuts raw and unsalted and then toast them myself. I find very good nuts at farmers' markets.

Olive Oil (and Other Oils)

Taste olive oils every chance you get. Just as the flavor of wine varies from region to region and year to year, so does the flavor of olive oils.

I use three types of olive oil. My everyday extra-virgin olive oil is a relatively inexpensive Manzanillo oil blend from California. I buy this by the jug and pour it into smaller glass vessels with spout tops for easy pouring. I cook with this oil, even though some cooks prefer to save their extra-virgin olive oil.

I do save the pricier extra-virgin olive oils in my pantry for use as a condiment, drizzling it on steaks, white beans, or pasta, just before serving. For me, purchasing this kind of *finito* olive oil—the oil used for the final drizzle—is pure pleasure. I find finishing oils all over the world and enjoy sampling the array on my top pantry shelf.

A third type of olive oil, which used to be called "pure," has a lighter, milder flavor. Throughout this book, in each recipe I've noted whether you should use extra-virgin olive oil. If a recipe calls for olive oil (with no mention of extra virgin), look for a paler, straw-colored olive oil often found in a can. This oil can be heated to a higher temperature without smoking and adds a lighter flavor to foods that you don't want to overwhelm with a stronger olive oil.

You'll also want a few specialty olive oils in your pantry. There's *olio nuovo* (in Southern Italy; in Northern Italy it's called *olio novello*). This "new" oil is the first press each year, and it's much more raw, pungent, and rustic in character than older oil. At Katz and Company (which makes a good one), they call it December's New Oil, because that's the only month it's available. This is a finishing oil (don't cook with it), and it's fantastic with bruschetta or drizzled over white beans or a steak. You'll want to use it quickly before the flavor fades.

Late-harvest olive oils are more delicate, lighter in color, and fruitier. They're a good choice for seafood or other mild dishes.

Store big containers of olive oil in the refrigerator to keep the oil from going rancid.

Olives

These days, my favorite olives are grown locally and water-cured right here at Bottega. I also buy kalamatas from Greece, gaetas from Italy, and picholine olives from France. All three of those are brine-cured. I also like the wrinkly dry-cured (also called oil-cured) olives that you find throughout the Mediterranean. I gently heat these dry-cured olives in olive oil with some herbs, red pepper flakes, and a strip of orange or lemon zest and serve them warm with cocktails.

Except for the olives I buy for Crispy Blue Cheese–Stuffed Olives (page 209), I prefer olives with pits, because the pit helps preserve the olive's flavor and texture. Most olives can be pitted easily; if the pit is stubborn, smash the olive lightly with a cleaver to loosen its hold.

Pasta

No matter how good your sauce, if the pasta is limp or slippery, the dish will be a disappointment. I'm a pasta lover and make my own fresh pasta when I can, but I'm also a working dad who has dried pasta at the ready. I buy Italian brands from artisan producers such as Rustichella d'Abruzzo. Pasta made by Barilla, another Italian producer, can be found readily in grocery stores and is much better than most of what sits on the shelves. Both brands put their pasta through bronze dies instead of Teflon-coated ones; this gives the pasta a textured surface (you can see the texture under a magnifying glass). Both brands also dry their pasta very slowly for a final product that comes out of the water with some "chew." This gives the cook a little leeway: you can leave a high-quality pasta in the hot water for a few extra minutes while you perfect the sauce, and it won't lose shape or texture.

If you love pasta as much as I do, you'll want different pasta shapes in your pantry. I like seafood sauces with long noodles such as spaghetti, spaghettini, or linguine. I'll choose penne or rigatoni when I'm making a chunky sauce. *Riso*, *ditalini*, and *acini de pepe* are soup pastas, ideal for floating in broth. *Pastina* is, for me, the most comforting of pastas, and it's a natural for the Calabrian Wedding Soup on page 84.

Polenta

Polenta is merely ground dried corn. The flavor of your polenta relies on the flavor of the corn before it's dried and the fineness of the grind. The creamy, fantastic polenta at Bottega results in large part from good fortune: I was lucky to have found an heirloom corn that has been used in polenta for many generations. I'm hopeful that this polenta will soon be available to the home cook. For now, look for fine-ground polenta like the kind available from Anson Mills (see Resources). If you're buying polenta from a grocery store, look for Italian polenta, which is generally more finely ground. (Finely ground means smoother polenta.) Fresher grains mean better-tasting polenta, so keep opened packages in the refrigerator and make sure to use them within 6 months of opening.

Rice

I stock two short-grain rices for my risotto: Arborio and Vialone Nano. Arborio is available in most grocery stores; you may need to seek out Italian specialty stores to find Vialone Nano, or order it online. I use Arborio most of the time. When a risotto contains more subtle flavors, the plumper-grained Vialone Nano can really add to your dish.

Salt

Salt is the new olive oil and deserves the same attention; if you change only one ingredient in your kitchen, change the salt. Switching to gray salt will give a home cook the same positive effect as switching from corn oil to extra-virgin olive oil.

Salt is the only ingredient that goes in everything you cook and bake. The simpler your food, the more important it is that each ingredient be stellar, and this is especially true of your salt.

At home, I use gray salt for all salt added during cooking, but I use kosher salt for brining and for making preserved lemons (see page 34) or duck breast prosciutto (see page 32). I use gray salt in my pasta water, but I know many cooks prefer to use kosher salt. Basically, unless the flavor of the gray salt is too full for a dish, gray salt is what I use 99 percent of the time.

Because it's moist and coarse, gray salt is more of a challenge to distribute equally. I dry large quantities of it in a 200°F oven for 2 hours, then pound it or grind it in a spice grinder until it's medium-coarse. I keep it in a tin beside my stove. You can also buy ceramic salt grinders made explicitly for gray salt (see Resources).

Fleur de sel, the top layer of sea salt that forms during certain weather conditions, is a finishing salt, not a cooking salt. Use it as a condiment on foods just before serving.

Salumi

At Bottega, we make all of our own cured meats. I'm very proud that every ounce of prosciutto we use at Bottega comes from pork we cure and slice ourselves. To duplicate the flavors found at Bottega in your home cooking, use only imported prosciutto di Parma when a recipe calls for prosciutto.

In my own home, cured meats from Bottega and from Italy—mortadella, prosciutto, pancetta, and a selection of salami from Calabria—are always at the ready, because they make such a fine and easy antipasti. Serve a selection of cured meats with warmed olives, some bread sticks, and a good wine, and you're good to go for the most spur-of-the-moment gathering. Don't buy sliced salami—because the meat can dry once it's cut, slice it yourself just before serving.

Scott—unpaid golfer, super-waiter

Spices

Fresher is always better where spices are concerned. Smell your spices, and if the aroma is faint you'll know the flavor has faded. Buy new spices in small quantities every 6 months or so, and purchase from a place that has quick turnover. We buy our Bottega spices from the Chefs' Warehouse (see Resources). The quantities are bigger than the home cook can use, but you can always buy with friends and divvy up the spices. A farmers' market is a great place to smell spices before you buy.

Tomatoes

I always have cans of whole San Marzano tomatoes in my pantry. In the summer, I don't use these often; I pick tomatoes off the vine as needed. But in winter, these cans are opened every week.

I never buy diced or puréed tomatoes and very rarely use tomato paste, preferring to push the whole canned tomatoes through a food mill just before cooking. It takes about 1½ pounds of fresh plum tomatoes to make 2 cups of puree. A 28-ounce can of whole Marzano tomatoes makes about 3½ cups purée.

I'm a big fan of Muir Glen's organic canned tomatoes. Because Muir Glen uses enameled cans rather than unlined tin, there's no worry about tinny flavors.

Truffle Oil

This ingredient has become a little passé in restaurant kitchens, but it never made a showing in the home pantry, which is a shame. Truffle oil lets you flavor everything from potatoes to prosciutto—just a few drops will change the tone of a dish. I prefer white truffle oil because it's lighter than black.

Vinegar

Invest in high-quality vinegars; the wrong vinegar can ruin a beautiful salad. Taste vinegars and find brands that you like. Bad wine vinegar (and there are a lot of bad vinegars out there) tastes harsh, with an unpleasant aroma. Good wine vinegar is fruity, aromatic, and mellow.

Balsamic vinegar is one of my kitchen essentials. I keep two balsamic vinegars in my pantry. The first is an aged *aceto balsamico tradizionale*, for sprinkling sparingly over Parmesan cheese or a grilled steak. I also stock a moderately priced, younger balsamic vinegar to use more freely in vinaigrettes and the like. Beware of inexpensive balsamic vinegar, it's often nothing more than wine vinegar and caramel. Look for reputable brands and find vinegars with rich, almost sweet flavor and depth.

Sherry vinegar and *verjus du Perigord* also have a place in my kitchen. For varietals, such as a Sauvignon Blanc vinegar or a Cabernet vinegar, I use Katz brand both at Bottega and in my home kitchen. They're worth seeking out (see Resources).

CHAPTER 1

Make Your Own

At Bottega, "make your own" could be an entire book. This chapter highlights the basic recipes that make so many dishes at Bottega unique. These stocks, sauces, condiments, and even prosciutto are the starting point, the *mise en place* that we have ready every morning before we begin cooking anything else. Most of these recipes freeze well, and on days when you're short of time, having a few of these in your freezer is like having a trusted sous-chef on hand.

I'm a big believer in a well-stocked pantry. I think all of us hold in our very cells a sense of well-being at the sight of food preserved and ready, come what may. Set aside one weekend morning every month and devote it to stocking your pantry, refrigerator, and freezer. You'll find yourself relying less on take-out food, you'll eat better, and the experience of making your own pantry items will add flavor to an already tasty meal.

Cooking doesn't have to be a solitary pursuit. Part of the joy of working in a restaurant kitchen is a camaraderie that makes work time fly. Try assembling your own kitchen crew: throw a stock-making party where three friends each brings a stockpot, one person brings the chicken, one brings the mirepoix, and so on. When you can talk and laugh as you work together, stocking your kitchen can be as satisfying as the sight of those jars and freezer containers, neatly stacked and ready for a rainy day. Most important, when you open one of those jars, you get the memories of good times spent with friends, and that can only make the food taste better.

A word about stocks and broths: I have always called liquid made with raw meat "broth" and liquid made with caramelized bones "stock"; thus the first recipe in this chapter is a basic chicken broth. The third recipe, the chicken stock we use most at Bottega, is a doubled, or rich, chicken stock, because we use broth in place of half the water. Try this at home and see how it changes your finished dish.

My mom's handwritten 3x5 recipe card

Faccia il vostri propri

Chicken Broth

MAKES ABOUT 5 QUARTS

There is an art to a well-made broth or stock. At one time, every restaurant had one person, the saucier, whose job it was to make the stocks and sauces the same way every day. Why is consistency important? If you want to repeat the flavors of a dish you love, you need to stay true to the details, right down to the vegetables you put in your stock. I like knowing how my stock will taste, and the only way to know is to use the same ingredients and quantities each time.

Please don't use your stockpot as a catch-all for veggie trimmings. You don't ever want to put a limp, sad vegetable into your stock. My rule of thumb: If I don't want to put it in my mouth, I don't add it to my broth. Beautiful, fresh, crisp vegetables add significant flavor, especially when they're coarsely chopped by cutting them on the bias into ½-inch pieces, because this exposes more cut surface to the water.

To my way of thinking, the best broths and stocks use the entire bird. The wings and feet contribute gelatin for better body, and the neck and the drumsticks both contribute more meaty flavor to the liquid. You want every bit of flavor that you can coax into the liquid. (A few extra chicken feet, if you can find them, are a real plus.)

Skimming stock is like trimming and weeding a garden. You're taking out the imperfections and leaving pure, clear flavors.

Add the chicken, vegetables, and water to the pot first. Always use cold, fresh water, not hot water from the tap. Add the herbs and spices after the first few skimmings, so you won't skim them off with the foam. This calls for a very large pot; you can halve the recipe if you like.

½ pound white mushrooms
2 pounds chicken necks
4 pounds chicken wings
  (cut each wing into 3 sections)
2 pounds chicken drumsticks
4 cups coarsely chopped yellow onions
  (about 4 large onions)
2 cups coarsely chopped celery (about 4 stalks)
2 cups peeled and coarsely chopped carrots
  (about 3 large carrots)
2 gallons cold water
1 cup packed coarsely chopped fresh
  flat-leaf parsley
¼ cup fresh thyme sprigs
2 tablespoons black peppercorns
12 lightly crushed juniper berries
6 bay leaves

In a large, heavy pot, crumble the mushrooms, using your hands, and add the chicken parts, all the vegetables, and the water. Over high heat, bring the liquid to a boil, then reduce the heat to medium-low and bring the liquid to a simmer. Watch the heat; a low simmer gives you better flavor than boiling your stock.

Cook for about 20 minutes, occasionally skimming off the foam that rises to the top. Add the parsley, thyme, peppercorns, and juniper berries. Add the bay leaves, crumbling them into the pot. Continue to simmer for 4½ hours.

Remove from the heat. Using tongs, transfer the chicken to a plate to cool. (Later, pull the chicken off the bone and reserve it for another use, such as chicken salad or chicken ravioli.) Strain the broth through a colander and then strain again through a fine-mesh sieve. Let cool completely.

Store in airtight containers in the refrigerator for up to 3 days or in the freezer for up to 3 months. If freezer space is tight, cook the broth to reduce it by about half and then thin with water as needed when you're ready to use the stock.

CHEF'S NOTE: I don't add salt to my broths and stocks for this reason: If I reduce a salted liquid significantly, it becomes too salty.

Vegetable Stock

MAKES ABOUT 5 QUARTS

At Bottega, we use this stock when we don't want to overpower the flavor of a dish by using chicken or veal stock.

Some cooks believe that vegetable stock is a way to use up the veggies in the fridge that are past their prime. I don't agree. I use beautiful, farm-fresh veggies for my vegetable stock every time. Don't forget to cut vegetables on the bias: the greater surface area means that more of the veggie's flavor infuses the liquid. And always begin with cold, fresh water for the best-tasting stock.

7 quarts cold water
4 cups coarsely chopped yellow onions
   (about 4 large onions)
2 cups split, rinsed, and coarsely chopped leeks
   (about 2 large leeks)
2 cups coarsely chopped celery (about 4 stalks)
2 cups peeled and coarsely chopped carrots
   (about 3 large carrots)
2 fresh Roma (plum) tomatoes, peeled, or 3 peeled
   whole tomatoes from a can (leave whole so juices
   don't cloud stock)
2 cups coarsely chopped cored fennel
   (about 2 large bulbs)
½ cup coarsely chopped fresh
   flat-leaf parsley, with stems
1 fresh thyme sprig
1 tablespoon black peppercorns
3 bay leaves

In a large, heavy stockpot, combine the water, onions, leeks, celery, carrots, tomatoes, and fennel. Bring to a boil over high heat. Reduce the heat and cook at a low simmer for about 20 minutes, skimming the foam occasionally. Add the parsley, thyme, peppercorns, and bay leaves and simmer for another 25 minutes. Using a slotted spoon, remove the tomatoes and strain the liquid through a fine-mesh sieve. Keep stock in an airtight container in the refrigerator for 3 days or in the freezer for up to 3 months.

Gardening with the li'l man

Roasted Chicken Stock

MAKES ABOUT 5 QUARTS

Adding roasted chicken bones and red wine
makes this stock rich, dark, and hearty.
You can use cold water instead of chicken
broth if you like, but I urge you to try
this double-chicken method for stock that
knocks your socks off. If you want to really
go the extra mile, double the Chicken
Broth recipe and use it for all the liquid in
this recipe, except for the red wine.

2 pounds chicken necks
4 pounds chicken wings,
    (cut each wing into 3 sections)
2 pounds chicken drumsticks
1 tablespoon olive oil (see Chef's Note, facing page)
½ cup chicken fat, saved from a previous stock,
    or olive oil
2 cups coarsely chopped yellow onions
    (about 1 large onion)
2 cups coarsely chopped celery (about 4 stalks)
2 cups peeled and coarsely chopped carrots
    (about 3 large carrots)
One 750-ml bottle dry red wine
1 cup water for deglazing, plus 1 gallon cold water
1 gallon Chicken Broth (page 16)
    or low-salt store-bought broth
1 cup packed coarsely chopped fresh flat-leaf parsley
¼ cup fresh thyme sprigs
2 tablespoons black peppercorns
12 juniper berries, lightly crushed
6 bay leaves

Preheat the oven to 450°F. Toss the chicken necks, wings, and drumsticks with the olive oil, arrange on two rimmed baking sheets, and roast until the chicken is golden brown, 15 to 20 minutes.

While the chicken bones roast, heat a large, heavy stockpot over medium heat, add the chicken fat, and then add the vegetables. Sauté the vegetables for about 20 minutes, or until nicely browned, and add the red wine. Increase the heat to high and cook until the wine has reduced to a syrup, 15 to 20 minutes. (Stay close by and don't cook it so long that the wine scorches.) Turn off the heat and let the pot cool.

When the chicken is brown, remove from the oven and transfer the chicken with tongs to a colander set on a plate, to let the fat drain. Set the baking sheets on the stove top over medium heat and add ½ cup water to each. Stir to scrape up the browned bits on the bottom of the sheets. Pour the contents of each sheet into the pot with the vegetables. Add the chicken pieces and then pour in the remaining 1 gallon water and the chicken broth. Cook over medium-high heat until the liquid barely boils, then reduce the heat and let the stock simmer for 20 minutes, skimming off the foam occasionally. Add the parsley, thyme, peppercorns, juniper berries, and bay leaves.

Using tongs, gently transfer the chicken to a plate to avoid clouding the liquid. (Later, pull the chicken off the bone and reserve it for another use, such as chicken salad or to toss with pasta.) Strain the stock through a colander and then strain again through a fine-mesh sieve. Let cool completely.

Store in airtight containers in the refrigerator for up to 3 days or in the freezer for up to 3 months. (Even when I plan to freeze the stock, I refrigerate it first; when it's chilled, I scrape off the fat that rises to the top and save it in plastic bags in my freezer for other uses.) If freezer space is tight, cook the stock over medium-high heat to reduce it by about half and then thin with water as needed when you're ready to use the stock.

CHEF'S NOTE: Extra-virgin olive oil is the type I use most often, but I also cook with a refined olive oil that isn't extra-virgin. Easily recognized by its light straw color, this type of oil used to be called "pure olive oil," but these days you rarely see "pure" on the label. If a bottle or can is labeled "olive oil" (with no mention of extra-virgin), this is the oil to use when you want a milder flavor.

In this book, I tell you where I use extra-virgin olive oil. If you don't see the words *extra-virgin* in an ingredient list, use this milder, straw-colored olive oil. Read more about oils in the Pantry section on page 11.

Shrimp Stock

MAKES ABOUT 3 QUARTS

I use this stock for many of Bottega's seafood and pasta dishes, including Solo Shrimp Pasta (page 100). When making shrimp stock, call ahead and ask your fishmonger to save shrimp shells for you; these add to the stock's flavor without adding much cost.

½ cup extra-virgin olive oil
¾ pound of the least expensive good fresh
    shrimp you can find, or ½ pound shrimp
    and ½ pound shrimp shells
4 cups coarsely chopped yellow onion
    (about 2 large onions)
2 cups peeled and coarsely chopped carrots
    (about 3 large carrots)
2 cups coarsely chopped celery (about 4 stalks)
1 cup Pernod
1½ cups Tomato Passata (see Note, page 214)
1 gallon fresh water
4 bay leaves
1 tablespoon black peppercorns

In a stockpot, heat ¼ cup of the oil over medium-high heat. Add the shrimp (or the combination of shrimp and shells) and sauté until the shrimp turns pink, 2 to 3 minutes. Empty the contents onto a baking sheet. Add the remaining ¼ cup olive oil to the pot and sauté the onion, carrots, and celery until lightly browned, about 5 minutes. Add any juice that's collected on the sheet under the shrimp. Add the Pernod, increase the heat to high, and cook until the liquid is reduced by about three-fourths. Add the tomato passata and return to a boil. Add the water, bay leaves, and peppercorns. Bring the liquid to a boil, then reduce the heat to a simmer. Return the sautéed shrimp (or the shrimp and shells) to the pot and cook for 45 minutes. Remove from the heat, let cool, and strain through a chinois or fine-mesh strainer.

Store in airtight containers in the refrigerator for up to 2 days or in the freezer for up to 1 month.

Fish Fumet

MAKES ABOUT 6 CUPS

For the Fisherman's Sauce (see page 60) alone as well as the Adriatic Brodetto (page 134), it's worth knowing how to make a fumet.

Ask your fishmonger for bones a few days before making a fumet, so you'll be sure to have them when you need them. Always rinse fish bones in cold water. If there's any blood, toss the fish bones with 1 tablespoon kosher salt and then rinse.

¼ cup olive oil (see Chef's Note, page 19)
1 cup coarsely chopped celery (about 2 stalks)
1 cup split, rinsed, and coarsely chopped leek
    (about 1 large leek)
2 cups coarsely chopped yellow onions
    (about 1 large onion)
1 cup coarsely chopped cored fennel
    (about 1 large bulb)
2 pounds fresh fish bones, well rinsed in cold water
¼ cup Pernod or Ricard
8 cups cold water
2 bay leaves
1 teaspoon black peppercorns
1 teaspoon fennel seeds

Heat a large pot over medium heat and add the oil. When the oil is hot, add the celery, leek, onions, and fennel and sauté until tender, about 12 minutes, stirring often; don't let the vegetables brown. Add the fish bones and the Pernod, increase the heat to high, and cook just until the alcohol burns off, about 1 minute. Pour in the water, but don't stir. Bring the liquid to a simmer and then add the bay leaves (crumbling them into the pot with your hands), peppercorns, and fennel seeds. Simmer over low heat for 30 minutes, skimming any foam from the top. Remove from the heat and strain through a fine-mesh sieve. Store in an airtight container in your refrigerator for 3 days or freeze for up to 3 months.

CHEF'S NOTE: You can tap the sieve gently to speed the liquid through, but don't use a spoon to push on the solids or you could make your fumet cloudy.

Tuna Conserva

MAKES ABOUT 5 CUPS TUNA AND 2 CUPS OIL

My mom would call this *tonno sott'olio*, which means "tuna in oil." When she pickled vegetables, she would always add a chunk of this tuna conserva to the canning jar before she put in the veggies and the hot brine. This is old-school Italian and worth trying.

Ask your fishmonger to get you a tuna loin and to remove the skin for you (and maybe take him or her a bottle of wine or something home-baked by way of thanks).

1 albacore tuna loin, about 2 pounds
6 tablespoons kosher salt
1 bay leaf
2 large garlic cloves
10 black peppercorns
Cold, fresh water
2 cups extra-virgin olive oil,
　　plus more as needed

Cut the tuna loin crosswise into three pieces and place them in a large, heavy pot. Pour in the salt and add the bay leaf, garlic, and peppercorns. Add cold water to cover by at least 2 inches. (The fish will poach slowly for 3 hours, so be sure you start with enough water; the tuna should stay submerged for the entire cooking time.)

Bring the liquid to a boil and then reduce the heat to a low simmer. Monitor the heat so the liquid never boils. After 3 hours, turn off the heat and line a platter with paper towels. Using a large spatula or a fish spatula, lift the tuna out of the liquid and place it on the paper towels to cool and dry for 1 hour. The tuna will break into smaller chunks, and that's fine.

Remove any debris, skin, or blood vessels from the tuna using your fingers. Divide the tuna among 5 or 6 pint-sized canning jars and pour enough olive oil into each to completely cover the tuna. Refrigerate the jars for up to 1 month, or follow the canning jar manufacturer's directions for longer storage.

My girlfriend
Eileen
(she also goes as my wife)

My Napa Style
merchant bud
Brooks

Super mother-in-law
Judy

My father-in-law Denis (Aiden calls him "Goofy")

The Support of a Family

Before we opened Bottega, I was like a kid watching a soccer game from the wrong side of the fence. I wanted to open another restaurant but knew the toll this would take on my family. My youngest daughter, Giana, who was very young when I worked at Tra Vigne, told me, "Go, Dad. Open your restaurant. Your family supports you."

My wife, Eileen, understood and wholeheartedly supported me. She not only gave me her blessing but helped us set the tone for Bottega in so many ways: She chose the lighting, finishes, chairs, and fabrics. Eileen created the link between the design, the visual experience, and the food. Her thoughtfulness shows in so many of the details of Bottega that whenever I glance around the room it feels like an embrace from her.

Baby Giana with friends

Salsa di Pomodoro della Nonna
(My Grandmother's
Old Hen Tomato Sauce)

MAKES ABOUT 4 CUPS

I remember the day my grandmother Vicencina proved to me that an ornery chicken made the best-tasting *brodo*. While my grandmother gathered eggs, one bird made the fatal mistake of pecking her ankle, poking a hole in her thick brown support hose. I was small, but even I knew that the bird's hours were numbered. I don't know if the sauce my grandmother made that day was so good because revenge added its own seasoning or just because it was that hen's time, but the flavor of that rich chicken has stayed in my memory all these years.

My mom made this sauce often for gnocchi, and whenever she did, she would pull the hen out of the sauce at the last minute, keep it warm, and then serve it as the *secondi*, or second course, with fresh-chopped parsley and a little basil. I suggest you try this, too.

¼ cup extra-virgin olive oil

One 4-pound chicken, quartered

Kosher salt and freshly ground black pepper

¼ cup peeled and finely diced carrot

¼ cup finely diced celery

½ cup finely diced yellow onion

1 teaspoon minced garlic

1 teaspoon minced fresh rosemary

1 bay leaf

½ cup dry red wine

Two 28-ounce cans San Marzano tomatoes,
    put through a food mill, with juice reserved
    (see Chef's Note, at right)

¼ cup torn fresh basil leaves

Preheat the oven to 300°F. Heat a large Dutch oven over medium-high heat and add the oil. Season the chicken with salt and pepper. Add the chicken to the pot and lightly brown on all sides, about 4 minutes per side. Using tongs, transfer the chicken to a plate.

Place the Dutch oven over medium-high heat and sauté the carrot, celery, onion, and garlic until tender, about 8 minutes. Add the rosemary, bay leaf, and red wine. Stir to scrape up the browned bits, then return the chicken to the pot. Cook to reduce the wine until the pot is almost dry. Pour in the milled tomatoes and season the sauce with salt and pepper.

Make a sweating lid to fit the pot (see Chef's Note, at right). When the sweating lid is in place resting on top the chicken, slide the pot into the oven and cook for about 1 hour, or until chicken is cooked through. (You can use a regular pan lid if you don't want to cut a sweating lid from parchment, but allow a little more cooking time.)

Using tongs, transfer the chicken pieces to a plate. You can keep the chicken warm and serve it as a second course, or let cool, wrap, and refrigerate for another use. Add the torn basil leaves to the sauce and use this in place of any marinara sauce.

CHEF'S NOTES: Tomatoes put through a food mill have the right consistency for the sauces I make. If you don't have a food mill, you could pulse tomatoes just 3 or 4 times in a food processor (don't overprocess them), but to get the same velvety consistency of the sauces we serve at Bottega, a food mill works much better, and is an inexpensive addition to your kitchen tool set.

Cooking under a sweating lid reduces the circulation of the air in the pot and, by holding in the steam, keeps the food moister. There are two ways to cut a sweating lid: Trace the lid for the pot you'll be using on parchment paper and then cut the paper a little smaller, so the parchment fits inside the pot. The other way to make a sweating lid—the chef's way—is to tear off a piece of parchment larger than the pot. Holding one point of the parchment sheet toward you, fold the parchment into a fan, starting at the left side and folding back and forth to create accordion pleats. Hold the parchment fan over the pot with the tip of it dead center, then use kitchen shears to snip off the fat end in a curve. The sweating lid will fit down inside the pot and sit right on top the bird as it cooks, keeping it moist and flavorful.

Salsa Verde

MAKES ABOUT 2 ½ CUPS

What pesto was for me in the '90s, this salsa verde is now. Chef de Cuisine Nick Ritchie created this blend, and I love it for its subtle underlying flavor notes; it doesn't take over, whereas pesto sometimes can overwhelm with its raw bite of garlic. I still use pesto, but I turn to this recipe just as often to drizzle on soups, over grilled bread or simple pasta, and especially with seafood such as octopus (see page 128).

Use any hearty artisan bread here; this is a fine way to use a few slices of day-old bread.

¼ cup white wine vinegar
2 slices white country bread, crust removed
6 to 8 cornichons
2 teaspoons capers, preferably salt-packed capers
    rinsed and soaked for 30 minutes
2 to 3 anchovies, preferably salt-packed anchovies
    soaked for 30 minutes and bones removed
1 cup packed fresh flat-leaf parsley
1 coarsely chopped hard-boiled egg
    (see Chef's Note, below)
1 cup extra-virgin olive oil,
    plus up to ½ cup more if needed

In a small bowl, pour the vinegar over the bread, flipping the bread slices so each side gets a vinegar soak, and set the bowl aside.

In a food processor, combine the cornichons, capers, and anchovies, pulsing until finely chopped but not a paste. Add the bread slices and pulse. Add the parsley and hard-boiled egg and pulse 2 or 3 times. Scrape down the sides of the processor bowl. With the machine running, gradually drizzle in the 1 cup olive oil through the feed tube. Turn off the machine and taste the sauce. It should be spreadable; if it's too thick, turn the machine on again and slowly drizzle in as much of the remaining ½ cup of olive oil as needed.

I like to use this the same day I make it, but you can cover it and refrigerate for up to 2 days.

CHEF'S NOTE: A good hard-boiled egg makes a difference in this sauce. To cook eggs without making the whites rubbery, place the eggs in a saucepan of cold water. Bring the water to a boil, then reduce the heat to a simmer and cook for 12 minutes. While the eggs cook, set up an ice bath. When the 12 minutes are up, use a slotted spoon to transfer the eggs to the ice bath and let them cool for 5 to 10 minutes. To make them easier to shell, transfer them back into the pot of hot water for a minute or so.

Blanched-Basil Pesto

MAKES ABOUT 1 CUP

This pesto is vibrant in color as well as flavor. Powdered vitamin C—also called ascorbic acid—is my secret for keeping pesto a fresh, appetizing green. The herbs go in boiling water and then straight into an ice bath, so I like to use a large sieve or colander to transfer all the herbs in one smooth move.

Pesto freezes well, so when basil is abundant, make a few batches to keep in your freezer for up to a month.

3 cups lightly packed fresh basil leaves

1 cup lightly packed fresh flat-leaf parsley leaves

½ cup olive oil (see Chef's Note, page 19)

1 tablespoon pine nuts, toasted
   (see Chef's Note, at right)

1 teaspoon minced garlic

½ teaspoon fine salt, preferably ground sea
   or gray salt

¼ teaspoon freshly ground black pepper

⅛ teaspoon powdered ascorbic acid
   (see Resources)

1 cup freshly grated Parmesan cheese

Set up a large bowl of ice water. Bring a large saucepan of water to a boil. Place the basil and parsley leaves in a sieve or colander that fits inside the pan. Lower the sieve full of herbs into the boiling water and use a spoon to push the leaves under so the herbs cook evenly. Blanch for 15 seconds, then transfer the sieve to the ice bath to stop the cooking process. Let the herbs cool in the ice bath for 10 seconds. Remove the sieve, let drain, and then squeeze any water that you can from the herbs. Transfer them to a cutting board and coarsely chop.

In a blender, purée the herbs with the oil, pine nuts, garlic, salt, pepper, and ascorbic acid until well blended and somewhat smooth. Add the cheese and whir for a second or so to mix. Transfer the pesto to a bowl; taste and adjust the seasoning.

Press plastic wrap directly on top of the pesto to keep it from turning brown and store in the refrigerator for up to 1 week, or freeze it for up to 1 month.

CHEF'S NOTE: Toast pine nuts in a small dry skillet over low heat, shaking the pan frequently. Heat for just 1 to 2 minutes; as soon as you smell the fragrance of the pine nuts, slide the nuts out of the pan and onto a plate so they don't burn.

Basil Oil

MAKES ABOUT 1⅓ CUPS

Follow these same steps with any fresh leafy herb, such as parsley, cilantro, or tarragon, that's abundant and at its peak. I first made this oil from basil in the '90s when a farmer backed up to the restaurant, his truck bed brimming over with fresh basil. We were making so much pesto it was inevitable that someone would overlook a batch and leave it out overnight. Disgusted with the waste, I decided to try to salvage something from the basil leaves, and this oil was born.

This is a condiment oil, something to drizzle on at the last second; don't try to cook with it because heat will destroy all those garden-fresh flavors.

4 cups firmly packed fresh basil leaves
2 cups olive oil (see Chef's Note, page 19)

In a blender, purée the basil and olive oil until completely smooth. Pour the mixture into a medium saucepan. Bring the oil to a simmer over medium heat; when you see small bubbles, let it cook for 45 seconds, then pour it through a fine-mesh sieve into a bowl. Tap the sieve lightly to coax the oil through but don't press on the solids with a spoon.

Let the oil cool for about 15 minutes, but strain it while it's still warm, because warm oil passes through the filters faster. While the oil cools, layer three coffee filters inside each other in a large sieve or strainer and set the sieve securely over a heat-proof container. Ladling from the top, transfer the oil into the layered filters and let it drip through. When most of the oil has gone through, pick up the filters and use your fingers to squeeze out the remaining oil, taking care not to tear the paper.

Let the filtered oil stand for a few hours and then pour it slowly into a clean container, leaving any sediment or cloudy liquid behind. Kept in an airtight jar in a cool, dark place, this oil will hold its bright flavor for at least 1 month.

Smoky Paprika Oil

MAKES ABOUT 5½ CUPS

Oil infused with *pimentón de la Vera*, a special smoked Spanish paprika, has a full-bodied flavor and gorgeous color. When making this blend, don't allow the oil to get too hot, or the spice will scorch, infusing the oil with a bitter flavor.

Try this same method with other spices such as cinnamon (for brushing a pie crust) or black pepper (to drizzle on steaks).

Most specialty grocers stock pimentón de la Vera, but if you have any trouble finding it, see Resources.

1 cup pimentón de la Vera (smoked Spanish paprika)
6 cups olive oil (see Chef's Note, page 19)

In a blender, mix the paprika and olive oil until completely smooth. Pour the mixture into a stockpot and cook over medium heat, watching carefully until the mixture begins to bubble not just on the perimeter of the pan but also in the center.

Immediately reduce the heat to low and simmer for 1 minute. If the oil gets too hot, the paprika will scorch, so keep the heat down. Do not stir the oil. Remove from the heat and let the paprika solids settle to the bottom of pan.

Layer three coffee filters inside each other in a large sieve or strainer set securely over a heat-proof container. It's best to strain the oil through the filters while it's still hot, because it'll strain more quickly. Ladling from the top, transfer the oil about 1 cup at a time into the filters and let it drip through before ladling in another cup. (This is to speed up the filtration; if you pour in all the oil and spices, the spices will clog the filter and it will take a long time to drain.) Finally, when all the oil has dripped through, spoon the paprika from the pot and let it drip down all its oil, too. When most of the oil has gone through, pick up the filters and use your fingers to squeeze out the remaining oil, taking care not to tear the paper.

Kept in an airtight jar in a cool, dark place, this oil will hold its sultry, smoky flavor for at least 1 month.

Basil Oil

Smoky Paprika Oil

pre-service lineup

Duck Prosciutto

MAKES ABOUT 1½ POUNDS
DUCK PROSCIUTTO

There is nothing like creating your own prosciutto to make you feel like the master of your kitchen. Yes, this will cure in your refrigerator for 6 weeks, but for all that, it requires a surprisingly small amount of effort from the cook.

There may be patches of light or dark mold on the cheesecloth. Don't worry about this. Just brush the prosciutto with grappa or any hard alcohol; this adds flavor while killing any mold on the surface of the duck.

Hudson Valley Moularde ducks are a cross between Muscovy and Peking and have the best breast meat for curing; you can buy these from D'Artagnan, or try Heritage Foods (see Resources).

As with prosciutto made from pork, this begs to be sliced very thinly. One way to get the thin slices is to take the whole finished duck prosciutto to your butcher and offer to trade a few slices if he or she agrees to slice it for you.

After the 42 days of curing, if this duck is wrapped in cheesecloth and hung in a cool, dry place, it will keep for about 5 weeks.

CURING SALT
½ cup plus 2 tablespoons kosher salt
1 teaspoon coarsely ground black pepper
3 juniper berries, finely chopped
Pinch of ground cloves
2 dried bay leaves

1 whole Hudson Valley Moularde duck breast
Grappa for brushing

FOR THE CURING SALT: In a large bowl, combine the salt, pepper, juniper berries, cloves, and bay leaves and mix them, crumbling the leaves with your hands. Set the mixture aside while you prepare the duck.

Remove the cartilage from between the duck breasts and cut the breasts in half to separate them. Lightly season the meat side of each half with the curing salt. Then press the two halves together in a sort of yin-yang formation, with the thick end of one breast against the thin tip of the other, with the two meat sides touching.

Using kitchen twine, tie the breasts together tightly. (See Chef's Note, at right, for directions on tying a butcher's knot.) Line a roasting pan with cheesecloth and spoon in half of the remaining salt. Lay the tied duck breasts on top the salt and then press on the last of the curing salt. Cover with plastic wrap and refrigerate for 21 days, turning the duck on the salt bed every 3 days and rubbing the salt into the duck's skin on each side. If the duck gives off any liquid, just use a paper towel to wipe it away. Every duck has a different moisture content, so this will be slightly different each time you make the prosciutto.

After the first 9 days, make up a new batch of curing salt and discard the used salt in the roasting pan. Twelve days later (when the 21 days are up), transfer the duck to a platter, discard the plastic wrap, and use a dampened paper towel to wipe the duck all the way around. Brush the duck with grappa and then roll it tightly inside a length of cheesecloth slightly longer than the duck. Tie the ends of the cloth together with a piece of kitchen twine or string at either end so the cheesecloth hugs the duck all the way around, and then trim off any extra cloth from the ends. Tie another length of twine to one end. Use this to hang the duck from a rung of a refrigerator rack toward the back, and place a dish or drip pan beneath it. The duck will lose about half its weight during the curing process.

After 21 more days, when the refrigerator part of the curing is complete, rub the prosciutto once more with grappa and hang in a cool, dry place. Use it within 30 to 40 days. Once you've cut it open, cover it in plastic wrap and refrigerate until ready to use.

CHEF'S NOTE: To tie a butcher's knot, start with a 2-foot length of kitchen twine. Bring it around the duck (which is sitting on your work surface so the tips point left and right) so the back length of twine and the front length are about even when you pull them taut above the duck. Hold the back length of twine still, while looping the front length of twine around it. With the front length of twine, form a loop and thread the same length through this loop from behind. When you've tightened this knot, continue holding the front length of twine with one hand while pulling taut the back length of string through the knot. Once again, bring the front length of twine around the back length and form another loop; pull the front length of twine through this loop from the back and tighten to hold the knot in place.

Roasted Lemons

I love lemons, but the wines I serve aren't always helped by the acidity. Grilling and roasting lemons mellows their flavor and lets you serve both lemons and wine without any fighting.

4 lemons, halved
1 teaspoon sea salt, preferably gray salt,
    or kosher salt
Freshly ground black pepper
2 teaspoons extra-virgin olive oil

Heat a grill pan over high heat, prepare a hot wood or charcoal fire, or preheat a gas grill on high. Toss the lemon halves in a bowl with the salt, pepper, and olive oil. Preheat the oven to 350°F. Grill the lemons all the way around just long enough to get clear grill marks, 30 seconds per side. Transfer them to a baking sheet and roast in the oven until softened, about 10 minutes.

These are best served the same day they are made. Store in the refrigerator for no more than 24 hours.

Preserved Meyer Lemons

I use this intensely flavorful lemon in almost every menu: to stuff a fish, with sautéed spinach, in gremolata. I even mince it to line the rim of a cocktail glass as a twistier twist for a martini. Packed in salt, these lemons must rest in your pantry or refrigerator for at least a month before you open the jar.

CURING SALT
4 cups kosher salt, plus more if needed
1 cup granulated sugar
1 teaspoon red pepper flakes
1 tablespoon black peppercorns
1 tablespoon juniper berries
1 teaspoon fennel seeds

12 lemons, preferably Meyer

FOR THE CURING SALT: In a large bowl, combine the 4 cups salt, the sugar, red pepper flakes, peppercorns, juniper berries, and fennel seeds. Stir to blend.

Score the lemons from top to bottom by cutting through the rind to the flesh. (Don't cut all the way through the lemons.) Pack the salt mixture into the cuts in each lemon and place the salted lemons into a large jar, until the jar is full. Pack the remaining salt mixture in the jar so the space around the lemons is taken up by salt. (If you run out of curing salt, just pour in extra kosher salt until the jar is full and every lemon is submerged in salt.) Seal the jar and store in a cool, dark place or in your refrigerator for 30 to 40 days.

When you're ready to cook with a preserved lemon, pull it from the jar, scoop out and discard the flesh, and use just the rind. Once you open the jar, store it in your refrigerator.

Crème Fraîche

MAKES ABOUT 1¾ CUPS

You can buy tubs of crème fraîche in high-end groceries, but it's the easiest thing in the world to make. It's just a matter of combining cream and buttermilk and letting them sit on your countertop at room temperature for up to 24 hours. That's all there is to it. Live cultures in the buttermilk react with the cream, creating a light, thin version of sour cream that's delicious and heat-stable.

I make this in a large, clean glass jar. After pouring in the cream and buttermilk, I cover the jar with two layers of cheesecloth, secure it with a rubber band, and just let it do its thing. I use crème fraîche often, so I make it in a quart-sized jar and double this recipe.

1 ⅔ cups heavy cream
1 tablespoon buttermilk

Whisk together the cream and buttermilk and pour into a glass jar. Cover it with two layers of cheesecloth and store at room temperature for up to 24 hours. After that, seal the jar with plastic wrap and refrigerate if you don't plan to use the crème fraîche right away. It will keep for up to 1 week in the refrigerator.

Dried Bread Crumbs

MAKES ABOUT 4 CUPS

I sometimes buy Progresso bread crumbs, and I also buy panko crumbs because they make crispier fried foods. But my mother always saved her stale bread and never, ever bought bread crumbs, so when I'm able to make my own crumbs from leftover bread, I think it adds something to the dish.

Stale bread makes better crumbs. You need a good amount of bread for the processor to do its job, but bread crumbs freeze beautifully; seal up any extra bread crumbs in small freezer bags.

2 loaves (1 pound each) country-style bread

Cut the bread into cubes about 1 to 2 inches wide. Leave the crust—don't slice it off. Spread the bread cubes on trays and let them air dry for several days, until the bread is very dry. In damp weather, you may need to heat the cubes in a 200ºF oven for an hour to reduce moisture. Let the bread cool completely before you grind it.

Working in batches, place the cubes in a food processor and whir until the bread is reduced to fine crumbs. Seal in freezer bags any crumbs that you don't need and freeze for up to 1 month.

CHAPTER 2

Tantalizing Snacks

STUZZICHINI

Stuzzichini are foods eaten out of hand, snacks that tease and tantalize. The Italian version of tapas, stuzzichini are meant to stimulate your appetite. At Bottega, we serve them as bar food or as a small bite while you read the menu and decide what you'd like for dinner. To me, they symbolize a kind of graciousness, a warmth at the start of the meal. At home, I make them as hors d'oeuvres to pass before the meal; they're wonderful for a cocktail party. Pick one of our cocktails—I'd go with the Negroni, on page 206—and make a party of it.

When I'm at Bottega, I can't help thinking about Belle and Barney Rhodes. Perhaps more than anyone, they encouraged this valley's growth. As Napa wines became known worldwide, the valley's vintners realized they needed to learn world-class entertaining. Twenty-five years ago, there were few restaurants here, and none of the caliber we have today. When Belle helped found the Napa Valley Cooking Class, chefs came from all over the world to teach which foods best complemented our Napa Valley wines. It's incredible to see how the valley has changed since those first cooking and wine classes. I'm inspired by the thought that Bottega is located where it all began.

I dined with Belle and Barney in their home many times, and one detail stands out in my memory: Most dinners ended with warm pistachios and the passing of a port decanter. The decanter had a round bottom—it couldn't be set down—so the bottle had to be passed from hand to hand. We felt contented after the meal, with Barney often dozing in his chair. The conversation was relaxed, and the passing of port and pistachios sealed the circle that had begun around the table, connecting us once more before the evening came to an end.

Stuzzichini can be as simple as warm pistachios. It's the passing from hand to hand that matters.

Stuzzichini

Chicken Wings Agrodolce

SERVES 6 TO 8

This is Bottega's answer to kung pao chicken: crisp outside, juicy inside, with a sweet-spicy sauce that makes it hard to stop reaching for another. *Agrodolce* is Italian for "sour-sweet," but this is more about the Calabrian chile paste than the sour. While I tested batch after batch, looking for just the right blend of spices, the entire waitstaff hovered on the other side of the counter, tasting. This is the final version, and it got a big "thumbs up" from everyone in the restaurant. You get two bonuses with this recipe: good stock and tender chicken.

COURT BOUILLON

2 cups diced yellow onions (about 2 large onions)
1 cup diced peeled carrot
1 cup diced celery
8 cups cold water
10 black peppercorns
1 ½ tablespoons sea salt, preferably gray salt,
    or kosher salt
1 fresh thyme sprig, or ½ teaspoon dried thyme
2 pounds chicken wings

AGRODOLCE SAUCE

1 cup Champagne vinegar or white wine vinegar
½ cup sugar
½ cup finely chopped red onion
½ teaspoon fennel seeds, toasted
    (see Chef's Note, page 189)
Pinch of sea salt or kosher salt
½ teaspoon Calabrian chile (see Resources),
    or ¼ teaspoon red pepper flakes

Corn, peanut, canola, or any neutral oil
    for deep-frying
2 cups buttermilk
Fritti Flour (page 71)

FOR THE COURT BOUILLON: In a stockpot, combine the onions, carrot, celery, water, peppercorns, salt, and thyme and bring to a boil over high heat. As soon as it boils, reduce the heat to medium-low and simmer for 10 minutes.

Add the chicken, reduce the heat to the lowest setting, and simmer for 30 minutes. Remove from the heat and let the chicken stand in the liquid until cool, at least 30 minutes. (See Chef's Note, below.)

FOR THE AGRODOLCE SAUCE: In a medium saucepan, combine the vinegar and sugar and bring to a boil over high heat. Stir until the sugar is dissolved. Add the onion, fennel seeds, and salt; reduce the heat to medium-low; and simmer until it reaches the consistency of maple syrup, about 10 minutes. Remove from the heat and stir in the Calabrian chile. Taste and add more chile if you like it very spicy. Set aside.

In a large, heavy pot, heat 3 inches of oil over high heat until it registers 375ºF on a deep-fat thermometer. Pour the buttermilk into a shallow bowl and the fritti flour in another shallow bowl.

Dip each chicken wing into the buttermilk and then roll in the fritti flour to coat. Cook about 6 coated chicken wings at a time in the hot oil until just slightly darker than the color of honey all the way around, about 4 to 6 minutes. Using tongs, transfer the wings from the oil to the agrodolce sauce and turn them to coat evenly. Shake off the excess and transfer the wings to a plate. Repeat to cook the remaining wings. Serve hot.

CHEF'S NOTE: Don't be in a hurry to pull the chicken from the court bouillon. If you let the chicken cool in the liquid, it will absorb the liquid and stay tender and juicy. If you pull the chicken out before the liquid is cool, the chicken will be dry.

Pesto Arancini
Stuffed with Mozzarella

MAKES 16 ARANCINI; SERVES 4

Arancini, or rice-balls filled with melting cheese, are for leftover-risotto days. I never make the rice from scratch when I'm making arancini at home. If you don't have leftover risotto, you can make these balls from cooked Arborio rice, but be sure to add a teaspoon or two of salt while the rice cooks. (Honestly, you're better off making a big pot of risotto—see "The ABC's of Risotto," page 117—and then making arancini the next day.)

Arancini remind me of my friend Mariano Orlando. He always made arancini the Sicilian way, his rice balls the size of oranges. We talked once about arancini and he kept saying in Italian, "telephone wire," making a motion with his hands as if to stretch a length of cord. "What are you saying?" I asked him. "Why are you talking about telephone wire?" The cheese, Mariano said, should stretch like a telephone wire when you take a bite from a perfect arancini and pull it away from your lips.

Our arancini don't have that same telephone wire of cheese; we use a little less cheese in the middle and a lot more cheese in the risotto. You can add more cheese to the middle if you want to go for the *telefono filo* effect. If you want to make these a few hours ahead, pour panko crumbs into a baking dish and rest the arancini on the panko before covering the dish in plastic wrap and refrigerating.

3 cups leftover risotto
   or cooked Arborio rice, cooled
1½ cups Blanched-Basil Pesto
   (page 27, double the recipe)
4 ounces fresh mozzarella, preferably bocconcini
2 cups all-purpose flour
3 large eggs, lightly beaten
2 cups panko (Japanese bread crumbs)
Peanut oil, corn oil, or canola oil for frying

Line a platter with parchment paper. In a large bowl, stir the risotto and pesto together until blended. Divide the rice into 16 more-or-less-equal portions.

Cut off about ½ teaspoon of mozzarella and then, with your hands, ball up one serving of rice around the cheese so it's completely encased in rice. Gently place on the prepared platter. Repeat to form 16 arancini. Slide the platter into the freezer for 30 minutes to allow the balls to firm up.

Before you take the rice balls from the freezer, set up your dredging station. Pour the flour into a shallow bowl; the eggs into another shallow bowl; and the panko into a third shallow bowl.

In a large, heavy pot or Dutch oven, heat 3 inches of oil over medium-high heat until it registers 375°F on a deep-fat thermometer. While the oil heats, dredge each rice ball in flour and lightly shake off the excess. Dip each rice ball in the egg and then in the panko. Gently drop 4 to 6 balls into the oil and cook until lightly browned, 60 to 90 seconds. Don't overcook them or the cheese will leak out into your oil. Using a slotted spoon or wire skimmer, transfer the arancini to paper towels to drain. Repeat to cook the remaining arancini. Serve at once.

CHEF'S NOTE: If you like, you can fry the day before, refrigerate overnight, and reheat with great success. To reheat, bake at 375°F for 10 to 15 minutes.

Location, Location, Location

My first thought in looking for a location for Bottega was, "Where could I possibly go after the villa-like setting of Tra Vigne?" I couldn't imagine a restaurant without that same kind of heritage. When I came to view this old building in Yountville, memories rushed over me. This portion of the building was once the Chutney Kitchen, started by French Laundry founders Don and Sally Schmitt in the 1970s. When I first came to the Napa Valley in the 1980s, I was introduced to it by Belle and Barney Rhodes, whom I still consider the royalty of Napa even though they've both left us in the past few years.

As you settle into your seat at Bottega, exhale your day, and begin to experience our hospitality, you can't help but be drawn in by the history of our building. The old brick walls and the deep crack in one of the beams overhead tell a story; it's like the European experience of knowing a place has had many lives before you ever arrived there. After we added some reinforcement, I left the cracked beam and brick walls exposed, in the hope that the stories we tell at Bottega will join the stories already here and the stories yet to come.

Bruschetta Trio: Tomatoes and Basil; Pepperonata; and Carrot, Onion, and Eggplant Caponata

SERVES 6

This is my answer to the luncheon sandwich—all the flavor on three half-slices of bread. Make the bruschetta slices small, from baguettes, and this becomes an hors d'oeuvre.

Bruschetta tells you something about the cook. Oven-dried slabs of bread don't count as bruschetta in my book. Aim for a crisp brown exterior, but make sure your bruschetta still has some tenderness inside.

I prefer to grill my bread slices over a flame and season them with sea salt and pepper and a good brush of olive oil after they've got the good grill marks. If you don't want to fire up your grill, you can use a grill pan to toast your bread slices or just put them on the rack in your oven preheated to 375°F and take them out when they're browned to suit your tastes.

For this presentation, I make bruschetta from large slices of bread cut in half, but baguette-size slices work, too.

If you have good tomatoes but don't feel like sautéing the garlic, skip it: chopped heirloom tomatoes and finely shredded basil, salt and pepper, EVOO (extra-virgin olive oil), and you're good to go. If you don't have fine summer tomatoes, don't bother with the tomato part of this trio; you have a wide world of options for topping your bruschetta. Try asparagus or artichoke hearts, fork-crushed fava beans or oven-roasted squash—all of these get a little spotlight shone on them when they sit atop a crunchy half-slice of good bread.

CHOPPED TOMATOES AND BASIL

4 Roma (plum) tomatoes

4 tablespoons extra-virgin olive oil

1 teaspoon minced garlic

2 tablespoons chopped fresh basil

Sea salt, preferably gray salt, or kosher salt

Freshly ground black pepper

PEPPERONATA

3 red bell peppers, roasted, peeled, and julienned
(see Chef's Note, at right)

1 teaspoon capers, preferably salt-packed capers
rinsed and soaked for 30 minutes

1 tablespoon finely shredded fresh basil

1 tablespoon sherry vinegar

2 tablespoons extra-virgin olive oil

Sea salt, preferably gray salt

Freshly ground black pepper

BRUSCHETTA

9 slices from a large country-style loaf of bread,
each ¾ inch thick, cut in half

2 tablespoons extra-virgin olive oil for brushing,
plus more for drizzling

Sea salt, preferably gray salt

Freshly ground black pepper

Carrot, Onion, and Eggplant Caponata (page 171)

12 to 18 heirloom tomato slices

6 to 12 whole basil leaves

FOR THE CHOPPED TOMATO AND BASIL: Bring a small pot of water to a boil and set up an ice bath. Cut a small X in the bottom of each Roma tomato and blanch in the boiling water for 10 seconds—just until the skin begins to curl at the X. Immediately shock the tomatoes by plunging them into the ice bath. The X at the bottom should show four curling corners; pull on those to peel the tomatoes. (If you don't mind a little skin, skip the peeling step.) Halve, seed, and dice the tomatoes and slide them, juice and all, into a medium bowl.

In a small saucepan, heat 2 tablespoons of the olive oil over medium-high heat. Add the garlic and stir until it begins to turn light brown, about 30 seconds. Pour the hot garlic oil over the diced tomatoes. Toss and add the basil and remaining 2 tablespoons of olive oil. Season with salt and pepper. Set aside.

FOR THE PEPPERONATA: In a medium bowl, combine the bell pepper strips, capers, and basil. Toss with the vinegar and oil, then season with salt and pepper.

(This is a great accompaniment to grilled steaks or roasted chicken.)

FOR THE BRUSCHETTA: Prepare a hot fire in a charcoal grill, preheat a gas grill to high, heat a grill pan over high heat, or preheat an oven to 375°F. Grill the bread slices for about 30 to 45 seconds on each side, or until well grill-marked, or toast in the oven on the oven rack for 2 to 3 minutes, using tongs to turn each slice as it begins to brown. Remove from the heat and brush the slices on one side with the 2 tablespoons olive oil, then sprinkle with salt and pepper.

Spread about a tablespoon of each topping, including the Carrot, Onion, and Eggplant Caponata, on six bruschetta pieces, so each person gets a full trio of the toppings. For the tomatoes and basil bruschetta, top the bread with heirloom tomato slices and whole basil leaves before adding a spoonful of the chopped tomato mixture. If you like, spoon more of the toppings into ramekins and pass extra at the table.

CHEF'S NOTE: You have lots of ways to roast peppers—in the oven, on your grill, or over the flame of your gas burner. I prefer to roast them under my broiler because I don't have to monitor them as closely. Just cut them in half, put them on a baking sheet, cut-side down, put the tray right under the heat source, and fire them up until the pepper skins are blackened all the way across.

When they come out of the oven, put them in a bowl and cover with plastic wrap. The steam will loosen the pepper skins, making it easier to peel them once they're cool.

Prosciutto-Wrapped Truffle Fries

SERVES 6

My wife inspired this dish one night when she was dining at Bottega with her girlfriends. I wanted to put something new on their table, something Eileen hadn't seen before that I knew she'd like: thin-cut, perfectly cooked golden fries, Parmesan, prosciutto, and—the final touch—a shimmer of truffle oil. Truffle oil is one of those flavors that, if you love it, puts you immediately in an amorous mood. At least that's what I was hoping for when I slid these onto the table.

Mission accomplished. This melding of sexy flavors got me exactly the attention I wanted at the table. It's impossible to eat these bundles politely. You have to open wide, it's messy, it's fantastic. I probably should just stop while I'm ahead.

Peanut oil, canola oil, or corn oil for deep-frying
1½ pounds russet potatoes, peeled and cut into
⅓-inch-thick lengthwise slices and then into
⅓-inch-wide sticks (you can also use
a good-quality frozen fry, such as Alexia's)
1 tablespoon minced fresh flat-leaf parsley
1 teaspoon truffle oil
2 tablespoons freshly grated Parmesan cheese
Sea salt, preferably gray salt
Freshly ground black pepper

6 thin prosciutto slices
6 ripe figs (optional)

In a large, heavy pot, heat 3 inches of oil over high heat until it registers 375°F on a deep-fat thermometer. In batches, fry the potatoes until golden brown, about 4 minutes. Using a wire skimmer or tongs, transfer the potatoes to paper towels to drain.

In a heat-proof bowl, toss the hot fries with the parsley and truffle oil. Add the Parmesan and toss once more, taste, and season with salt and pepper.

Spread a slice of prosciutto on a work surface. Gather up a small bundle of fries as if you're gathering pencils to put in a jar. Place the fries on the prosciutto and gently wrap. *Tear* each fig (if using) into four sections (don't wuss out and use a knife). Plate the bundles with the torn figs and serve while warm. Don't put any utensils on the table; this is for fingers and mouths only. Napkins are a good idea.

SIMPLE VARIATION: The truffle fries alone, without the prosciutto wrap, are still outstanding. You can change the seasoning: use just herbs, or just cheese, or try flavored oils such as Basil Oil (page 28) with dried Jack cheese, Smoky Paprika Oil (page 28) with manchego cheese, orange oil with sage. This is a good place to experiment with flavor combinations because fries are inexpensive and easy to make.

CHAPTER 3

Before the Meal

ANTIPASTI

The strength of any Italian restaurant lies in its antipasto. For a chef, antipasto is *the* chance to wow a guest before the wine kicks in and everything gets slightly blurry. At Bottega, we concentrate on making this the dish that blows the lid off the meal. When the server brings out a polenta "under glass," or our warm pecorino cheese budino, or our famous fritto misto, everybody at the table sits forward, eager to taste. That's how it should be with this course.

We also introduce the idea of whimsy in this chapter. Serving polenta "under glass" is an example. Used judiciously, these small, unexpected touches can add their own flavor to the experience.

I lean toward serving a number of antipasti, family style. At home, I serve them in two waves, bringing out the simpler antipasti, then another round of more complicated flavors.

Almost all of our antipasti can serve as one-course suppers or can morph into an entrée for two or four people. Make pasta for the polpettini and you have a great dinner. Add a plate of sliced tomatoes to the "Angry" Ahi Tuna Crudo and you have a satisfying luncheon dish.

This chapter shares my fritto misto technique. Once you learn this method, you can make the best calamari (tender inside and crisp on the outside), as well as onions or even a crispy blue cheese–stuffed olive for your martini (see page 209). People shy away from deep-frying, but this is still a fast, easy way to make a good bit of fish, soft-shell crab, or potato taste even better. I don't eat *fritto* every day (nobody should!), but having a great *fritto misto* on occasion makes me very happy.

Green Eggs and Ham

SERVES 6

I'm a big Dr. Seuss fan, and I must have read *Green Eggs and Ham* hundreds of times when my daughters were young and now again with my son. I find myself saying those much-loved words, "Would he? Could he?" at our dinner table, and Aiden can't stop chuckling. This dish is my "get over yourself" reminder; it's just food, after all. Tomorrow you'll cook and eat again, so let yourself have some fun with it.

I've always gone for the California hint-of-crunch asparagus; this is an old-school cooking method of cooking each stalk completely through so it has a little give when you pick it up and shake it, like a medium-stiff diving board. To snap off an asparagus end, before poaching hold the spear in both hands and bend it until it breaks. It will snap off at the point where the spear becomes tough.

You can poach the asparagus the day before and reheat in the poaching liquid, but I think the texture is better if you poach the spears just before serving.

Wine Pairing: Sauvignon Blanc or Ribolla Gialla

PROSCIUTTO BITS

1 ½ teaspoons extra-virgin olive oil

½ pound prosciutto, finely diced (1 generous cup)

CAMBOZOLA SAUCE

8 ounces Cambozola cheese

⅔ cup heavy cream

½ teaspoon finely minced fresh thyme

1 pound asparagus (about 2 bunches)

½ cup extra-virgin olive oil

½ cup water

½ teaspoon sea salt (preferably gray salt)

CRISPY EGGS

6 large eggs

Peanut, corn, or canola oil for deep-frying

2 cups all-purpose flour

2 cups buttermilk

2 cups panko (Japanese bread crumbs)

FOR THE PROSCIUTTO BITS: In a small nonstick skillet, heat the olive oil over medium heat. When it's hot, add the diced prosciutto and reduce the heat to medium-low. Stir and toss occasionally, and cook until the prosciutto is very crisp, 10 to 15 minutes. With a slotted spoon, transfer the prosciutto to paper towels to drain. (Reserve the fat in the pan for another use.) Prosciutto bits may be made up to 1 week in advance and kept in an airtight jar in the refrigerator or frozen for up to 1 month. If frozen, heat briefly in a 300°F oven before using.

FOR THE CAMBOZOLA SAUCE: Cut off the cheese rind and cut the cheese into small chunks. Add it to a saucepan with the cream. Whisk the mixture over medium heat until there are no lumps. If you like, strain the mixture to remove the "veins," and pour it back into the pan. Add the thyme and simmer another 2 minutes, whisking continually. Take it off the heat and cover to keep warm.

After snapping the end off each stalk, line up the asparagus and trim so they're all the same length. In a large sauté pan, combine the olive oil, water, and salt and bring to a boil over high heat. Lower

the heat to medium-high and then poach the asparagus, working in batches and using a spatter screen: Cook the asparagus in a single layer, simmering just until tender, 3 to 4 minutes. Don't overcook, because it will continue cooking when it's off the heat. Transfer the asparagus to a sheet pan to cool. When you've poached all the asparagus, reserve the poaching liquid, keeping it warm in a small pan on the stove.

FOR THE EGGS: Prepare an ice bath large enough to hold all 6 eggs. Bring a large pot of well-salted water to a rolling boil. Put the eggs in a pasta basket or a sieve and lower it into the water. When the water just barely returns to a boil, set the timer for 4 ½ minutes (5 minutes if using larger brown eggs). When the time is up, transfer the basket to the ice bath and let the eggs chill for least 20 minutes. Carefully peel the eggs, starting at the larger, rounded end of the shell.

In a large, heavy pot, heat 3 inches of oil to 375°F on a deep-fat thermometer. Pour the flour, buttermilk, and panko into separate bowls. Dip each egg first in the flour, then in the buttermilk, and finally in the panko. Be sure to coat well with the panko. Using a wire skimmer, add 3 eggs at a time to the hot oil and deep fry until golden brown, just 60 to 90 seconds. Using the skimmer, transfer the eggs to paper towels to drain.

Divide the asparagus evenly between 6 warmed plates. Drizzle the spears with a spoonful of the warm poaching liquid. Place one crispy egg per serving on top the spears, drizzle with cambozola sauce, and top with a teaspoonful of prosciutto bits.

Burrata Three Ways

Burrata is the Italian word for "buttered," and that's fitting for a cheese that's as soft, delicate, and creamy as this one. Among Italian cheeses, burrata is a baby, first made in Puglia in the 1920s but not appearing throughout Italy until the 1950s.

How does burrata differ from mozzarella? Burrata is much creamier. The technique for burrata is to shape the hot cheese strands into a pouch, stuff it full of mozzarella, and then top it off with cream before pinching the pouch closed. At Bottega, burrata appears on our menu in so many ways, we had trouble choosing just a few of our recipes to include in the book.

We don't make our own burrata at Bottega. We buy ours from Vito Girardi, who owns Gioia Cheese Company with his wife, Monica. Here in California, Vito and Monica have been making burrata every day for a decade, so there's no shame in saying that they make it better than I do. This is a funny, full-circle situation, because at Tra Vigne, we couldn't find good mozzarella to buy and had to make our own. If Tra Vigne had been in Italy, I would never have made cheese. We got a reputation for cheese making, and it hit a nerve in the stratosphere. In 1987, I couldn't find one person to sell me curd. These days, you could probably throw a rock and hit three people who can supply you with the curds you need to make mozzarella.

Burrata is a different story. The Italian tradition is to buy from local artisans. The artisanal food movement here in the States has worked a little differently, often with chefs making a hard-to-find ingredient until the small-scale producers turn up to help keep the restaurant walk-ins full. Buying my burrata means I can turn my focus to other products that I've had trouble finding, such as fresh-cured olives, jams made without pectin, sun-dried tomato conserve . . . and the list goes on and on.

I know that domestic burrata will be more widely available in a few years, but until then you can order directly from Vito and Monica by calling them at (626) 444-6015. Their cheese is expensive because it's fragile and requires overnight shipping. Vito doesn't like taking credit cards, so be prepared to prepay or have your burrata shipped C.O.D. For imported burrata, try the A.G. Ferrari stores.

Burrata tastes best within 48 hours of being made; after 72 hours it will have lost some of its fresh, delicate flavor, so when it arrives don't wait to cook with it.

Torn Figs and Burrata

SERVES 6

This is a perfect example of how having burrata on hand means you don't need a recipe: You just need to figure out what else you want on the plate.

Wine Pairing: Pinot Grigio

¼ cup extra-virgin olive oil,
    plus more for drizzling
3 fresh rosemary sprigs
About 18 ripe figs, preferably Mission
12 ounces (3 balls) burrata
Sea salt, preferably gray salt
Freshly ground black pepper

Heat a small saucepan over medium heat, add the ¼ cup olive oil, and sauté the rosemary until crisp. Transfer the rosemary to a paper towel to drain and cool for at least 10 minutes. Strip the leaves from the stems (and discard the stems). Tear each fig into 4 pieces and divide among 6 plates. Tear each ball of burrata in half and add a half to each plate with the figs. Sprinkle crispy rosemary on top, season with salt and pepper, and drizzle with olive oil.

WATERMELON VARIATION: Substitute chunks of icy-cold watermelon or any melon for the figs.

Burrata Caprese with Heirloom Tomatoes, Basil Oil, and Balsamic "Caviar"

SERVES 6

Executive sous-chef Ryan McIlwraith helped me solve a problem that I've always had with a classic caprese. Normally, when you drizzle on the vinegar and then take that first bite, the wash of vinegar in your mouth blocks the more subtle flavors of the tomatoes and the cheese. But mix the balsamico with gelatin, and it's easy to create these wild little caviar bubbles of flavor. You take the first bite, fully taste the cheese and the tomatoes, and then get a tiny splash of vinegar at just the right moment. Pure balsamic exhilaration.

When I first set out to make the balsamic "caviar," I used medical equipment to get pearls the right size, but we've figured out an easier technique. I think of this as how your *nonna* would make these pearls if she were into molecular gastronomy. The pearls are easier than you'd expect, but if you'd rather not make the caviar, reduce some balsamic vinegar to a syrup and drizzle that over your caprese instead.

Wine Pairing: Falanghina, a white wine from Campania

10 to 12 heirloom tomatoes,
    preferably 4 large and 6 small,
    at peak of season (about 2 pounds)
12 ounces (3 balls) burrata
6 tablespoons Basil Oil (page 28)
Sea salt, preferably gray salt
Freshly ground black pepper
6 tablespoons Balsamic "Caviar" (facing page)

Cut the large tomatoes into ½-inch-thick slices and then cut the slices in half. Cut the smaller tomatoes into wedges and arrange on the plates so each serving shows a variety of colors and sizes, half-slices and wedges. Tear each burrata ball in half and place one half on each plate. Drizzle the tomatoes with basil oil and season with salt and pepper. Sprinkle a good amount of the "caviar" on each salad and serve.

BALSAMIC "CAVIAR"
MAKES 2 CUPS

You can buy a caviar maker shown below from Chef Rubber (see Resources) to help form the small pearls. If you don't have the caviar maker, use a squeeze bottle.

Gold gelatin sheets (also called *leaves*) are the key here; don't use the silver or bronze, because they bloom differently.

You can try various types of vinegar with this recipe. I've had great success with red wine vinegar and sherry vinegar. I've also made this from a good Cabernet, which is show-stopping.

You need a very light, neutral oil here that won't add flavor to the pearls. Grapeseed oil is best, but if you don't have that use canola oil. You can use any tall pitcher to chill the oil, but we find it's easiest to use a clean, empty half-gallon milk container. When you're done making the pearls, you can save the oil for another use.

6 cups grapeseed or canola oil
2 cups balsamic vinegar, sherry vinegar,
    or red wine vinegar
15 gold gelatin sheets (see Resources)
3 to 5 cups ice water

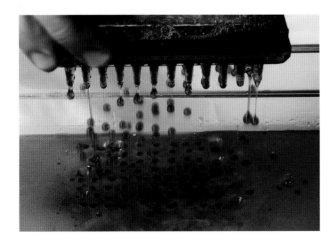

Pour the oil into a clean, empty, half-gallon milk carton. Put it in the freezer for about 1 hour. The oil will turn cloudy and almost become icy.

Bring the vinegar to a boil in a medium saucepan over medium-high heat. Reduce the heat and simmer for 1 minute. Turn off the heat.

Place the gelatin sheets in a stainless-steel roasting pan or a nonreactive rimmed baking sheet. Pour enough ice water over them just to cover. Let the sheets soften for about 5 minutes. Lift the gelatin from the water and squeeze out any water that you can. Discard the water left in the pan. Add the softened gelatin to the warm vinegar. Whisk gently over medium heat until the liquid returns to a boil, then remove from the heat. Pour through a fine-mesh sieve. Let stand for about 1 hour or until it's about room temperature, but don't let it turn solid. Don't try to speed the cooling with an ice bath. Just let the mixture cool naturally in a cool place.

If you have a caviar maker, place it in the pan with the vinegar mixture. Remove the cold oil from the freezer, pour the vinegar mixture into the caviar maker, and follow the instructions in the Chef's Note, below.

If using a squeeze bottle, make sure it has a narrow tip. Fill with the vinegar mixture and let it rest in the freezer for at least 2 minutes. Holding the squeeze bottle over the cold oil, very gently squeeze out one bead at a time, moving the bottle so the drops fall apart from each other. Transfer the container of oil with the vinegar bubbles to the freezer for 2 minutes.

Using a large fine-mesh sieve, gently strain the little beads, and then transfer them carefully into a shallow dish. Cover and refrigerate immediately. The "caviar" should be used the same day it's made.

CHEF'S NOTE: Our caviar maker is a device that's like sixty small squeeze bottles set in a large square attached to a syringe. When you squeeze the liquid into the square with the syringe, sixty little soon-to-be-caviar drops fall at the same time into the chilled oil. A squeeze bottle with a narrow tip does the exact same thing, but only 1 drop at a time. For the home cook making 6 to 10 servings, a squeeze bottle works fine; if you fall in love with caviar making (and you might), you may want to invest in the device.

Roasted Butternut Squash and Mushrooms with Burrata

SERVES 6

I love that burrata complements rich, caramel-ized autumn vegetables just as easily as it dresses up summer tomatoes, figs, or water-melon. Because it's so light, it adds the perfect fresh, creamy note to the plate. You can use any combination of mushrooms here. I like matsutakes, chanterelles, shiitakes, or morels but use what looks best at the farmers' market or in the produce section.

I give the squash a little heat on the stove top before I put it in the oven to roast.

Wine Pairing: A fruity Napa Valley Cabernet

2 tablespoons unsalted butter
2 tablespoons extra-virgin olive oil
5 cups 1-inch cubes butternut squash
   (about 2½ pounds)

BROWN-BUTTER VINAIGRETTE

6 tablespoons unsalted butter
1 tablespoon minced fresh sage
2 tablespoons balsamic vinegar
Pinch of sea salt, preferably gray salt,
   or kosher salt

2 tablespoons unsalted butter,
   plus ½ tablespoon if needed
2 tablespoons extra-virgin olive oil
3½ cups mushrooms, any variety, preferably wild
2 shallots, thinly sliced
Sea salt, preferably gray salt
Freshly ground black pepper
12 ounces (3 balls) burrata

Preheat the oven to 400°F. Heat a large ovenproof skillet over high heat and add the butter and the olive oil. When the butter foams, add the squash and cook, shaking the pan occasionally, until cara-melized and lightly browned, about 3 minutes. Slide the pan into the oven and roast until a deeper brown on the edges, about 20 minutes.

FOR THE VINAIGRETTE: Heat a small sauté pan over medium heat, add the butter, and when it foams, brown the sage for just a minute, and then pour in the vinegar and let it reduce by half. Don't stir or touch it. Just keep it at a simmer, gently reducing until thickened. When it's the consistency of a light syrup, add the salt. Turn off the heat but leave the pan on the stove while you sauté the mushrooms.

Heat a medium sauté pan or skillet over medium-high heat and add the 2 tablespoons butter and 2 tablespoons olive oil. When the butter foams, add the mushrooms and sauté until they begin to release their water, about 8 minutes. Add the shallots to the pan and sauté until brown, 3 to 4 minutes, tossing so they cook evenly. Season with salt and pepper and add another ½ tablespoon of butter if they look dry.

Divide the squash and the mushrooms evenly among 6 plates. Tear the burrata into pieces, scattering them over the vegetables. Drizzle with the vinaigrette.

CABERNET VARIATION: Make Cabernet caviar using Cabernet instead of vinegar in the recipe on page 55. Top each plate with 1 tablespoon of the caviar and some minced fresh chives.

"Angry" Ahi Tuna Crudo

SERVES 6

*a salt slab—
to season and keep cold*

In the United States, soy sauce and sushi are inseparable, but in Japan, sashimi would never get dunked in soy. At Bottega, we ignore the soy sauce, bring out the salt slab, and finish with an "angry" sauce of chiles, basil, garlic, and orange. Serving sashimi on a slab of salt seasons the fish—giving the underside a kiss of salt—while keeping the fish cold, because the salt acts as an insulator. See Resources if you can't find a salt slab, or put your plate in the freezer so it's extra cold before you serve the fish on it.

Ask your fishmonger to cut the tuna into brick-shaped rectangles, each about 2 inches long.

You can make the sauce up to an hour beforehand and keep it at room temperature.

Wine Pairing: Riesling

"ANGRY" SAUCE
⅓ cup extra-virgin olive oil
4 garlic cloves, finely sliced
1 tablespoon finely sliced seeded serrano chile
1½ cups fresh basil leaves
Sea salt, preferably gray salt
Freshly ground black pepper
1 tablespoon julienned orange zest

1 pound sashimi-grade bigeye
   or sushi-grade tuna, cut into 2-inch bricks
6 salt slabs for serving, or fleur de sel for sprinkling

FOR THE SAUCE: In a large sauté pan or skillet, heat the olive oil over high heat and add the garlic. As soon as it begins to color, add the chile and sauté for 10 seconds, then get ready to add the basil leaves. Basil leaves hold water, so they'll pop when you toss them into the hot pan. Stand back! Sauté until crispy, 1 to 2 minutes, either flipping or stirring the contents of the pan with a wooden spoon. Season with salt and pepper, remove from the heat, and stir in the orange zest.

Cut the tuna into ⅛-inch-thick slices and fan the slices on each salt slab or chilled plate. If not using salt slabs, season lightly with the best salt you have. Top with a little of the "angry" sauce.

The Four Key Relationships in Cooking

- Your produce guy (or gal)
- Your butcher (not your meat cutter)
- Your fishmonger
- Your wine merchant

If you want to put great food on your table, these are the relationships you need to nurture. It's not enough to recognize these people—know their names. Bring them something during the holidays. Ask their advice frequently. They'll tell you when something's great, they'll help you special-order, they'll teach you. If you don't have a relationship with these people, you will be limited in what you can buy.

Special-ordering is always smarter than going into the store the day you're cooking and choosing from the case. If you know you want to serve lamb to ten people, the first person to talk to is your butcher, days beforehand if possible.

Chiarello Vineyards wine maker Thomas Brown, one of Napa's huge young stars! also makes Rivers Marie, Outpost, and Schrader.

Swordfish Polpettini (Swordfish Meatballs with Fisherman's Sauce)

MAKES ABOUT 2 DOZEN POLPETTINI;
SERVES 6 TO 8

One of the great ways to enjoy pricey favorites like swordfish and not break the bank is to do what the Italians do—make meatballs! One pound of swordfish, which normally feeds three or four people, can now feed eight. Not only are these meatballs a big hit at Bottega, they helped me win my first quickfire challenge on *Top Chef Masters*. You can serve it the way we do at Bottega, with all the bells and whistles, such as my Calabrian Mayo, or make it simple and just serve the polpettini with the Fisherman's Sauce. This sauce is so good, you'll turn to it often for fillets, cooked crab and shrimp, and in the brodetto on page 134.

I prefer anchovies and capers that have been salt-packed; rinse the capers and soak both anchovies and capers in cold water for 30 minutes before using. These polpettini are versatile: try skewering them like the lamb spiedini on page 66, or topping them with tomato sauce and gently baking them in the oven. They even make a good lasagna if you use béchamel without any cheese and a seafood-based tomato sauce.

You can form and refrigerate these balls the morning you plan to serve them, but give them 30 minutes to come almost to room temperature before you begin cooking them.

Wine Pairing: Nero d'Avola

FISHERMAN'S SAUCE
¼ cup extra-virgin olive oil
1 yellow onion, thinly sliced lengthwise
4 garlic cloves, minced
6 minced anchovy fillets, preferably salt-packed anchovies, soaked in cold water for 30 minutes, drained, and bones removed before mincing
1 bay leaf
2 tablespoons capers, preferably salt-packed, rinsed and soaked in cold water for 30 minutes
Tomato Passata (see Note, page 214)

CALABRIAN MAYO
2 large egg yolks at room temperature
1 tablespoon fresh lemon juice, plus more to taste
1 cup extra-virgin olive oil at room temperature
1 to 2 teaspoons Calabrian chile paste (see Resources), or ¼ to ½ teaspoon red pepper flakes
½ teaspoon minced garlic
1 teaspoon sea salt, preferably gray salt
Freshly ground black pepper

POLPETTINI
2 pounds swordfish (preferably line caught) fillets or "trim"
2 cups Salsa Verde (page 26), plus more for garnish
¼ cup extra-virgin olive oil, plus more for garnish
1 large egg, beaten, plus 3 large eggs
1½ cups Dried Bread Crumbs (page 35)
1 teaspoon Calabrian chile paste, or ¼ teaspoon red pepper flakes
1½ teaspoon kosher salt or sea salt, preferably gray salt
½ teaspoon freshly ground black pepper
¼ cup grated pecorino cheese
2 tablespoons minced Preserved Meyer Lemons (page 34), or 1 tablespoon grated lemon zest
1 cup all-purpose flour
1½ cups panko (Japanese bread crumbs)
Peanut, corn, or canola oil for deep-frying
Coarsely chopped fresh flat-leaf parsley for garnish

hot-water process it, according to manufacturer's instructions for your canning jars.

FOR THE CALABRIAN MAYO: With a hand-held mixer or whisk, beat the egg yolks with the 1 tablespoon lemon juice until frothy. Gradually beat in the olive oil just a few drops at a time until the mixture begins to emulsify, then beat in the remaining oil in a steady stream. Beat in 1 teaspoon of the chile paste, then taste and decide if you'd like more. Blend in the garlic, add the salt, and season with pepper. Set aside. If covered and refrigerated this keeps for 2 days.

FOR THE POLPETTINI: With your fingers, coat the swordfish pieces with 1 cup of the salsa verde. Heat a large sauté pan or skillet over medium-high heat, add ¼ cup of the olive oil, and when the oil is hot, add the coated swordfish pieces. Shake the pan occasionally to prevent the fish from sticking. When the fish is cooked halfway through, after about 4 minutes, use a metal spatula to lift each piece and turn it, cooking the other side for about 3 minutes. Transfer to a baking sheet and spread the pieces out to cool. When cool enough to handle, transfer the fish to a large bowl and squash the fish with your hands, but don't overdo it. You still want to see some distinct fish pieces. Add the 1 beaten egg, the bread crumbs, chile paste, salt, pepper, cheese, lemon, and the remaining 1 cup salsa verde and stir with your hands or a spoon until well blended. Divide the fish mixture into chunks the size of a golf ball and roll into balls. Refrigerate for 15 minutes.

While the fish chills, set up a dredging station, pouring the flour, the remaining 3 eggs, and panko into separate shallow containers. Beat the eggs lightly. Dip each fish ball first in the flour, then the egg, and finally the panko and set on a platter.

In a large, heavy pot, heat 3 inches of oil to 375°F on a deep-fat thermometer. Cook 6 to 8 polpettini at a time for 3 to 5 minutes, or until they're a deep golden brown. Using a wire skimmer or a slotted spoon, transfer to paper towels to drain. Spoon the fisherman's sauce onto individual plates, add 3 or 4 piping hot polpettini, top with salsa verde, use a pastry bag or a squeeze bottle to place a few ribbons of Calabrian mayo over the top, drizzle olive oil around the plate, and finish with a sprinkling of parsley.

FOR THE FISHERMAN'S SAUCE: Heat a large sauté pan or skillet over medium heat and add the olive oil. Add the onion and garlic and sauté until the onion gives off its liquid, about 3 minutes. Reduce the heat to low and let the mixture cook for about 6 minutes; do not brown.

Add the anchovies, bay leaf, and capers and cook over medium-low heat until the anchovies have melted into the onion, about 4 minutes, stirring occasionally. When you add the tomatoes, the onion will stop cooking, so taste and be sure it's completely tender first. Add the passata and simmer for 20 to 30 minutes. Taste for seasoning, but be careful about adding more salt, because even soaked anchovies bring salt to the sauce. Return to a boil, then reduce heat and simmer for another 20 minutes. Remove from the heat and let cool. Once it's cool, you can refrigerate it for up to 5 days. At this point, you can also freeze it or

Budini di Pecorino Fulvi
with Oven-Roasted Rapini

SERVES 6

This dish starts with a food that is sometimes viewed as humble and elevates it to a higher plane. Pecorino is a "low-cotton" food, meaning it's what you eat when you're not dressed in your finest clothing. But made into a cream-laden pudding, it's black-tie worthy, and the salty, satiny *budino* set against the rapini is an ideal contrast.

Wine Pairing: Vermentino

BUDINI
Butter for preparing soufflé cups
3 cups 1-inch cubes pugliese bread
   (about 3 ounces bread, crust removed)
1 cup whole milk
1 cup heavy cream
1 cup grated pecorino cheese, preferably Fulvi
3 large egg yolks

RAPINI
2 bunches rapini (broccoli rabe), about 2 pounds,
   the bottom 3 to 4 inches trimmed
¼ cup extra-virgin olive oil
2 garlic cloves, minced
2 teaspoons Calabrian chile paste,
   or ¼ teaspoon red pepper flakes
½ teaspoon red pepper flakes
Sea salt, preferably gray salt
Freshly ground black pepper
Juice of ½ lemon

BRUSCHETTA
Six ¾-inch-thick slices country-style bread
Extra-virgin olive oil for brushing
Sea salt, preferably gray salt
Freshly ground black pepper

FOR THE BUDINI: Butter six 4-ounce soufflé cups. Have ready a roasting pan in which you can fit the soufflé cups. Put the bread cubes in a bowl. In a medium saucepan, combine the milk and cream and bring to a boil over medium heat. Whisk in the grated cheese. Strain through a coarse-mesh sieve into the bowl of bread cubes. Let the bread rest in the cream mixture until it comes to room temperature, about 30 minutes.

Preheat the oven to 280°F. Using an immersion blender or in a regular blender, blend the bread and cream. While blending, add the egg yolks one at a time, blending after each. Pour into the buttered soufflé cups. Set the cups in the roasting pan and pour in hot water to come halfway up the sides. Bake until the budini are set and just beginning to puff, 30 to 35 minutes. Siphon some of the hot water out of the pan, then remove it from the oven. Carefully take the soufflé cups from the water and allow the budini to cool for 15 minutes. These are best served warm; if made earlier, reheat by pouring boiling water into the roasting pan; place the soufflé cups in the hot water and heat in a 300°F oven for about 20 minutes.

FOR THE RAPINI: Preheat the oven to 375°F. Bring a large pot of water to a boil and add 1 tablespoon of salt per quart of water. Add the rapini and cook for 4 minutes; stop while it's still crunchy. Drain and squeeze out the excess water with tongs. Spread the rapini out on a sheet pan to cool.

Heat a large ovenproof sauté pan or skillet over medium heat. Pour in the oil and, when it's hot, sauté the garlic just until golden. Stir in the chile paste and red pepper flakes, then add the rapini to the pan. With tongs, turn the rapini to coat evenly. Season with salt and pepper. Transfer to the oven and roast for 10 minutes. If too dry, add 1 teaspoon water. Serve the rapini at room temperature, or heat in the oven before serving. Give it a squeeze of lemon juice just before you eat it.

FOR THE BRUSCHETTA: On a grill or under your broiler, toast the bread slices on both sides. Brush with olive oil and sprinkle with salt and pepper.

Carefully run a knife around the edge of each soufflé cup to loosen the budini. Place a plate over the top and turn over swiftly. Gently shake the cup if the budino doesn't slide right out. Serve with the bruschetta and rapini on the side.

Cooking as a Team Sport

The kitchen at Bottega is small, and in a way that's a good thing, because there's a close bond within a restaurant crew that makes me glad to come to work. Is there yelling? Yes, sometimes. Is there laughter? Yes, every day. In the nine years since leaving Tra Vigne and coming to Bottega, this is what I missed the most: a camaraderie, a shared goal of making sure that the people sitting at our tables this evening want to be here and nowhere else on the planet. This is not an easy thing to pull off, but when you come to Bottega and see the warmth and the dedication of the Bottega team, you will understand why I am so proud of them.

Bring camaraderie into your kitchen, too. The rainy afternoons I spent sitting at the table talking to my mom stay with me even though she is no longer here. Pull friends and family into the kitchen with you; the time will fly and the food will be fantastic.

Murph - Northern California waiter legend

Grilled Lamb
Spiedini Agrodolce

MAKES 10 SPIEDINI PLUS 1 TEST FOR THE COOK;
SERVES 4 TO 6

The flavors in these spiedini are intense and beautiful. This is one of my favorite dishes, inspired by Francis Mallmann, a world-famous chef from Argentina. I've roasted onions in coals before but never eggplant. The roasted eggplant is puréed, and the silky mixture is folded into the meat, which is shaped onto skewers. This technique seemed a natural for a dish of Middle Eastern spices, lamb, and wine-soaked raisins—a Southern Italy combination that reflects the flavors of the ancient spice route.

I grew up next to Assyrians who made a variety of lamb kabobs using whole chunks of meat but also spiced ground lamb shaped around the end of a twig like a hot dog on a stick, so this idea brought back flavors from my childhood. For this technique, wide, flat skewers work better because the spiedini is less likely to slip off into the fire.

The next time you have after-dinner coals still glowing and eggplant and onions right there in your kitchen, bury the vegetables in the coals with their skins on (pierce the eggplant first) and let them cook. Then, when cool, pass the eggplant's flesh through a sieve for a rich, silky purée that's folded into the ground lamb. The lamb has a smokiness that's both inside the meat, from the eggplant purée, and outside, from the grill. You'll want some brightness against all that smoky sultriness, and the watercress salad is exactly right.

This is food best cooked outdoors, in hot but dying coals in your grill, but you can also cook them in your oven on a baking sheet. You can't roast them over a wood-burning fire or they'll taste smoldery. You want to bury them in the hot embers. You could cook them under a 500°F broiler too, but they won't

have the same depth of flavor. If you don't want to stand outside grilling in the dead of winter, try roasting the vegetables for these meat skewers in your fireplace. Some of my best dinner parties have taken place on the floor in front of the hearth.

Wine Pairing: Russian River Pinot Noir

ROASTED-VEGETABLE PURÉE
2 Italian eggplants with stems, unpeeled
1 large yellow onion, unpeeled
2 tablespoons extra-virgin olive oil
1 teaspoon minced fresh thyme
1 tablespoon sea salt, preferably gray salt
Pinch of freshly ground black pepper

SPIEDINI
¼ cup dry white wine
¼ cup raisins
1 pound ground lamb, or a combination
    of ¼ pound ground pork and ¾ pound
    ground lamb
Sea salt, preferably gray salt
Freshly ground black pepper
⅓ cup reserved roasted-vegetable purée
Extra-virgin olive oil for drizzling

WATERCRESS SALAD
1 tablespoon extra-virgin olive oil
2 teaspoons grated lemon zest
1 teaspoon fresh lemon juice
2 packed cups watercress sprigs
Sea salt, preferably gray salt
Freshly ground black pepper

roast in the oven until a skewer slides easily into the eggplant's center. Remove the vegetables from the coals or oven and set aside until cool to the touch. Cut the eggplants in half lengthwise and scoop out the center, being careful not to get any ash into the flesh; place the flesh in a food processor. Peel the onion and add it to the food processor as well; purée until smooth.

Heat a large sauté pan over medium-high heat and pour in the oil. When it's hot, add 2 cups of the purée, the thyme, salt, and pepper and sauté until almost dry, cooking out the excess liquid. Strain the mixture through a sieve, pushing the flesh through with the back of a large spoon and occasionally cleaning the sieve. (This is a pain, but worth the effort for the silky result.) Reserve ⅓ cup of the purée for the spiedini.

FOR THE SPIEDINI: Prepare a hot fire in a charcoal grill, preheat a gas grill to high, or preheat a broiler to 500°F. Soak eleven wooden skewers in water for 30 minutes (one skewer is for testing). Pour the wine over the raisins and let them soak for at least 15 minutes.

In a large bowl, combine the meat, ½ teaspoon salt, ½ teaspoon pepper, and the ⅓ cup vegetable purée. Add the wine-soaked raisins and mix until well incorporated. Shape about 2 tablespoons of the meat mixture into a small torpedo around one end of a skewer; season with salt and pepper.

Cook the meat skewer gently on the grill or under the broiler for about 4 minutes, turning to cook about 1 minute on each of the four sides; this is your test skewer. Taste and adjust the seasoning of the meat mixture if necessary. Shape the remaining 10 spiedini, drizzle each with olive oil, and season with salt and pepper. Gently grill all the spiedini on all four sides, about 1 minute per side.

FOR THE ROASTED-VEGETABLE PURÉE: Let a charcoal fire or wood fire burn down to glowing coals that are just beginning to lose their red color, or preheat the oven to 500°F. Pierce both eggplants with a fork so you don't run the risk of an eggplant explosion. Push the eggplants and onion into the hot embers so they are completely buried and cook until the eggplants are soft (test with a skewer), 20 to 40 minutes depending on the heat of the coals. Or, place them on a rimmed baking sheet and

FOR THE WATERCRESS SALAD: Whisk together the olive oil, lemon zest, and lemon juice and toss with the watercress sprigs. Season with salt and pepper.

Spoon some of the purée off-center on each plate. Rest 2 skewers on top, just touching the purée. Nestle some of the watercress salad to one side.

CHEF'S NOTE: Exceptional watercress can be hard to come by. At Bottega, we use Sausalito Springs watercress (see Resources).

Ancient-Grain Polenta "Under Glass," with Mushrooms and Balsamic Sauce

SERVES 6

When we first opened Bottega, there was a group of women dining one night, spanning a few generations. (I happen to find that incredibly sexy: a group of strong, beautiful women of all ages.) I brought them this polenta just to taste; they each took a bite, then they looked at each other and ordered three more.

"Why polenta under glass?" one of the women asked. A glass dome used to be one way to glorify rare, costly dishes, like pheasant under glass. To me, polenta—that most peasant of all peasant foods—is just as glorious. This recipe gives polenta its due. This is creamy like you've never known creamy—it's almost like a warm, savory, textured crème brûlée with a light, thin crust of cheese instead of sweetness. Add caramelized wild mushrooms and a dark, deep sauce and you have a sexy, sexy combination . . . but still no match for that group of women. (Note to self: If I could make a dish that sexy, I'd really have my game on.)

Instead of a fancy glass dome, I serve this in a glass canning jar because it reminds me of the skill and resourcefulness of all the women in my life who've made royalty-worthy food from simple backyard ingredients.

The polenta is best made an hour or two before you plan to serve it; cover it with a sheet of waxed paper smoothed onto the surface. If you'd like to make it the day before, you might need to add some liquid when you heat it. Definitely make the balsamic sauce the day before, so you can chill it overnight and lift off the fat; then rewarm it and add a final touch of butter just before serving. The Parm crostini can be made a day or two ahead of time as well.

Wine Pairing: Sangiovese

BALSAMIC SAUCE
2 cups balsamic vinegar
1 shallot, chopped
¼ cup extra-virgin olive oil
2 cups coarsely chopped yellow onions
1 cup coarsely chopped carrots
1 cup coarsely chopped celery
2 bay leaves
3 cups dry red wine
8 cups Roasted Chicken Stock (page 18),
    or veal or rabbit stock
6 black peppercorns
4 tablespoons unsalted butter

ANCIENT-GRAIN POLENTA
1½ cups heavy cream (see Chef's Note, facing page)
3 cups cold water
Pinch of sea salt, preferably gray salt
1 cup fine-ground polenta
½ teaspoon freshly grated nutmeg
½ cup shredded fontina cheese
¼ cup freshly grated Parmesan cheese

MUSHROOMS
3 tablespoons extra-virgin olive oil,
    plus more if needed
10 ounces cultivated or wild mushrooms
    such as shiitakes, chanterelles, and morels,
    cleaned and trimmed (stem shiitakes)
Pinch of sea salt, preferably gray salt
Freshly ground black pepper
½ teaspoon minced garlic
½ teaspoon minced fresh thyme
1 teaspoon minced fresh flat-leaf parsley

PARM CROSTINI
1 cup freshly grated Parmesan cheese

FOR THE BALSAMIC SAUCE: In a small saucepan, combine the vinegar and shallot. Bring to a simmer over medium heat and cook until reduced by half, about 10 minutes. (Watch this, because at the end, the reduction process speeds up.) Remove from the heat and set aside.

In a large saucepan, heat the olive oil over medium-low heat and add the onions, carrots, celery, and bay leaves. Cook, stirring occasionally, until

any hint of grittiness, 15 to 20 minutes. Remove from the heat and stir in the nutmeg, fontina, and Parmesan.

FOR THE MUSHROOMS: Heat a large sauté pan or skillet over high heat, add the 3 tablespoons oil, and heat until it shimmers. Add the mushrooms but no more than two deep anywhere in the pan; if you pile them on, they will steam instead of brown. Cook the mushrooms in two pans if you have to, using about 2 tablespoons oil per pan. Mushrooms over heat can be temperamental: don't stir them, don't salt them, and don't turn them until the bottom layer is brown, about 2 minutes. Reduce the heat to medium and season with salt and pepper. Stir in the garlic and sauté until the garlic shows a light brown color. Add the thyme, and listen to it crackle in the pan. Add the parsley and toss. Remove from the heat and set aside. You can cook the mushrooms up to 1 hour before serving.

FOR THE PARM CROSTINI: Preheat the oven to 425°F. Line a baking sheet with a silicone mat or parchment paper. If you have them, place six 3-inch ring molds on the prepared pan. Inside each ring mold, evenly spoon about 2 tablespoons grated Parmesan. (To make without ring molds, spoon 6 mounds of Parmesan about 2 inches apart, and spread into thin, even rounds. The free-form crostini won't fit as smoothly on the top of your polenta as the ring-molded ones, but just angle them in or trim to fit.)

Slide the pan into the oven and bake until the Parmesan is melted into disks that are just beginning to brown, 3 to 5 minutes. Store these stacked in an airtight container for up to 3 days.

Spoon ½ cup polenta into each of 6 half-pint French glass canning jars with attached lids. Place 1 Parmesan crostini on top, either neatly resting on the surface of the polenta or slid into the surface at an angle. Divide the mushrooms among the jars. Serve the balsamic sauce at the table and let guests pour a few tablespoons of it per serving. Pour any remaining sauce into small creamers or pitchers so guests can pour on more sauce as they wish.

CHEF'S NOTES: Consider the polenta recipe a template; you can substitute any liquid for the cream. Try it with chicken stock, tomato sauce, or vegetable juice.

the vegetables are a deep brown, about 20 minutes. Add the red wine and reduce the heat to medium-low. Cook to reduce by half, about 10 minutes.

While the vegetables are cooking, pour the stock into a stockpot, add the peppercorns, and cook over high heat until the liquid is reduced by half, about 15 minutes. Pour the reduced stock into the pan with the red wine and vegetables. Cook for 5 minutes over medium heat. Add the reduced balsamic vinegar. Remove from the heat, stir in the butter, and set aside.

FOR THE POLENTA: In a large, heavy saucepan, combine the cream, water, and salt. Bring to a boil over high heat and then reduce the heat to medium. Gradually whisk in the polenta in a slow, steady stream. Whisk until the liquid boils again and the grains are suspended in the liquid. Keep whisking so the polenta doesn't scorch. Once it comes to a simmer, switch to a wooden spoon and stir every few minutes until the polenta is creamy without

Fritto Misto di Calamari with Aioli Nero

SERVES 6

Made with the ink of squid, garlic, egg yolk, and lemon juice, *aioli nero* completes the flavor of the calamari. The ink is salty, so you probably won't need to add more salt to the aioli.

If at all possible, use fresh calamari and ask the fishmonger to clean them for you. You can buy squid ink from your fishmonger or grocery stores such as Whole Foods, although you may have to order in advance.

Wine Pairing: Prosecco, Champagne, or a vintage California sparkling wine

AIOLI NERO
1 cup dry white wine
1 shallot, finely sliced lengthwise and julienned
¼ teaspoon black peppercorns
1 bay leaf
1½ tablespoons squid ink (see Resources)
2 egg yolks
1 teaspoon Dijon mustard
1½ teaspoons fresh lemon juice
1½ teaspoons Calabrian chile paste (see Resources), or ¼ teaspoon red pepper flakes, plus more for top of aioli (optional)
1 teaspoon minced garlic
1½ cups extra-virgin olive oil
1 to 2 tablespoons room temperature water, if needed

Peanut, corn, or canola oil for deep-frying
1 pound calamari
¾ cup buttermilk
1½ cups Fritti Flour (facing page)
Lemon halves for squeezing

FOR THE AIOLI: In a small saucepan, combine the wine, shallot, peppercorns, and bay leaf. Bring to a simmer over medium heat and cook until almost all the liquid has evaporated, about 5 minutes. Add the squid ink and heat just until it begins to simmer, to take the astringent edge off. Remove from the heat and strain the liquid. Set aside and let cool.

In a medium bowl, whisk together the egg yolks, mustard, lemon juice, chile paste, and garlic. Once it emulsifies, you can whisk in the oil in a slow, steady stream. If it gets too oily or separates, stop adding oil and whisk while adding the water just a few drops at a time until it comes back together. Whisk in the squid ink mixture until smooth and even in color. Spoon the aioli into small ramekins and top with a spoonful of Calabrian chile paste, if you like. Refrigerate until the calamari is cooked.

Rinse the calamari under cold running water and lightly pat dry with paper towels. With your fingers, locate the beak and make an incision behind it. Pull out the beak and discard. Use a knife to remove the backbone. Remove the flipper and scrape both sides of the squid inside and out with your knife blade. Cut the calamari in half, removing the head with one slice while leaving the tentacles still attached together at one end. Slice the tentacles into rings. Slice into the body but don't cut it all the way through; you just want to open, fold it back, and scrape both sides. Cut in half, then rinse in cool running water and pat dry again.

In a large, heavy pot, heat 3 inches of oil to 375ºF on a deep-fat thermometer. While the oil is heating, combine the calamari and buttermilk in a large bowl. Put the calamari in a sieve and shake off the excess buttermilk. Sprinkle with the fritti flour to cover and shake off the excess. Resprinkle and shake two more times.

Add a dozen pieces or so of calamari to the hot oil and cook for 45 seconds, or until light brown but still quite tender and soft. Using a slotted spoon or wire skimmer, transfer to paper towels to drain. Serve at once, with lemon halves for squeezing.

CHEF'S NOTE: When I'm making a mayonnaise, I roll up a dish towel and place my bowl in the center; this helps keep the bowl in place and makes whisking easier. You can also use a hand-held mixer or immersion blender to blend while you slowly add the oil.

Cauliflower Fritto

SERVES 6

Fritti Flour

MAKES 5 CUPS

Because this coating stays so crisp, it allows you to fry a little ahead of time and keep your food warm in a low oven. Buttermilk is my pre-dip of choice, because it gives some body without double dipping and adds a little tanginess that I like.

Don't halve this recipe. We've found it takes at least 1 cup of Arborio rice for the blender to grind the rice properly. Make the full recipe and store any leftovers in the freezer in an airtight container for up to 6 weeks.

1 cup Arborio rice
1 cup semolina
3 cups all-purpose flour
2 tablespoons table salt (yes, you read that right: table salt here, sea salt is too heavy for this blend)
1 teaspoon freshly ground black pepper

In a blender, grind the rice until very fine, about the consistency of powdered gelatin. Shake the ground rice into a large bowl and add the semolina, all-purpose flour, table salt, and pepper. Toss until well mixed.

Fritto Misto Flour—
The Story of One Man's Coating

One slow January at Tra Vigne, we took to grinding every single thing in our storeroom to see which ingredients might make the best coating. We ground corn and beans, white rice, brown rice, and black rice. The clear-on favorite was Arborio rice. Its sugar content gives a caramelization that can't be beat by any other coating we've tried.

This is a little different from our traditional fritto misto coating. Beer and sparkling water make the batter lighter and fluffier, which works well for the cauliflower or any cruciferous vegetable.

Beer Pairing: A toasty Italian ale or Anchor Steam

4 cups cauliflower florets
    (about ½ large head or 1 ½ pounds)
2 egg whites
1 cup all-purpose flour
1 teaspoon sea salt, preferably gray salt
Pinch of freshly ground black pepper
½ cup beer
½ cup sparkling water
1 tablespoon extra-virgin olive oil
1 teaspoon Calabrian chile paste (see Resources), or ¼ teaspoon red pepper flakes
1 ½ tablespoons chopped fresh flat-leaf parsley
Corn, peanut, or canola oil for deep-frying

In a large pot of salted boiling water, cook the cauliflower until crisp-tender, 3 to 4 minutes. Using a slotted spoon or wire skimmer, transfer to a baking sheet to cool.

In a medium bowl, beat the egg whites until stiff, glossy peaks form. Set aside. In a large bowl, combine the flour, salt, and pepper; whisk to blend. In another bowl, mix the beer, sparkling water, olive oil, chile paste, and parsley. Add half of the liquid to the dry ingredients and whisk until smooth. Add the remaining liquid and whisk again until smooth. Gently fold the beaten egg whites into the batter.

In a large, heavy pot, heat 3 inches of oil to 375°F on a deep-fat thermometer. When the oil is just about ready, add the cauliflower to the batter and gently toss until each floret is coated.

Add a batch of the battered cauliflower to the hot oil and cook until the florets turn a light to medium brown, 4 to 5 minutes. Using a wire skimmer, transfer to paper towels to drain. Continue frying until all the cauliflower has been cooked.

CHAPTER 4

Soups and Salads

MINESTRE E INSALATE

I treat soup and salad as part of antipasti even though, in Italy, soup traditionally is served in place of risotto or pasta. At Bottega, this is what you eat while you decide on a main course.

Soup is a great first course for home cooks so you can save time to work on a killer second course like gnocchi or a whole roasted pig. Most soups let you do the prep work ahead of time, which makes life easier when you're hosting.

Soup, for me personally, often means lunch or a simple supper with some salami, cheese, and bread. A bowl of my mother's Calabrian meatball soup makes the rest of the day better. We never called it "Wedding Soup" when I was a kid; we called it "I've been a good boy soup," because the brother who was in less trouble than usual was the one who'd try to talk my mom into making it.

Salads can embrace a wide variety of dishes; don't limit yourself by thinking of salad as only leaves. Salads are a good place to step into new territory. If you treat Brussels sprouts as tiny cabbage heads and shave them, then toss them with fried Marcona almonds and sieved eggs, you have a salad like nothing you've tried before. I love that this salad is finely chopped, so each bite has a good mix of crunch and salt, egg and citrus without a leaf in sight.

Grilled radicchio is another salad that steps outside the box. The trick is to soak the radicchio in ice water, then get it on the grill when drained but still cold. I love to bite into the hot, grilled outer leaves while the inside is still fresh, crisp, and cool. Add my Tuna Conserva, which has been a part of my family's life for generations, and some perfectly cooked potatoes, and you have a salad that's traditional, satisfying, and still exciting.

Minestre e Insalate

Zuppa di Melone con Zeppole
(Melon Soup with Zeppole)

SERVES 6 TO 8, DEPENDING ON
THE SIZE OF THE SOUP CUPS

Salt makes the most of a perfect summer melon. The saltiness of the prosciutto and the Parmesan on the *zeppole* act as a trampoline, bringing up the fruit's flavor so it's bolder and more intense. Because every melon is different, you'll want to add honey, lemon juice, grappa, and salt; taste the soup; and then add more sweet, tang, or salt to suit your preference. I use cantaloupe here, but any ripe melon can be made into a beautiful soup.

What is zeppole? A savory treat from my bud Chef Dena Marino. If a donut hole were given the option, it would choose to be zeppole, an airy, savory—not sweet—Parmesan-dusted puff ball. I serve this by pouring the soup into a small bowl or glass that's been chilling in the freezer. I set the bowl on a medium oval platter and lay out thin sheets of the prosciutto. On top of that go paper-thin slices of nectarine or peach or a good sprinkling of pomegranate seeds. Finish with a good sprinkle of fresh-ground black pepper. To eat, wrap a sheet of prosciutto around the zeppole, being sure to include a fruit slice or two. Take a big bite. Put down the zeppole and sip the soup. (The extremes are appealing to me: big messy bite, small delicate sip.)

You can make this soup the night before and make the zeppole dough up to 5 hours before you'd like to cook it. Keep the dough in the refrigerator until 15 minutes before you're ready to begin cooking, and keep the soup refrigerated until you're ready to plate.

Wine Pairing: Prosecco

ZUPPA DI MELONE

8 cups 2-inch cubes cantaloupe
   (about one 5-pound melon)
2 tablespoons honey, plus more to taste
¼ cup fresh lemon juice, plus more to taste
1½ tablespoons grappa, plus more to taste
2 teaspoons sea salt, preferably gray salt,
   plus more to taste

ZEPPOLE

⅔ cup warm water (105° to 115°F)
1 teaspoon active dry yeast
1 teaspoon sugar
2 tablespoons all-purpose flour, plus 1 cup
Pinch of sea salt, preferably gray salt
1 scant teaspoon chopped fried rosemary leaves
   (see Chef's Note, facing page)
1 cup freshly grated Parmesan for rolling
Peanut, corn, or canola oil for deep-frying

18 to 24 slices prosciutto or artisan domestic ham
   for garnish
2 ripe nectarines or peaches, peeled, pitted,
   and cut into thin slices for garnish
½ cup fresh pomegranate seeds
Freshly ground black pepper
Late-harvest olive oil for drizzling (optional)

FOR THE ZEPPOLE: In a medium bowl, combine the warm water, yeast, and sugar. Stir to dissolve the yeast. Let stand for 10 to 15 minutes, or until foamy. Stir the 2 tablespoons flour into the yeast mixture and let stand for another few minutes. Whisk in the remaining 1 cup flour. Whisk in the salt and rosemary, cover with plastic wrap, and let stand in a warm spot for 15 to 20 minutes. (Use now, or cover and refrigerate the dough for up to 5 hours; remove from the refrigerator 15 minutes before you begin cooking the zeppole.)

Line a platter with paper towels. Pour the Parmesan onto a plate or into a shallow bowl.

In a large, heavy pot, heat 3 inches of oil over medium-high heat to 375°F on a deep-fat thermometer. Oil an ice-cream scoop or two large serving spoons. (The dough is sticky; without the oil coating, it's impossible to coax it off the scoop or spoon and into the cooking oil.) Scoop up about 1 tablespoon of dough and carefully drop it into the hot oil.

Add 3 to 5 more dough balls to the hot oil, making sure they're not too crowded. Cook for about 2 minutes on each side, or until golden. Using a slotted spoon, transfer them to the prepared platter to drain for a minute or so. Then roll them in the Parmesan. (Save the remaining Parmesan in your fridge for another use.)

Ladle the soup into each of 6 to 8 small, chilled bowls. Fan the prosciutto slices onto oval platters, 3 slices per serving. Top with paper-thin slices of nectarine or peach and a sprinkling of pomegranate seeds. Grind black pepper over the fruit and prosciutto (but not over the soup). If you like, drizzle a late-harvest olive oil over the soup, and serve.

CHEF'S NOTE: At Bottega, we deep-fry small branches of rosemary to remove its slightly soapy aftertaste and make this herb a little more versatile. You can either deep-fry (if you have a fryer set up), or heat 2 tablespoons of olive oil in a small sauté pan, add the rosemary still on the stem, and sauté until it begins to crisp, 30 seconds to 1 minute. Let the rosemary drain on paper towels. Strip the leaves from the stems, discard the woody stems, and blot the leaves again with paper towels. Keep any extra in an airtight jar in your pantry for up to 1 week or freeze it for a few months.

FOR THE SOUP: Purée the melon in a food processor or blender until smooth. (You may need to do this in batches if you don't have an extra-large food processor.) Pour the puréed melon into an 8-cup container. Stir in the 2 tablespoons honey, the ¼ cup lemon juice, the 1½ tablespoons grappa, and the 2 teaspoons salt. Taste and add more honey, lemon juice, grappa, or salt if needed. Refrigerate for at least 1 hour or overnight.

Shaved Brussels Sprouts Salad with Marcona Almonds and Pecorino

SERVES 6

Chef de Cuisine Nick Ritchie and I were looking for a winter salad that was more than mixed greens. He came up with the idea of shaving the Brussels sprouts. If you never thought you'd take to Brussels spouts, this will be better than the best coleslaw you've ever had.

Six dozen Brussels sprouts seems like a lot to shave, but with a mandoline this goes quickly. At Bottega, we've got both the expensive ones and the small thirty-dollar plastic version, and for this job, the inexpensive mandoline works great.

A full-flavored citrus vinaigrette ties it all together. In France, I learned that citrus peel is just as important as the juice. I've been making this dressing for decades, and it never disappoints. The trick is to use a juice extractor, which lets you juice the whole fruit, peel and all. (If you don't have one, ask the person at the juicing machine of a specialty produce market to juice the lemons and oranges for you, making sure they juice the whole fruit.) Feel free to make the vinaigrette a day or two in advance.

Marcona almonds from Spain add the crucial crunch to this salad. You can fry your own blanched almonds in a few tablespoons of olive oil with a pinch of sea salt, but it's easier to buy them already cooked in olive oil and salted.

If you don't have a sieve for the egg, don't go out and buy one: improvise. My mom was a master at using one tool for another job; try a box grater, a slotted spoon, or a colander. At home, I use my mini-chopper on the eggs.

This salad tastes best if the shaved Brussels sprouts, egg, and vinaigrette are all well chilled before you start.

Wine Pairing: Sauvignon Blanc

WHOLE-CITRUS VINAIGRETTE

2 lemons, preferably Meyer lemons
½ navel orange, or 1 small orange
1 large shallot
1½ cups olive oil (see Chef's Note, page 19)
1 teaspoon sea salt, preferably gray salt
½ teaspoon freshly ground pepper

1 dozen large eggs, hard cooked
 (see Chef's Note, page 26)
6 dozen (8 to 9 cups) Brussels sprouts
3 dozen (¾ cup) Marcona almonds, finely chopped
¼ cup grated Pecorino-Romano

FOR THE VINAIGRETTE: Use a juice extractor to juice the lemons, orange, and shallot, using the entire fruit with peel. Pour the juices into a small bowl and gradually whisk in the olive oil in a thin stream to form an emulsion. Season with the salt and pepper. Taste and adjust the seasoning. Whisk again, cover, and refrigerate for at least 30 minutes or up to 3 days. You should have about 2 cups.

At Bottega, we push the hard-cooked egg whites through the sieve, then sieve the yolks and layer the two separately when serving. If it's easier, you can sieve the whole eggs and not bother separating whites from yolks.

Using a mandoline, carefully shave each Brussels sprout, holding the stem end. You should have about 9 cups when they're all grated. In a large bowl, toss together the shaved Brussels sprouts, sieved eggs, and chopped almonds. Pour on about ¾ cup of the vinaigrette and toss again. Spoon into chilled small bowls and top with the pecorino. Top with a little more of the vinaigrette.

SUMMER VARIATION: Substitute 9 cups of julienned sugar snap peas for the shaved Brussels sprouts.

Grilled Radicchio Salad with Tuna Conserva

SERVES 6

This dish brings together parts of my child-hood and my adult life. The tuna conserva, or *tonno sott'olio* as my mother called it, was a staple, ready in our pantry at all times when I was growing up. Grilling radicchio definitely reflects how I cook today. I love how well the two flavors meet in the middle. This salad takes a page from salade niçoise, but its flavors are bolder and the presentation is more interesting.

Grilling radicchio is a technique you have to nail. Soak the radicchio in ice water for at least 30 minutes to take out some of its bitterness. In Italy, bitterness is a flavor that is acknowledged and respected. Here in the States, we tend to shy away from anything bitter; soaking removes the bitterness without robbing the radicchio of its flavor. Keep the radicchio in a bowl of ice water in the refrigerator until you're ready to grill. You'll grill the radicchio until almost black outside but still cool inside—the contrast is fantastic. You can grill this indoors in a cast-iron pan, but it's worth firing up your grill even in the dead of winter to get that smoky flavor. You'll be tempted to overgrill the wedges, but resist the urge. One minute per side on a hot, hot grill is about all it takes.

Wine Pairing: Unoaked Chardonnay

PICKLED RED ONION
½ large red onion
2 teaspoons red wine vinegar

½ pound unpeeled small fingerling potatoes

GRILLED RADICCHIO
3 heads radicchio, stems intact, cut into quarters
4 tablespoons extra-virgin olive oil, plus extra
    for brushing grill
2 tablespoons thinly sliced garlic (about 3 cloves)
6 minced anchovy fillets, preferably
    salt-packed anchovies soaked for 30 minutes,
    drained, and bones removed before mincing
2 teaspoons Calabrian chile paste, or ½ teaspoon
    red pepper flakes (see Resources)
2 teaspoons chopped capers, preferably salt-packed
    capers rinsed and soaked for 30 minutes
¼ cup sherry vinegar
2 tablespoons chopped fresh flat-leaf parsley

3 cups Tuna Conserva (page 21)
3 tablespoons extra-virgin olive oil for drizzling
1 tablespoon red wine vinegar for drizzling
Chopped fresh flat-leaf parsley for garnish

FOR THE ONION: Quarter the onion, then cut into thin slices. Toss the onion slices with your fingers to break apart. Pour on the red wine vinegar, toss again, and let stand for at least 15 minutes or up to 30 minutes. This is a very quick pickling to just smooth away a little of the onion's sharpness.

In a medium saucepan of salted boiling water, cook the potatoes until fork-tender, about 8 minutes. Drain the potatoes and cut them into quarters. Set aside.

FOR THE RADICCHIO: Soak the radicchio in ice water to cover for 30 minutes to 1 hour. Light a hot fire in a charcoal grill, preheat a gas grill to medium-high, or have ready a grill pan on the stove.

Heat a medium sauté pan or skillet over medium-high heat and add 2 tablespoons of the olive oil. When the oil is hot, add the garlic, reduce the heat to medium, and sauté until light brown, about 3 minutes. Add the anchovies and chile paste and let the anchovies melt, about 1 minute. Add the capers and sauté for another 30 seconds. Add the sherry vinegar and cook until the liquid is reduced by half. Remove the pan from the heat and gradually add the remaining 2 tablespoons olive oil while stirring. Add the parsley and let cool.

Gently squeeze the excess water from the radicchio quarters and drain on paper towels. Preheat a grill pan, if using, over high heat; brush the pan or the grill grids with oil. Use your fingers to push some of the dressing between the radicchio leaves while keeping the wedges intact. Grill the radicchio for about 1 minute on each side, or until charred. Remove from the heat and set aside.

This is not a composed salad but has a masculine edge to it, so don't get too fussy with the plating. Slide a wedge of grilled radicchio onto each plate. Top with tuna conserva so it covers part of the radicchio wedge. Add the quartered potatoes and pickled onions to the conserva. Finish with a drizzle of olive oil, a drizzle of red wine vinegar, and a light sprinkling of chopped parsley.

Roasted Beet Salad with Blue Cheese Cream

SERVES 6

You may think you've had every beet salad, but this one is different. First, roasting the beets in white wine gives them another layer of flavor; second, a blue cheese cream and an outstanding creamy pistachio vinaigrette let you come back to the beet salad without the slightest chance of boredom.

I think this vinaigrette is possibly the best dressing I've ever tasted anywhere. You can use it on many different salads.

Roast the beets the morning you plan to make this, and make the blue cheese cream and pistachio vinaigrette the day before, if you like. If the vinaigrette separates overnight in the refrigerator, use an immersion blender or standard blender to bring it back together just before serving.

Wine Pairing: Sauvignon Blanc

6 golden beets, about 1 ½ pounds
6 Chioggia beets, about 1 ½ pounds
¾ cup olive oil (see Chef's Note, page 19)
1 cup dry white wine, plus more if needed
2 teaspoons sea salt, preferably gray salt
½ teaspoon freshly ground black pepper

BLUE CHEESE CREAM
4 ounces mascarpone at room temperature
4 ounces blue cheese at room temperature
¼ cup heavy cream
Pinch of sea salt, preferably gray salt
Light grind of black pepper

CREAMY PISTACHIO VINAIGRETTE
¼ cup Champagne vinegar
2 teaspoons Dijon mustard
½ shallot, minced
2 teaspoons minced fresh thyme
2 egg yolks, plus 1 more if needed
1 cup pistachio oil (see Resources)
1 cup extra-virgin olive oil
1 tablespoon ice water, if needed
½ teaspoon sea salt, preferably gray salt
¼ teaspoon freshly ground black pepper

⅓ cup pistachios, toasted (see Chef's Note, page 188)
Chopped fresh flat-leaf parsley for garnish
1 tablespoon minced fresh tarragon for garnish
Microgreens such as micro arugula for garnish (optional)
1 tablespoon Champagne vinegar for drizzling
3 tablespoons extra-virgin olive oil for drizzling

← *Mega-talented exec. sous Ryan*

FOR THE BEETS: Preheat the oven to 400°F. Wash the beets, cut off their tops and tails, and put them in a roasting pan. Pour the olive oil over the beets and then pour in enough white wine so at least half of each beet is under wine. Season with salt and pepper. Cover the pan with aluminum foil and roast for about 1 hour and 20 minutes, or until a knife blade slips into a beet easily. Remove from the oven and set aside until cool to the touch. Slip the peels from the beets. When ready to serve, slice the beets into 1½-inch chunks. (The chunks don't have to be uniform for this salad.)

FOR THE BLUE CHEESE CREAM: In a stand mixer fitted with the paddle attachment, combine the cheeses and beat on low speed until blended. Add the cream, salt, and pepper and beat on medium speed until smooth.

FOR THE PISTACHIO VINAIGRETTE: In a blender, whir together the vinegar, mustard, shallot, thyme, and egg yolks until smooth. With the machine running, add the pistachio oil and then the olive oil, 1 tablespoon at a time. If the mixture gets too thick, add the 1 tablespoon ice water. You may want to stop if your blender gets warm, because you don't want your emulsion heated. (If the emulsion breaks, it's easy to fix: Scrape the vinaigrette out of the blender and set it aside. Cool the blender container in cold water, add another egg yolk and a couple of ice cubes, and then gradually add the broken vinaigrette back to the blender with the machine running.) Season with the salt and pepper.

Chill 6 salad plates, and spoon the vinaigrette into a squeeze bottle or a pastry bag fitted with a small plain tip. Spoon about 2 tablespoons of the blue cheese cream onto a chilled plate. Mound the beet chunks on top of the cream in an even mix of golden and Chioggia. Squeeze a circle of the vinaigrette around the periphery of the salad. Toss about a dozen toasted pistachios over the salad, very lightly sprinkle on the parsley and tarragon, and finish with a small mound of micro greens on the top if you like. Drizzle with vinegar and olive oil. Repeat for the other 5 salads.

Calabrian Wedding Soup
(Pastina Soup with Tiny Meatballs)

SERVES 8 TO 10

Tender bite-size meatballs and pastina make up this soup, which my mother cooked for me when I begged her long enough. Pastina is like pasta with training wheels, the first solid food a little Italian kid eats. I have such vivid memories of asking my mom to make this soup, and what goes around comes around: My daughter Giana is nineteen now and living in an apartment, but sometimes when she visits she'll say, "Papa, please, please make me pastina soup." Having this soup as a link between my mother and my daughter makes it even more soul-soothing.

Yes, the meatball-making can be tedious if you're doing it alone. Don't sit there by yourself; have at least one of your children or a friend—anyone you like talking with— sitting across from you and rolling, too. For me, decades later, the time I spent rolling meatballs with my mom is time that I look back on with gratitude.

My mom always used a lot of liquid in her meatballs; this will seem like too much water when you're adding it, but it will work out just right for supremely tender meatballs. I like using homemade bread crumbs, but you can always buy crumbs if you like.

Bright spinach gives this soup some color. In the autumn, I switch to mustard greens. Don't sprinkle Parmesan on this soup; it calls for first-rate pecorino and tiny dishes of Calabrian chile paste as a condiment for anyone who wants some. Serve each bowl with a thick slice of toasted country-style bread that's been brushed with olive oil.

Wine Pairing: Rosé Champagne

MEATBALLS

⅓ cup cold water
⅓ cup Dried Bread Crumbs
    (page 35) or store-bought bread crumbs
1 pound ground beef, about 20 percent fat
1 large egg, beaten
⅓ cup grated pecorino
3 tablespoons minced fresh flat-leaf parsley
1 teaspoon minced garlic
½ teaspoon sea salt
½ teaspoon freshly ground black pepper
1 teaspoon kosher salt

PASTINA SOUP

¼ cup extra-virgin olive oil
2 large yellow onions, diced
3 celery stalks, cut into 3-inch pieces
2 large carrots, peeled and cut into 3-inch pieces
8 cups Chicken Broth (page 16) or store-bought
    chicken stock or water
1 chicken, about 4 pounds
2 fresh thyme sprigs
3 bay leaves
One 14-ounce can whole peeled tomatoes,
    with their juice
½ pound pastina
1½ cups julienned spinach leaves

6 slices bruschetta (see page 44) for serving
Grated pecorino cheese for serving
Calabrian chile paste for serving

FOR THE MEATBALLS: In a medium bowl, pour the water over the bread crumbs and let stand for 5 minutes while you season the meat. In a large bowl, mix together the meat, egg, pecorino, parsley, garlic, sea salt, and pepper. (I use my hands, but you can use a wooden spoon if you like.) Pour in the bread crumbs and water and mix that in too. Don't let it worry you that the mixture seems wet.

Divide the meat mixture in half and roll one half into a cylinder about 1 inch in diameter, the size of a rope. Cut into 1-inch pieces and roll each piece into a small ball about the size of a marble. Set each meatball on a baking sheet. When you've finished shaping half the meat, repeat with the second half. You should have about 80 meatballs all together.

Pour 3 cups of water into a large saucepan. Add the kosher salt and bring to a gentle simmer. Gently add about two dozen of the meatballs and cook for 2 minutes. Using a slotted spoon or wire skimmer, transfer the meatballs to a baking sheet. Add another two dozen meatballs to the pan, cook for 2 minutes, and continue this way until every meatball is poached.

FOR THE SOUP: Heat a large soup pot over medium-high heat, pour in the olive oil, and when it's shimmering, sauté the onions, celery, and carrots until browned, about 10 minutes. Add the chicken broth, chicken, herbs, tomatoes, and tomato juice. Bring to a strong simmer, then reduce the heat and simmer until the chicken is tender, about 1 hour. Remove from the heat and let cool to the touch. Transfer the chicken to a baking sheet. Save the chicken for another use, or serve for a second course. (My mother always kept the bird warm and served it as a second course.) Strain the soup into a large pot.

In a large pot of salted boiling water, cook the pastina until al dente, about 10 minutes. Drain the pastina and add to the soup. Add the spinach and meatballs, heat for 1 minute, and serve in bowls accompanied with bruschetta. Set small bowls of grated pecorino and Calabrian chile paste on the table as condiments.

Joe & Ashley Criscione— dear friends and great customers

The Importance of Small Details

How much does temperature matter? I would say that having food at the perfect temperature when it's placed in front of you is critical and nonnegotiable. At Bottega, we warm all our plates (except for salad and dessert plates, which are chilled) so that your gnocchi is perfectly warm to the last bite, and your salad crisp and cool. You can do this in your home kitchen. Warming and chilling plates and glasses is a small touch that makes a big difference.

How about your chair? Is it comfortable? (At Bottega, our chairs are supremely comfortable thanks to the careful choices of my wife, Eileen.) You will spend some of the best moments of your life at the table, and my hope is your chair enhances the experience.

The cup that holds your coffee at Bottega is fine china, because I finally realized that my mother was right, and coffee does taste better from a china cup. We pull out the china at home as well; nothing contributes to a meal like the stories that come with serving pieces, silver, or decanters passed down through generations. If your grandmother's china doesn't match your color scheme, then throw out your color scheme. Story is the most important detail of all.

allan
"the Badger"
with hairs
on his neck up

Pappa al Pomodoro
(Tomato-Bread Soup)

SERVES 6

This soup is the definition of Tuscan food, made from great tomatoes that aren't cooked too long, mixed with old bread, and milled for texture. You won't find versions like this in Southern Italy. I like the combination of fresh and canned tomatoes, but you can use all fresh if you like; just aim for about 6½ pounds of tomatoes. If you don't have a food mill, by all means use your food processor, but for a true *pappa al pomodoro* a mill is key. This soup is all about the texture: the word *velvety* comes to mind, not because this soup is smooth but because the combination of good tomatoes and stale bread has a mouthfeel that's rich and satisfying. It's the most rustic food, and yet it doesn't feel simple or rustic in your mouth. Darrell Corti, who calls himself a grocer, is actually a wine merchant and food expert and also one of the smartest guys I know. He makes a pappa al pomodoro even thicker than mine, and it's like a breath of new air.

You can spoon this onto a plate as a sauce and top it with grilled sardines, fried calamari, or slices of grilled steak.

Wine Pairing: Sangiovese

5 pounds fresh Roma (plum) tomatoes
One 28-ounce can peeled whole tomatoes
4 cups extra-virgin olive oil
1 tablespoon minced garlic
4 cups diced crustless bread, preferably from
  a slightly stale country-style loaf
Sea salt, preferably gray salt
Freshly ground black pepper
½ cup chopped fresh basil

Core each fresh tomato (see Chef's Note, below), mark a shallow X in the opposite end, and blanch in a pot of boiling water for 30 seconds. Transfer to cold water to cool briefly, then peel the tomatoes. Cut the tomatoes in half, scoop out the seeds with your fingers, then chop. (I prefer to squish the pulp into a large bowl.) Drain, reserving the liquid in a bowl. Empty the pulp into another bowl. Open the can of tomatoes and drain, adding the liquid to the reserved fresh tomato liquid and the canned tomatoes to the fresh tomato pulp.

Heat a large stockpot over medium heat, add 1 cup of the olive oil, and sauté the garlic until golden and aromatic, about 30 seconds. Pay attention because it colors quickly, and dark garlic can be bitter. Pour the tomato liquid into the pan and cook to reduce by half, about 3 minutes. Add the chopped tomatoes and pulp and cook until they give off their juices, about 30 minutes. Add the bread and cook for 2 more minutes, stirring to break down the bread.

To get the best texture, pass the soup through a food mill; don't expect it to be satin smooth but it should be even in consistency, with no lumps of bread. If you don't have a food mill, whisk the soup until the bread is broken up and then whir it in a blender. Season with salt and pepper, then add the basil. Whisk in the remaining 3 cups olive oil. Divide among warmed soup bowls.

CHEF'S NOTE: Good tomatoes are like gold at Bottega, and we don't waste a bit of them. When you core the tomatoes, take out as little flesh as possible. Then cut a shallow X in the opposite end of the tomato, and when it goes into the hot water, the skin will curl into four little corners, making it easier to peel.

CHAPTER 5

Pastas and Risottos

PASTE E RISOTTI

Pasta wants to be simple. The best pastas have a primary flavor and a secondary flavor, like the mind-bending Solo Shrimp Pasta in this chapter. The first flavor is shrimp, the second is salt water; it's the ocean brought to life in your mouth.

Just because a pasta dish is simple doesn't mean it's easy. Often when the flavors are simple, the technique requires some effort. Take our gnocchi. Mostly made of ricotta, these gnocchi are so light they'd float off the plate if they weren't held down by my grandmother's velvety, classic "old hen" tomato sauce. There's a saying in the restaurant business that if a dish's ingredients cost two dollars, and you're charging ten dollars, there'd better be at least three dollars' worth of labor involved. Gnocchi is worth about twenty dollars of labor. Gnocchi this light requires technique—it has to be made repeatedly until your fingers have a muscle memory of how the gnocchi takes shape. Until you have the technique down, you're in apprentice mode. Make it the same way again and again until the steps are second nature.

The same holds true for risotto: Make a basic risotto until you know when to add more stock and how quickly to stir. When your basic risotto is great and you're confident in your pasta-making skills, then you can go in new directions. Try black rice risotto, or smoke the flour for your pasta in your grill. But until your technique is sound, don't mess with the recipe. Follow it faithfully step by step until you've got the steps down.

I see pasta-making as similar to Buddhism; it's not a destination but a journey. To that end, I'm building a pasta kitchen at Bottega to expand the scope of my own journey. Making good pasta is not difficult, and you can easily substitute a good dried pasta for almost any of the fresh ones. When it comes to making filled pastas, you may be able to find fresh sheets of pasta to aid the process, but I also encourage you to try making pasta from scratch. There are few things that bring me as much pleasure as pasta.

Ricotta Gnocchi
with Salsa della Nonna

SERVES 6 TO 8 AS A MAIN COURSE;
MAKES 72 TO 84 GNOCCHI

This dish is the work of two of my favorite people. Nick Ritchie, Bottega's chef de cuisine, created these cloudlike gnocchi. The rich traditional sauce is my grandmother's old recipe. The combination is now a "can't remove" mainstay of the Bottega menu.

The lightness of this gnocchi is due to Nick's competitive streak. Nick trained with Carmen Quagliata at Tra Vigne, and the whole "who's got the lightest gnocchi" battle has gone on between Nick and Carmen for years.

These gnocchi have just four ingredients: ricotta, flour, egg yolks, and salt. Use a very good ricotta, such as Bellwether Farms' sheep's milk ricotta. This gnocchi needs a 48-hour lead time because you'll let the ricotta drain overnight the day before you make the gnocchi and then you'll freeze the gnocchi for 24 hours before cooking. Drain the ricotta by lining a colander with cheesecloth and setting it in the sink. My mom used to make a little sling out of the cheesecloth and hang it right from the kitchen faucet.

You want your work surface to be cool. Marble is ideal—a marble pastry slab or countertop is best. If you don't have marble, try laying a few ice packs on the countertop while you make the dough. When you're ready to roll, put the ice back in the freezer and wipe down the work surface so it's dry.

The sauce recipe makes about 4 cups, which is more than you'll need. You can't cut the recipe in half, because the chicken needs a good amount of sauce to simmer in, but having my nonna's sauce in your freezer is never a bad thing.

Wine Pairing: Zinfandel

3 pounds whole-milk ricotta, drained overnight

6 egg yolks

2 teaspoons sea salt, preferably gray salt

¾ cup all-purpose flour, plus extra for sprinkling and dusting

Best-quality extra-virgin olive oil for drizzling

Salsa di Pomodoro della Nonna (page 24) for serving

Grated Pecorino-Romano for sprinkling

Using the back of a large spoon, press the ricotta through a fine-mesh sieve into a large bowl. Add the egg yolks and sea salt and mix with a rubber spatula. Gently fold in the ¾ cup flour; the less you work the dough, the lighter and more tender the gnocchi will be. Cover and refrigerate for 30 minutes.

Lightly sprinkle your work surface and two baking sheets with flour. Pull off about a quarter of the gnocchi dough and gently roll it into a rope about 1 inch wide.

Using a dough scraper or a sharp knife dipped in flour, cut individual dumplings from the rope into 1-inch pieces. Gently transfer each piece to a prepared baking sheet and dust with flour so it's lightly coated. Repeat with the remaining gnocchi. Slide the pans into the freezer and freeze for at least 24 hours or up to 1 month. (Gnocchi have a better texture if they go right from the freezer to the pot.)

Heat a pot of salted water (see note, at right), and, while the water heats, put the sauce on the stove over a simmering flame so it's warm when the gnocchi are cooked.

When the water comes to a boil, cook two dozen frozen gnocchi for 3 to 3 ½ minutes, or for 30 to 45 seconds after they rise to the surface. Using a slotted spoon or a wire skimmer, transfer the gnocchi to a warmed plate. Add another two dozen gnocchi to the pot and, while they cook, finish plating the batch of gnocchi you just took out of the pot.

Spoon about a dozen gnocchi per serving onto a warmed plate. Drizzle with olive oil. Spoon a little of the warm tomato sauce on top and finish with a sprinkling of pecorino.

Note: Salting Pasta Water
The Italians have a saying: "The pasta water is salted enough when it tastes like the sea." If you can't taste the salt in the water, you haven't used enough. The basic rule is 1 tablespoon of kosher or sea salt for every 1 quart of water. Always reserve a bit of pasta water. If your pasta seems dry, spoon on a little pasta water and toss just before serving.

Potato Gnocchi Ravioli with Egg Yolk and Sage Brown Butter

MAKES 6 LARGE RAVIOLI; SERVES 6

I was in my twenties when Lidia Bastianich taught me this trick for using gnocchi dough to make ravioli. Lidia filled her ravioli with nettles, which she called *ofelia*. Instead of nettles, my recipe shows you how to slip the most perfect, most organic, most free-range, golden egg yolk you can find inside each ravioli and seal it up. Your guests' eyes will open wide when they cut into the ravioli and the yolk runs onto their plate.

As with the tiny meatballs in the Calabrian Wedding Soup (page 84), this is another labor-of-love dish. It's a pasta dish that inspires delight and awe—it's a Saturday-night dish, a dish for close friends. Finish with a simple sage brown butter and Parmesan, then sit down and watch as your guests discover the treasure.

Wine Pairing: Ribolla Gialla

SWISS CHARD FILLING

2 pounds Swiss chard or fresh spinach, stemmed
1 pound whole-milk ricotta, such as
    Bellwether Farms, drained for 30 minutes
    in a cheesecloth-lined colander
½ teaspoon freshly grated nutmeg
½ teaspoon sea salt, preferably gray salt,
    or kosher salt
¼ teaspoon freshly ground black pepper
2 egg yolks

GNOCCHI DOUGH FOR RAVIOLI

1 pound large unpeeled russet potatoes,
    preferably from Idaho
3 egg yolks, plus 1 extra if needed
½ cup freshly grated Parmesan
1 cup all-purpose flour, plus extra
    for dusting work surfaces

6 egg yolks
1 egg beaten with 2 tablespoons water

SAGE BROWN BUTTER

2 tablespoons unsalted butter
3 tablespoons finely shredded fresh sage
Sea salt, preferably gray salt, or kosher salt
Freshly ground black pepper

4 to 5 tablespoons freshly grated Parmesan
    for sprinkling

FOR THE FILLING: Set up an ice bath. In a large pot of salted boiling water, blanch the chard for 3 minutes. Drain, then plunge it into the ice bath; drain again and squeeze out as much water as possible. Coarsely chop the chard and transfer it to a food processor.

Using the back of a large spoon, press the ricotta through a fine-mesh sieve into a bowl. Add the sieved ricotta to the food processor with the chard. Pulse a few times and then add the nutmeg, salt, pepper, and 2 egg yolks. Taste the filling and make sure it's well seasoned with salt and pepper, then spoon it into a pastry bag fitted with a ½-inch round tip and refrigerate while you make the dough.

FOR THE DOUGH: Preheat the oven to 375°F. Pierce the potatoes and bake until tender when pierced with a knife, about 70 minutes. Remove from the oven and let cool just enough to handle; the interior should still be hot.

Cut each potato in half, scoop out the flesh, and put through a food mill into a bowl. (If you don't have a food mill, push the warm potatoes through a coarse-mesh sieve or a ricer.) You should have about 2 cups. On a lightly floured board or work surface, make a mound of the potatoes. Push a well into the center of the mound with a spoon. Add the 3 egg yolks and the Parmesan to the well and mix until smooth. Add the flour, ½ cup at a time, and gently knead just until the dough becomes a cohesive mound, about 3 minutes. If the dough seems too dry, add another yolk or 2 teaspoons of water. The dough should feel firm but yielding. To test, pinch off a piece of dough and roll it on a floured surface into a rope about ½-inch in diameter. If the rope holds together, the dough is perfect. If not, add more flour, knead, and test again. Cover the finished dough with a cloth and let it rest for 30 minutes.

On a floured surface, roll the dough until it forms an oval about ¼ inch thick. With a 5-inch round pasta cutter, or a small bowl about 5 inches across, cut 12 rounds from the dough. If you need to, push together the dough scraps and reroll until smooth. Sprinkle a baking sheet with flour.

On 6 of the dough rounds, pipe a ring of the chard filling about ½ inch from the edge. Leave the center without filling; that's where the egg yolk will fit. With your fingers, place a whole egg yolk in the center of each dough round. Brush the egg-water mixture around the edges of each dough round. Top with another dough round and, with your fingers, seal it all the way around, gently so you don't break the yolk inside. Transfer the ravioli to the floured sheet and refrigerate for at least 30 minutes or up to 2 hours.

FOR THE BUTTER: Heat a small saucepan over medium heat, add the butter, and cook until it just begins to brown, about 2 minutes. Add the sage and season with salt and pepper; remove from the heat and set aside.

Gently add the ravioli to a large pot of salted boiling water (see Note, page 93) and cook for 3 minutes, or until they float to the surface. Don't overcook these. Using a large slotted spoon or a wire skimmer, transfer the cooked ravioli to individual warmed plates. Spoon on the sage brown butter and finish with a sprinkle of Parmesan.

Compressed-Tomato Ravioli with Shrimp and Tomato Water

SERVES 6

The essence of tomato fills this pasta. The dish is finished with tomato water (the juice left behind when you cut and core the tomatoes, and compress them) and barely poached prawns with a kiss of pesto. Serving this with the light, refreshing tomato water instead of a heavier tomato sauce means you can really appreciate the texture of the pasta and the beautiful red filling. The shrimp oil adds another layer of flavor, and the combination is unexpected and yet exactly right.

Ask your fishmonger for the shrimp shells; most stores that carry loose shrimp will have shells if you call in advance. Otherwise, use ¾ cup of the least expensive shrimp you can find in place of the shells.

Save this dish for the summer; winter tomatoes don't provide enough juice.

Wine Pairing: Pigato, a white wine from Liguria

TOMATO FILLING

6 pounds Roma (plum) tomatoes
1 tablespoon sea salt, preferably gray salt
1 cup extra-virgin olive oil
¼ cup chopped garlic
3 cups chopped fresh basil leaves
1 large egg
½ cup freshly grated Parmesan
Freshly ground black pepper

SHRIMP OIL

1¼ cups olive oil (see Chef's Note, page 19)
1 cup chopped yellow onion
½ cup peeled and chopped carrot
½ cup chopped celery
2 cups shrimp shells, or ¾ cup small shrimp
2 tablespoons tomato paste

All-purpose flour or semolina for dusting
1 pound fresh egg pasta sheets (see page 106)
  or store-bought
24 large shrimp (about 1½ pounds)
2 tablespoons Blanched-Basil Pesto (page 27)
1½ cups halved cherry tomatoes (about ¾ pint)
2 tablespoons freshly grated Parmesan cheese

FOR THE TOMATO FILLING: Peel, core, and quarter the tomatoes, taking care to catch and reserve all their juice. In a large, nonreactive pot, combine the tomatoes and salt. Bring to a boil over medium-high heat, then reduce the heat to medium-low and simmer until the tomatoes release most of their water, about 15 minutes.

While the tomatoes simmer, line a large colander with two layers of cheesecloth and place it over a heatproof container large enough to hold the colander steady. The cheesecloth should be long enough to extend over the sides of the colander. Pour the hot tomatoes into the colander. Fold the cheesecloth over the tomatoes and weight them down with a sturdy plate and a few clean, heavy cans. Let the tomatoes sit overnight to force out as much liquid as possible. Add the liquid that falls through the cheesecloth to the tomato juice reserved when you chopped the tomatoes. Cover and reserve in the refrigerator. You should end up with about 1½ cups of liquid.

CONTINUED

When you're ready to cook, heat a large, heavy pot over medium-high heat, add the olive oil, and heat just until it begins to smoke. Add the garlic and cook until golden brown, about 1 minute. Add the basil and stir until wilted, about 30 seconds. Add the compressed tomato solids to the pan and cook, stirring frequently, until there's very little liquid left, about 5 minutes. Transfer the tomato mixture to a platter to cool to room temperature, at least 30 minutes.

In a blender or a food processor, combine the egg and tomato mixture and blend, in batches if necessary, until smooth. Add the Parmesan in three additions, blending after each addition until smooth. Season with pepper. Set aside and let cool completely. The tomato filling can be made the day before and refrigerated if you like.

FOR THE SHRIMP OIL: Position a rack in the center of the oven and preheat the oven to 400°F. Heat a large, ovenproof sauté pan or skillet over high heat, add ¼ cup of the olive oil, and sauté the onion, carrot, and celery until the vegetables begin to show some color, 8 to 10 minutes. Add the shrimp shells and tomato paste. Stir well and transfer the pan to the hot oven. Let it cook until the tomato paste melds with the vegetables, about 10 minutes. Remove from the oven and pour the contents into a blender, working in batches if necessary. Add the remaining 1 cup oil and blend until smooth. Line a colander with flat-bottom coffee filters and strain the oil into a bowl. Transfer the oil to a squeeze bottle, or cover the bowl. Refrigerate.

Spoon the tomato filling into a pastry bag. Dust a baking sheet with flour. Gently place one sheet of the pasta dough onto a lightly floured surface and cut it into two long sections. Before you begin piping the filling onto the dough, envision folding over one half of the dough sheet length-wise to encase the filling into individual raviolis. Pipe filling into 8 small mounds (each about 2 teaspoons filling) separated on the dough by about two fingers' width. Fold the dough over the filling, gently pressing down between each ravioli, and then use a ravioli cutter or a knife to cut the strip into 8 individual raviolis, each about 3 by 2 inches. Gently crimp the edges of each ravioli all the way around. (Reserve any extra pasta pieces, seal in a

plastic bag, and add them to soups.) Repeat with the remaining pasta dough and filling. You'll end up with ninety-two 2-inch ravioli. If you'd like to make these ahead, store them in the freezer in plastic bags for up to 1 month.

Bring a large pot of salted water to a boil (see Note, page 93). While the water heats, pour 3 cups of the reserved tomato water into a large, nonreactive sauté pan or skillet. (Gently warm the remaining tomato water and pour into a decanter, preferably clear glass, for the table.) Taste and add more salt and pepper if you like. Bring the liquid to a simmer over medium-low heat, add the 24 shrimp, and poach until they turn pink, 2 to 3 minutes. With tongs, turn over each shrimp, add the cherry tomato halves, and cook for 1 minute.

When the pasta water boils, add the ravioli and cook for 2 to 3 minutes. Drain.

Spoon 8 or 10 ravioli into each bowl and top with 4 shrimp and some tomatoes. Spoon on the tomato water and drizzle with shrimp oil at room temperature. Top each serving with about 1 teaspoon pesto and sprinkle with Parmesan. Let guests pour more tomato water from the decanter if they like.

Garganelli with Rabbit Sugo and Mushrooms

SERVES 6

Maybe the most popular pasta at Bottega, this old-school version of garganelli with slow-braised rabbit, sautéed chanterelles, and a spoonful of just-made ricotta is as perfect as pasta can be. Rabbits are underused by Americans, but they are more widely available than ever. Talk to your local butcher about ordering rabbit, or see Resources.

Wine Pairing: A super Tuscan

1 ounce dried porcini mushrooms
1½ cups warm water
One 3- to 3½-pound rabbit
Sea salt, preferably gray salt, or kosher salt
Freshly ground black pepper
2 tablespoons extra-virgin olive oil
1 cup diced yellow onion
½ cup diced peeled carrot
½ cup diced celery
2 teaspoons minced garlic
2 cups dry red wine
1 fresh sage sprig
One 28-ounce canned whole
    San Marzano tomatoes, juice reserved
8 cups Roasted Chicken Stock (page 18)
1½ pounds garganelli, penne, ziti,
    or other tube pasta
1 cup whole-milk ricotta

In a small bowl, soak the porcini in the warm water for 30 minutes.

To prepare the rabbit, remove the front and back legs and then cut in half from front to back. Remove the liver and kidneys, chop them finely, and set aside. Season the rabbit with salt and pepper. Heat a Dutch oven or large, heavy sauté pan over medium-high heat, add 1 tablespoon of the olive oil, and sear the rabbit pieces until well browned on all sides. Using tongs, transfer the rabbit to a plate. Add the onion, carrot, and celery to the pan and sauté until crisp-tender, about 10 minutes. Increase the heat to high and sauté the vegetables until lightly browned. Reduce the heat to medium, add the garlic, and sauté, stirring occasionally, for 10 more minutes.

Drain and squeeze the liquid from the porcini, reserving the liquid. Strain the liquid through a fine-mesh sieve and set aside. Chop the mushrooms coarsely. Add them to the pan with the vegetables. Cook for 3 to 4 minutes. Add the chopped liver and kidneys and cook for a few more minutes. Add the red wine, sage, and reserved mushroom soaking liquid. Increase the heat to medium-high and cook for 4 minutes to reduce the liquid.

Using your hands, crush the tomatoes right over the pan. Add the reserved juice from the tomatoes and the chicken stock and bring to a boil. Reduce the heat to low and return the rabbit to the pan. Completely submerge the rabbit by pushing it under the cooking liquid with a spoon. At Bottega, we make a parchment paper lid (see Chef's Note, page 25) and push it down inside the pot so it rests on top the cooking liquid. If you prefer, you can use a standard pan lid, but the liquid will take longer to reduce. Gently simmer until the rabbit leg meat can be pulled from the bone, about 2 hours. Transfer the rabbit to a plate and let cool. Pull the meat from the bones and chop into 1-inch pieces. Discard the bones. Continue to cook the stock until it has reduced by half. Return the chopped meat to the sauce and remove from the heat.

In a large pot of salted boiling water (see Note, page 93), cook the pasta according to the package directions, usually 8 to 10 minutes, or until al dente. Drain. Spoon the pasta into warmed shallow bowls. Top with a good amount of the sauce and then finish with a spoonful or two of the ricotta.

Solo Shrimp Pasta

SERVES 6

Barcelona, Positano, Venice, and the Amalfi Coast—all of these places exceeded my expectations, despite all the tourist hype. The shrimp I ate while sitting next to the Mediterranean also topped my expectations. I created this dish for Bottega when I found shrimp here in the United States that was just as good. One fisherman in Louisiana supplies us with all our shrimp; he ships live shrimp to us three times a week in containers filled with seawater, and we save just a little of that water for the pasta.

This isn't a pasta you put together from frozen seafood. Solo shrimp means "just shrimp," and when you find the best shrimp you've ever had, this is how to cook them.

Wine Pairing: Chardonnay

¾ cup extra-virgin olive oil
24 large, perfect Gulf Coast shrimp
   with heads on (about 2 pounds)
Sea salt, preferably gray salt, or kosher salt
Freshly ground black pepper
2 tablespoons sliced garlic
2 teaspoons Calabrian chile paste (see Resources),
   or ½ teaspoon red pepper flakes
10 cups Shrimp Stock (page 20)
1 pound chitarra pasta
3 tablespoons finely shredded fresh basil
2 tablespoons minced fresh tarragon
6 tablespoons minced fresh flat-leaf parsley
4 tablespoons unsalted butter

Set a large pot of salted water to boil for the pasta (see Note, page 93).

Heat a very large sauce pan or Dutch oven over high heat and add the olive oil. Season the shrimp with salt and pepper and add 8 to 12 shrimp to the pan. Cook just until they turn pink, 1 to 2 minutes. Take one out and taste it; as soon as they're cooked through, transfer the shrimp to a plate using a wire skimmer or slotted spoon. Repeat with the second batch of shrimp. When the second batch has cooked, transfer to the plate and add the garlic to the pan. Cook until golden, then add the chile paste. Add the shrimp stock and cook to reduce by half, about 10 minutes.

While the sauce reduces, add the pasta to the boiling water. Cook for half the time suggested on the pasta package; drain. Using tongs, add the pasta to the pan with the sauce, gently tossing, and cook for 2 to 3 minutes. (It still has another 2 minutes to cook with the herbs, so don't overcook the pasta in the sauce.) Add the basil, tarragon, and parsley and stir in the butter and season with salt and pepper. Return the shrimp to the pan and cook for 2 minutes. Remove from the heat and divide among pasta bowls to serve.

CHEF'S NOTE: Remember that pasta (like meat) will continue to cook after you take it off the heat. Read the directions on your pasta package. If the package advises 10 minutes, cook it for 5 minutes in the water and for another 3 minutes in the pan. I always leave a hint of crunch to my pasta for some room to let it finish cooking in the sauce.

Zinfandel Spaghettini
with Spicy Rapini

SERVES 8 AS A FIRST COURSE,
4 AS A MAIN COURSE

This pasta is a celebration of one of my favorite grapes, Zinfandel. Seldom is Zinfandel given the respect I think it deserves. This dish lets you kneel at the altar of Zinfandel, a glass of it at your right hand, an entire plate of it on your left. The pasta is barely cooked in water, and then it's finished in Zinfandel until deep purple in color. Paired with a little rapini and some pecorino, this is a dish that is simple and yet extravagant.

It's a great crowd pleaser, but one that might need explanation. Spaghetti and spaghettini are expected to be doused in tomato sauce; this dish shows that they have a wider range than you might imagine.

Wine Pairing: Zinfandel

1 ½ pounds rapini (broccoli rabe)
1 pound spaghettini or spaghetti
One 750-ml bottle dry red wine, preferably Zinfandel
1 tablespoon sugar
⅓ cup extra-virgin olive oil
2 tablespoons sliced garlic (about 4 cloves)
1 teaspoon Calabrian chile paste (see Resources),
    or ¼ teaspoon red pepper flakes
1 teaspoon kosher salt or sea salt, preferably gray salt
½ teaspoon freshly ground black pepper
½ cup grated Pecorino-Romano

In a large pot of salted boiling water, cook the rapini for about 3 minutes. Using a wire skimmer, transfer the rapini to a baking sheet and spread it out to cool. In the same boiling water, cook the spaghettini, stirring occasionally, for 2 minutes if fresh, 3 to 5 minutes if dried. (Cook spaghetti for 2 minutes if fresh, 6 to 8 minutes if dried.) You'll do the second half of the cooking in the Zinfandel. Reserve 1 cup of the pasta water and then drain the pasta and set it aside. Return the empty pasta pot to the stove.

Add the wine and sugar to the pasta pot. Bring to a boil over high heat and cook to reduce by half, 8 to 10 minutes. Add the pasta to the pot and shake the pot to prevent the pasta from sticking. Gently stir with tongs until coated and boil over high heat, stirring occasionally, until most of the liquid is absorbed and the pasta is al dente (about 3 minutes for spaghettini and 4 or 5 minutes for spaghetti. Again, tasting tells you when your pasta is ready better than the clock can).

While the pasta cooks in the wine, heat a large, deep sauté pan or skillet over high heat. Add the oil, reduce the heat to medium-low, and sauté the garlic until pale golden, about 3 minutes. Add the chile paste, blanched rapini, salt, and pepper and cook, stirring occasionally, for 1 to 2 minutes. Pour in ½ cup of the reserved pasta water, or more if desired. Add the rapini mixture to the pasta, toss gently, and transfer to individual pasta bowls or one big platter. Sprinkle with the pecorino.

Tagliatelle with Bread Crumbs, Mint, and Tomato Carpaccio

SERVES 6

This is a country dish, simple to put together, but the flavors are surprisingly satisfying. A fresh carpaccio of tomato lines the serving dish, providing just the right juicy, cool complement to the buttery, garlic-bread-crumb-coated pasta. Mint sparks it up a little and gives it a fresh finish.

Taglia means "to cut," so if you don't have a pasta machine and just want to cut a sheet of pasta, the fact that it's *deformatta*—not precise and even—is an attribute. I like pasta that has clearly been cut by hand. This is a fast, easy dish to make with dried pasta on a weeknight, so don't turn the page just because you're not in a pasta-making mood at the moment (just use 1 pound of your favorite dried pasta).

Wine Pairing: Vernaccia

EGG PASTA
4 large eggs, plus 3 egg yolks, lightly beaten
1 tablespoon plus 1 teaspoon extra-virgin olive oil
1 teaspoon finely ground sea salt, preferably gray salt
2½ to 3 cups *doppio zero* pasta flour (see page 10)
   or all-purpose flour, plus extra for rolling
   and sprinkling

6 large ripe tomatoes, thinly sliced
3 tablespoons extra-virgin olive oil
Sea salt, preferably gray salt
Freshly ground black pepper

GARLIC BREAD CRUMBS
4 tablespoons unsalted butter
2 teaspoons minced garlic
1¼ cups Dried Bread Crumbs (page 35)

2 tablespoons chopped fresh mint,
   plus 3 to 4 mint leaves, finely shredded
¼ cup finely grated Pecorino-Romano

FOR THE PASTA: In a stand mixer fitted with the dough hook, combine the eggs and egg yolks, olive oil, and salt. Add 1 cup of the flour and mix on medium-low speed. Add the remaining flour 1/2 cup at a time, stopping several times to scrape down the sides of the bowl, until the dough forms into a ball; don't add any more flour after this point. Beat the dough for another 3 to 4 minutes, or until smooth and slightly misshapen. Transfer to a lightly floured surface and knead by hand for 60 seconds, until smooth. Wrap it in plastic wrap and allow it to rest in the refrigerator for at least 1 hour.

Press the dough into a disk and cut it in half. Place one half of the dough on a floured surface and lightly sprinkle the top of the dough with flour. Using the heels of your hands, press the dough into an oval that's thin enough to pass through the pasta machine.

Feed the dough into the pasta machine, and then gently take the dough from underneath the machine and fold it into thirds lengthwise, pressing it down with the heel of your hand. Feed the dough back into the machine so it presses the three layers together. Change the setting of the rollers, decreasing it by one setting. Lightly flour the dough and run it through the machine again. Change the machine's setting again, lowering it by two settings, lightly flour the dough, and run the dough through again. Repeat three more times, decreasing the width of the roller setting and flouring the dough each time before rolling. (Altogether, you'll pass the dough through the machine six times, adjusting the setting for pasta thickness each time. Lightly flour the dough after each pass; if the dough is sticky it can tear while going through the machine.) Gently lay the dough on a lightly floured surface and cover it with a barely damp, clean towel. Let rest for 10 minutes. Cut the pasta with the pasta machine, or roll it up and cut it by hand, into 1/4-inch-wide ribbons.

Lay the tomato slices on a large serving platter, overlapping them in concentric circles. Drizzle the olive oil over the tomato slices and season with salt and pepper. Set aside.

FOR THE BREAD CRUMBS: Heat a small saucepan over medium heat and add the butter. When it foams, add the garlic and sauté until golden, about 3 minutes. Add the bread crumbs and stir until well mixed. Remove from the heat and set aside.

Bring a large pot of salted water to a boil (see Note, page 93). Add the pasta and cook for 3 minutes, or until al dente. Reserve 1 cup of the pasta water and drain the pasta.

In a large bowl, toss together the pasta, bread crumbs, and chopped mint. Add 1/2 cup of the reserved pasta water, or more if needed. Using tongs, transfer the pasta to the platter on top of the seasoned tomato slices. Sprinkle with the shredded mint and pecorino. Serve, making sure each person gets tomato slices with his or her pasta.

A Yelp Star

The most entertaining part of reading about
Bottega online is discovering what diners
have to say about our staff. Joël Hoachuck,
Bottega's general manager, gets a lot of online
commentary. Although many folks can't
resist discussing Joël's moustache, eventually
you'll read words like *welcoming, warm*, and
hospitable. I love these comments because
that's how I see Joël, too. He has embodied
the spirit of hospitality since he walked onto
the floor at Tra Vigne fifteen years ago.

Joël has managed Thomas Keller's
fantastic Bouchon, has been a key figure at
Auberge du Soleil, and was general manager
at Dean & Deluca. Each and every time we
bumped into each other, he has embodied
that warm, welcoming spirit. When Joël heard
I was opening a restaurant, he opened up that
wonderful heart of his for Bottega.

The quality of Joël's work goes unmatched.
He never complains and never argues. (And
for a chef to not argue with his G.M. is almost
unheard of.) Best of all, Joël truly welcomes
the people who come to Bottega and extends
to them a sincere interest that (judging
from all those online comments) stays with
them long after they've left the Napa Valley.
Because of Joël, we have the best service of any
restaurant that I've been involved with.

G.M. Joël working his French magic

Tagliarini with Manila Clams and Calabrese Sausage

SERVES 6 TO 8

In different incarnations, this has been a part of my repertoire for twenty-five years. It's one of my all-time favorites, and all it needs is a jet-cold glass of Pinot Grigio or a Bianco from Friuli to make it sing. Add some blanched rapini (broccoli rabe) to round out the meal.

Like many of my favorite dishes, this one began with fishermen. They brought dried sausages on their boats, caught clams, and cooked the two together for supper. You'll find variations of this shellfish-and-cured-pork idea in China, Portugal, Spain—in just about every fishing village around the world.

You can use either cherrystone or Manila clams. Manilas open faster than cherrystones, within about four minutes. If you don't own a sauté pan large enough to hold a pound of pasta and a lot of clams, a big roasting pan set right on the burners of your stove will work in its place, or you can use a Dutch oven. Taste before adding any salt; the sausage has a good amount of salt and you may not need any extra.

Wine Pairing: Greco, Pinot Grigio, or Friuli Bianco

24 Manila or cherrystone clams (1 pound), scrubbed
¼ cup extra-virgin olive oil
¼ cup sliced garlic
3 cups dry white wine
½ cup chopped fresh basil
¾ cup peeled and diced Calabrian sausage
    or any spicy salami or chorizo
½ teaspoon freshly ground black pepper
1½ pounds fresh egg pasta (see page 106) or
    store-bought, cut into tagliarini (⅛-inch-wide
    ribbons),or 1 pound dried tagliarini
½ cup chopped fresh flat-leaf parsley
¼ cup late-harvest extra-virgin olive oil for tossing

Toss out any clams that aren't tightly closed. Bring a large pot of salted water to a boil over high heat.

Heat a large sauté pan, roasting pan, or Dutch oven over medium-high heat. Add the olive oil and, when it's hot, add the garlic. Sauté until the garlic is light brown. Immediately add the clams and cook until you hear them popping, no more than 1 to 2 minutes. Remove the pan from the heat and pour in the wine.

Increase the heat to high, place the pan on the heat for just 30 seconds, then reduce the heat to medium-high. (If using cherrystone clams, you'll need to cover the pan.) Using tongs, transfer the opened clams to a baking sheet. Shake the pan to redistribute the remaining closed clams. (If cooking cherrystone clams, lift the lid every 30 seconds or so and take out any opened clams.)

After 5 minutes, give any clam that has not opened a good tap with a pair of tongs or a metal spoon, and put it back in the liquid, cooking for another minute to see if it will open. Discard any clams that do not open. Increase the heat to high and bring the liquid to a boil, cooking for about 1 minute to reduce the liquid. Add any clam juice from the baking sheet to the pan, along with the basil, sausage, and black pepper.

Cook the pasta in the boiling water for about 6 minutes, or until not quite al dente, because you'll finish cooking it in the pan used to cook the clams. (Again, the clock isn't as important as tasting to tell when the pasta is ready.) Reserve 2 cups of the pasta water, then drain the pasta.

Add the pasta to the sauté pan and toss for 1 minute. Add the clams and the parsley and toss. If the pasta is dry, add ½ cup of the pasta water, or more if needed. Cook until the pasta is al dente, about 2 minutes more for fresh pasta or 3 to 4 more for dried. Taste to tell when the pasta is perfect. Toss with the late-harvest olive oil and serve right away.

The ABC's of Pasta Making

The flour you use determines how supple your pasta dough will be. You can use all-purpose flour, but it's better to seek out special flours developed just for pasta making. In Italy, flours are labeled by how finely they're ground. *Doppio zero* ("double zero") is super-fine flour, almost the consistency of talcum. (Flour also comes labeled as *zero* or *uno*.) See Resources for pasta flour.

Whether a pasta dough contains only flour and water or flour, water, egg yolks, and salt, choose the best of each ingredient. Seek out organic farm eggs with yolks that are a deep, vibrant yellow.

A pasta machine is necessary to make dough as thin and even as you need it to be. The good news is, you can buy a pasta machine for a lot less than you'd pay for tools that you have to plug in, like a food processor. If you find you love pasta making, you can check out pasta-making tools such as a ravioli cutter or the chitarra maker. Fashioned like a harp strung with wires, this very low-tech tool makes instant ribbons of a sheet of pasta when you press the dough against the strings.

The best pasta-making tools are your hands. I think there's a real beauty in *pasta rustica*—sheets of pasta that you cut with a knife to any width you like. The more often you make pasta, the more you find to admire in the process.

Pasta "Bezza" with Robiola and Braised Asparagus Sauce

SERVES 6

Handkerchief pasta is also called *bezza*, which means "rag" in the Calabrian dialect. Sicilians might call these *mopin*, or "moppings." Growing up, my brothers and I each had a table *bezza*, a torn sheet that my mother had cut and stitched into a napkin. She washed the napkins once a week on washday. Just as I did, my kids eat with cloth napkins every night. (We do wash our napkins more than once a week, fortunately.)

These are easy, just sheets of pasta cut into squares. The pasta gets its due under the clean flavors of asparagus, olive oil, and *robiola* cheese. You can substitute other soft ripened cheeses, but if you can find robiola, try it, especially in the spring when you can really taste the grassy notes. If you can't find robiola, try this with *cana de oveja*. This is my favorite late-night pasta when asparagus is in season.

Wine Pairing: Vernacchia

1 pound fresh egg pasta sheets
   (see page 106) or store-bought
2 pounds asparagus
½ cup water
½ cup extra-virgin olive oil
1 teaspoon minced fresh thyme
1 tablespoon sliced garlic
Sea salt, preferably gray salt, or kosher salt
¾ pound *robiola, cana de oveja,*
   or other soft ripened cheese
Freshly ground black pepper

Cut the pasta sheets into about 3 dozen 4-by-6-inch rectangles. Bring a pot of salted water to a boil over high heat (see Note, page 93).

Bend each asparagus spear until it breaks naturally at the point where the spear becomes tough. Discard the tough ends. Cut the asparagus on the bias into 2-inch pieces.

In a large sauté pan, combine the water, olive oil, thyme, and garlic. Season with salt. Add just enough asparagus to the pan as can fit in a single layer. Bring the liquid to a boil over medium heat, reducing the heat as necessary to keep it at a simmer. Cook the asparagus until crisp-tender, 4 to 5 minutes. Remove from the heat. Using tongs, transfer the asparagus to a plate and keep warm. Repeat with the remaining asparagus.

When the pasta water boils, add the pasta and cook for 3 minutes or according to the package directions; drain. Transfer the cooked pasta to a serving dish and drizzle with some of the pan juices from the asparagus, tossing the sheets with tongs to keep them from sticking to each other. Top with the braised asparagus and about half of the soft cheese. Allow 1 or 2 minutes for the cheese to melt over the pasta, then top with a generous amount of black pepper. Serve the remaining cheese at the table for guests who'd like more (and most will).

CHEF'S NOTE: Have everyone at the table ready to eat before you add the cheese to the pasta. You want to have it on the plates in front of them while the cheese is still melting.

Butternut Squash and
Fontina Risotto with Squab Ragù

SERVES 6 AS A MAIN COURSE

Although risotto is usually a first course in Italy, a risotto this opulent is a main course at Bottega and deserves all the respect of the meal. This should be followed by nothing—except maybe a simple dessert, an hour after the dinner is through.

I can't say it enough, you will dramatically change your cooking for the better if you find a real butcher who works in a shop where the meat isn't all wrapped in plastic. Ask your butcher, with whom you're now on a first-name basis, to bone the squab and grind the meat for you, setting aside the livers and giving you the bones. (You can use them for stock.) Don't forget the bottle of wine as a small thank-you. If your butcher can't grind squab (sometimes their machinery is too big for this kind of work), you can grind it yourself. Get out your food processor and pulse until the meat is the consistency of ground beef.

You may want to read "The ABC's of Risotto," page 117, before starting.

Wine Pairing: Nebbiolo

SQUAB RAGÙ

2 squabs, each about 1 pound (livers reserved), boned, skinned, and finely ground, (see head note)
½ ounce dried porcini mushrooms
1½ cups warm water
2 tablespoons unsalted butter
¼ cup extra-virgin olive oil
½ cup finely chopped yellow onion
½ cup finely diced peeled carrot
¼ cup thinly sliced scallions, white part only
1 tablespoon minced garlic
Sea salt, preferably gray salt
Freshly ground black pepper
1 tablespoon minced fresh thyme
1 tablespoon minced fresh rosemary
3 thick slices apple-smoked bacon, finely chopped
2 cups dry red wine
2½ cups peeled fresh tomatoes, milled or puréed in a blender until smooth (see Chef's Note, page 25)
2 cups squab stock or Roasted Chicken Stock (page 18), or store-bought low-salt chicken broth
1 bay leaf
¼ cup minced fresh flat-leaf parsley
¼ cup unsalted butter at room temperature

ROASTED SQUASH

2 cups 1-inch cubes butternut squash (from a 4-pound squash)
½ cup (1 stick) unsalted butter
2 tablespoons finely shredded fresh sage, or 2 tablespoons minced garlic
¼ cup balsamic vinegar
2 tablespoons brown sugar
Sea salt, preferably gray salt
Freshly ground black pepper

RISOTTO

About 6 cups squab stock, Roasted Chicken Stock
    (page 18), mushroom stock, or
    Vegetable Stock (page 17)
3 tablespoons extra-virgin olive oil
1 cup finely chopped yellow onion
2 cups Arborio rice
1 tablespoon minced garlic
1 cup dry white wine
1 tablespoon finely shredded fresh sage
3 cups shredded fontina cheese (not packed)

About ¼ cup freshly grated Parmesan cheese
3 tablespoons minced fresh flat-leaf parsley
    for garnish

FOR THE SQUAB RAGÙ: Using a chef's knife, finely chop the squab livers and set aside. In a small bowl, soak the dried mushrooms in the warm water for 30 minutes. Lift the porcini out of the liquid with a slotted spoon and chop finely. Strain the soaking liquid through a fine-mesh sieve to catch any grit. Reserve the porcini and liquid separately.

Heat a large, heavy saucepan over medium heat, add the butter and olive oil, and heat until the butter foams. Add the onion, carrot, scallions, and garlic. Season with salt and pepper and cook the vegetables, stirring frequently, until soft, about 12 minutes. Add the thyme and rosemary and sauté for about 1 minute.

Add the chopped porcini mushrooms and chopped squab livers and sauté until livers are cooked through, about 3 minutes. Add the bacon and the ground squab, season with salt and pepper, and cook over medium heat, stirring occasionally to break up large clumps and to scrape the meat from the bottom of the pan, until it's cooked through, about 10 minutes. Add the wine and cook for 1 minute, stirring to scrape up the browned bits from the bottom of the pan. Add the reserved porcini liquid, stir to combine, and cook to reduce until the pan is almost dry. Add the tomatoes and bring to a simmer. Add the stock and bay leaf and simmer, uncovered, for about 30 minutes. Just before serving, stir in the parsley and butter.

FOR THE SQUASH: Preheat the oven to 350°F. Line a baking sheet with aluminum foil. Put the squash chunks into a large heatproof bowl.

Heat a large sauté pan or skillet over medium-high heat and add the butter. When it begins to brown, add the sage (or the garlic, one or the other but not both), followed by the vinegar and brown sugar. Stand back, as the mixture may spatter. Season with salt and pepper and simmer for 1 to 2 minutes, stirring gently to dissolve the sugar. Pour the mixture over the squash and toss well.

Arrange the squash on the prepared sheet, cover with aluminum foil, and bake until very tender and caramelized, about 40 minutes. Remove the foil and increase the oven temperature to 425°F for 5 minutes to caramelize the squash further. Remove from the oven and baste the squash with the liquid on the sheet. Let cool briefly, then purée in a food processor until creamy.

FOR THE RISOTTO: In a medium saucepan, bring the stock to a boil over high heat. Reduce the heat to low and keep the stock at the barest simmer while you make the risotto.

Heat a large sauté pan or heavy medium saucepan over medium heat, add the olive oil, and cook the onion until soft, about 10 minutes. Add the rice and the minced garlic and cook, stirring frequently, until the rice is pearly white with a translucent outer layer. Add the wine and cook, stirring, until very little liquid is left in the pan. Ladle in 1 cup of the hot stock. Reduce the heat to medium-low, keep the rice at a gentle simmer, and stir frequently until almost all the liquid is gone. Ladle in ½ cup of the hot stock and repeat, ladling in ½ cup of stock each time most of the liquid has been absorbed. (You might not use all the stock.) You'll stir and cook for about 18 to 25 minutes after adding the first cup of stock. Taste the rice to decide when it's done: it should be creamy, firm in the center but without any hint of crunch. Stir in the squash mixture, remove from the heat, and stir in the shredded sage and the fontina.

Divide the risotto among shallow bowls. Top with the squab ragù. Sprinkle with the Parmesan and parsley before serving.

Sea Urchin Risotto

SERVES 5

Divers hunting abalone often bring back sea urchins as a backup plan; if the abalone is hard to find, the sea urchins are always there, clinging to the rocks along the shore. When I eat sea urchin, I think of the Italian fishermen in west Marin County who've fished all their lives and know how to eat. If one of these old fishermen had a pound of rice, what would he make? Sea urchin risotto. He'd pop the urchins open and suck the roe while stirring the rice. When I was a young chef, friends would bring urchins to the restaurant and be given this dish in payment. Twenty lucky customers that day would also get to taste this.

This adventurous dish celebrates the rugged coastline of Northern California. It's worth having live sea urchins shipped to you. (Catalina Offshore Products ships them in packages of five; see Resources.) If you buy cleaned sea urchin instead of live urchin, choose premium grade or better.

While deciding whether or not you want to attempt this recipe, consider the very first person who took on the prickles of the urchin and discovered a treasure inside. That could be you.

Wine Pairing: Verdicchio

5 sea urchins
6 cups Fish Fumet (page 20), Vegetable Stock
(page 17), Shrimp Stock (page 20),
or a combination of 3 cups chicken stock
and 3 cups water
3 tablespoons extra-virgin olive oil
1 cup finely chopped yellow onion
2 cups Vialone Nano or Arborio rice
1½ cups dry white wine
½ teaspoon sea salt, preferably gray salt,
or kosher salt
2 tablespoons minced fresh chives
1 teaspoon minced Preserved Meyer Lemons
(page 34)
About 2 teaspoons fresh lemon juice

Have ready a small bowl to catch the sea urchin juice and a plate to hold the roe. Using a kitchen towel to protect your hand, hold a sea urchin with the upper side pointing toward the ceiling. Using a sharp knife or kitchen shears, cut a wide circle around the top of the shell, sort of like cutting a lid in a pumpkin to make a jack-o'-lantern. Pour any juice from inside the urchin into the bowl and reserve. Using a knife or your fingers, remove the brown matter, which is mostly partially digested seaweed. Using a spoon, carefully transfer the yellow roe to the plate. It's okay if some of the roe breaks, but try to save it in good-size clumps. You should get about four clumps of roe from each urchin. Discard everything except the shells, roe, and juice. Very gently rinse the roe in cool water, using a sieve if you like, then set aside one good clump of roe for each serving of risotto (you'll use this as garnish). Push the rest of the roe through a sieve into a bowl and set aside. Under cool running water, gently clean the inside of each urchin shell with your fingers, leaving the prickles in place. At Bottega, we run the shells through a dishwasher without any soap. You can do that, or boil the empty shells in a stockpot of water for 10 minutes. Drain and set the shells upside down on paper towels to dry while you make the risotto.

In a medium saucepan, bring the stock to a boil over high heat. Reduce the heat to low and keep it at the barest simmer.

Heat a large sauté pan or heavy saucepan over medium heat, add the olive oil, and cook the onion until soft, about 10 minutes. Add the rice and cook, stirring frequently, until the rice is pearly white with a translucent outer layer. Add the wine and cook, stirring, until very little liquid is left in the pan. Ladle in 1 cup of the hot stock and add the salt. Reduce the heat to medium-low and keep the rice at a gentle simmer, stirring frequently, until almost all the liquid is gone. Ladle in 1/2 cup of the hot stock and continue in this way, ladling in 1/2 cup of stock each time most of the liquid has been absorbed. All together, counting from the first cup of stock, you'll stir and cook for 18 to 25 minutes, but don't go by the clock; taste the rice to decide when it's done. It should be creamy, firm in the center, with no hint of crunch. Add the reserved sea urchin juice and half of the strained roe, stirring until mixed. Taste and add more strained roe if you like. Add the chives, the preserved lemon, and a few spoonfuls of water if the rice looks dry. Add a squeeze of fresh lemon juice. Taste and adjust the seasoning.

Spoon the risotto into the clean, dry shells and top each serving with a clump of roe before serving.

CHEF'S NOTE: At Bottega, we give this a dramatic presentation by making a bed of sea salt on the plate before placing the sea urchin.

The ABC's of Risotto

Risotto is easy to make if you know what to look for at each stage of the game. First, keep more stock or broth at a low simmer than you think you'll need; you don't want to run out of hot liquid when the risotto is three-quarters done. If you add cool stock, the risotto will stop cooking and lose its creamy texture.

Almost every risotto begins with minced onion, cooked over medium heat until soft but not brown. Add the rice and stir the rice and onion together for about 1 minute. You'll know the rice is ready for wine when it's pearly white and the outer layer of most of the grains looks translucent.

At that point, pour in the wine and cook until the pan is almost dry. Reduce the heat so the rice stays at a low simmer. You don't want to cook too rapidly, or the liquid will evaporate instead of being absorbed into the rice.

Season when you add the first cup of stock. If you wait until later, the rice will taste flat. When the first cup of stock is almost all absorbed, add another 1/2 cup of the hot stock. At this point, you're in a Zen frame of mind, contentedly watching the rice, stirring, and adding another 1/2 cup of liquid as soon as most of the last liquid has been absorbed. From the time you add the first cup of stock to the last 1/2-cup addition should be 18 to 25 minutes. Don't go by the clock, but by how the rice tastes to you; when done, the grains should be al dente—a slightly firm center with an overall creaminess. As soon as the rice is done, stir in any cheese or additions.

CHAPTER 6

Fish and Shellfish

PESCE ED I MOLLUSCHI

My Italian ancestors were landlocked in the mountains of Calabria, so they ate only fish that could travel for three days. The Chiarellos/Aiellos would have walked a donkey down the mountain to the sea, caught their sardines and anchovies, salted them, and loaded them back on the donkey for the trip home.

Even though I was born in California, those traditions made their way through generations and flavored the fish that my family ate. We caught sardines and grass shrimp and had big fish only when someone went to Monterey and came back with a fresh catch. We went every year to Coos Bay, Oregon, where we met up with about fifty cousins to dig for clams, go crabbing, and can some albacore tuna (you can find *that* recipe, Tuna Conserva, on page 21). Crab was a big deal every Christmas, but that was because we were within a day's drive of San Francisco Bay.

The menu at Bottega shows a great respect for the big fish like salmon and swordfish, but it also reveals my fondness for the fish that Chiarellos have eaten for many generations. The brodetto, for example, is a fisherman's stew, humble in origin and yet sultry and sexy with its accents of Spanish paprika and saffron. This is a signature dish that our regular guests order again and again.

Bottega has also become known for octopus with a recipe I created while cooking for the king of Thailand in Bangkok. I like that these dishes are Italian in origin but they've been influenced by a wide variety of cultures.

The one thing that's changed since those Chiarellos of old salt-packed their anchovies—today we feel a responsibility to become better stewards of the oceans and marine life. I'm a big fan of the Web site www.seafoodwatch.org, maintained by the inspirational Monterey Bay Aquarium. Please check it before purchasing fish. Because I cook fish every day, I have a good idea of what's sustainable, but I still visit the site periodically to see what's new on their list.

Pesce ed i Molluschi

Grilled Swordfish "alla Barcaiola"

SERVES 6

This combination is one of my favorites: swordfish so thin it cooks almost as soon as it hits the grill, served with a polenta so good it doesn't require any cheese. Finish with a briny caper- and anchovy-laden sauce and a fresh, bright celery salad to bring it all together.

Nick Ritchie, chef de cuisine at Bottega, worked in a restaurant near Salò, a beautiful town on the shores of Lago di Garda in Italy, and he brought back this sauce. A *barcaiolo* is a boatman, and thus the simple sauce can be made from pickled peppers, onions, and salt-packed capers that can stay on the boat, ready for the boatman's *cena* (dinner) when the fishing is done.

Wine Pairing: Verdicchio

SALSA ALLA BARCAIOLA (SALÒ SAUCE)

1 cup whole pepperoncini, preferably Bruno's
   wax peppers (see Resources), drained
½ cup cocktail onions packed in vinegar,
   drained (16 onions)
3 tablespoons capers, preferably salt-packed
   capers rinsed and soaked for 30 minutes
5 anchovies, preferably salt-packed anchovies
   soaked for 30 minutes and bones removed
1 garlic clove, peeled
1½ cups extra-virgin olive oil, or as needed
2 tablespoons chopped fresh flat-leaf parsley
Squeeze of fresh lemon juice
Sea salt, preferably gray salt, or kosher salt
Freshly ground black pepper

CELERY INSALATINA

1 tablespoon extra-virgin olive oil
2 teaspoons grated lemon zest
1 teaspoon fresh lemon juice
1 cup packed fresh flat-leaf parsley leaves
1 cup thinly sliced celery

Olive oil for brushing
Six 6-ounce swordfish fillets, ¾ to 1 inch thick
Sea salt, preferably gray salt
Freshly ground black pepper
6 cups Ancient-Grain Polenta
   (page 68, double the recipe)

Prepare a hot fire in a charcoal grill, preheat a gas grill to medium-high, or set out a grill pan.

FOR THE SAUCE: In a 6-quart pot over medium heat, combine the pepperoncini, cocktail onions, capers, anchovies, and garlic. Add just enough olive oil to cover, bring to a simmer, and cook gently for 10 minutes. Transfer to a blender or food processor, in batches if necessary, and purée the mixture. Add the parsley and lemon juice and season with salt and pepper. Set aside.

FOR THE INSALATINA: In a medium bowl, whisk together the olive oil, lemon zest, and lemon juice. Add the parsley and celery and toss to mix. Set aside.

Brush the grill grids with olive oil and wipe with paper towels to ensure that the fish doesn't stick. Or, heat a grill pan over high heat and oil the pan. Lightly brush the fish with olive oil and season with salt and pepper on each side. Grill the fillets for 2 to 3 minutes on each side. The fish is done when you see its juices run white. Transfer to a platter.

Add about ¾ cup of the polenta to one side of each warmed plate. Top with a grilled fish fillet and a few spoonfuls of the sauce. Place a small mound of insalatina beside it and serve.

Halibut in Parchment with Grilled Artichokes and Fisherman's Sauce

SERVES 6

Folding parchment paper around fish is worth the extra effort for that moment when you unseal the bag at the table and the moist, tender flesh is revealed in a rush of fragrant steam. If you don't want to bag the fish, keep it moist by cooking it on top of a puddle of sauce, with sauce spooned over and a little more sauce on the plate.

Halibut isn't the only option; this recipe works well with any white-fleshed fish. If the fish is thinner than 1 inch, decrease the cooking time by a minute or two.

Normally, you keep a bowl of lemon water nearby while cutting artichokes so you can keep them from oxidizing and turning brown. Here, you'll skip the water dunk and put them right in the marinade, which serves the same purpose. If you don't want the extra work of cutting artichokes, leave them out and instead serve the fish with a simple spinach salad.

Wine Pairing: Sauvignon Blanc

2 teaspoons minced garlic
1 teaspoon minced fresh thyme
½ teaspoon sea salt, preferably gray salt
¼ teaspoon freshly ground black pepper
4 tablespoons fresh lemon juice
½ cup extra-virgin olive oil
6 artichokes

OLIVE PASTE
2 cups pitted Kalamata olives
1 tablespoon extra-virgin olive oil

Six 6-ounce halibut fillets, each about 1 inch thick
1½ cups Fisherman's Sauce (see page 60)
2 tablespoons minced fresh flat-leaf parsley

Preheat the oven to 375°F. Prepare a hot fire in a charcoal grill, preheat a gas grill to high, or have ready a grill pan or sauté pan. In a large ovenproof baking dish, combine the garlic, thyme, salt, pepper, lemon juice, and olive oil and stir to blend.

Prepare each artichoke by pulling off the small lower leaves. Snap off the larger leaves by holding the bottom of the leaf in place with your thumb while snapping the top of each leaf downward, leaving a fingernail's worth of leaf still in place on the choke. Using a paring knife, slice away the tough dark green leaves to reveal the paler green heart. Trim the base of the artichoke next to the stem and peel with a vegetable peeler. Use a teaspoon to scrape the fuzzy choke away from the heart. Cut each heart into quarters, add to the marinade, and toss to coat.

Using tongs, transfer the artichoke pieces to the grill or a grill pan or sauté pan heated on high heat (reserve the marinade) and cook for 1 to 1½ minutes on each side. Using tongs, return the artichoke pieces to the marinade. Cover with aluminum foil and bake in the oven for 20 minutes. Remove the foil and bake for an additional 5 minutes, or until tender throughout.

FOR THE OLIVE PASTE: In a food processor, pulse together the olives and olive oil until smooth. Set aside.

For each fillet, cut a sheet of parchment paper about 16 inches long. Spoon about ¼ cup of the Fisherman's Sauce just off-center on each piece of paper. Place a fish fillet on top of the sauce. Divide the olive paste evenly among the packets, spooning it on top of each fillet. Top each fillet with 4 pieces of the grilled artichoke hearts and sprinkle with parsley.

Fold the paper over the fish. Align the two cut ends of the paper and fold the edges together twice, tucking the folded edges of the paper underneath the packet. Starting at the side closest to you (at the fold) begin crimping the paper together, folding the two sides of the parchment down in folds about 2 inches long and then folding it under again in small, tight creases. The folds won't be exactly even, and that's fine. The goal is to seal the paper all the way around just by folding the two edges under and under again; in the end you'll have a half-moon shaped packet with the fish inside. Place the packets on a baking sheet. (Cook the fish now, or refrigerate for up to 4 hours, being sure to remove the packages from the refrigerator 20 minutes before cooking.)

Preheat the oven to 400ºF.

Bake the packets for 11 minutes, or until the fillets are opaque throughout. To check if the fish are done, open one of the packets and cut into the fish with a knife.

Ask everyone to take their place at the table. Place each packet on a warmed plate and serve. (The fish will continue to cook inside the paper, so as soon as everyone's seated—always the hardest part of cooking at my house—have them tear open the bags, and enjoy.)

Note: How to Buy Frozen Fish

At Bottega we buy only fresh fish, but at home you don't always have the luxury. If you've ever had frozen fish that cooked up mushy or mealy, the problem most likely wasn't the freezing process but the thawing process. Because fish is so delicate, if the ice crystals melt too quickly the cell structure of the fish contracts and can be damaged. Basically, the individual cells deflate. Allowing frozen fish to thaw slowly, a process called "slacking," keeps the individual cells intact and the fish firm.

The first question to ask your fishmonger is "How many days do you let your fish thaw?" If he looks you in the eye and says, "Three days," this is a person who knows how to thaw fine fish. You can work this angle for yourself, too: Buy a 5-pound block of fish ahead of time, ask for it to be slacked for three days, and then either divide the fish among your cook friends or throw a fish-fry party. If you want to slack the fish at home, clear room in your refrigerator, cover the fish with plastic wrap, and let it sit undisturbed for 3 days. Don't be tempted to bring it to room temperature until it's completely thawed.

Walt—
part of my waiter Trifecta
with Murph & Scotty

Salt-Roasted Branzino

SERVES 4 TO 6, DEPENDING ON
THE SIZE OF YOUR FISH

This is just as much a Bottega signature as the brodetto, but this fish is simple, fast, and good for a spur-of-the-moment gathering with friends. Make this with the best white-fleshed fish in the market—snapper, sea bass, and bream are all great cooked this way.

One of the most vivid memories of my life happened during a meal of *branzino*. My then-girlfriend and now-wife, Eileen, and I were in Brittany, tasting sea salt, and then having this salt-encrusted fish made for us in a tiny restaurant on the coast. We watched as the waiter cracked open the salt crust, and we tasted this wonderful fish. Eileen and I were about halfway through the meal when we heard that two planes had flown into the World Trade Center. We ran out the door to the point of the coast that jutted farthest into the ocean, trying and trying and trying to reach our families by cell phone.

When it became clear that we needed to gather our things, we found that the staff had packed up not just our fish but other foods as well. Every face held the same expression: shock, but also concern, empathy, caring. We weren't just Americans far from home; we were part of a very large group of people around the world feeling this loss.

You'd think I wouldn't want to make this dish again, given those circumstances, but in fact, when I make this, I think about the people in that restaurant putting a hand on my shoulder, handing me a bag full of food, wishing me a fast trip home, and sending out a prayer that my family was safe. I make this fish every time with a filled heart and much gratitude.

Wine Pairing: Champagne

1 whole fish, about 14 inches long (about 1½ pounds), or 1 smaller whole fish for each person
1 lemon, thinly sliced, plus 5 lemons, halved
Sea salt, preferably gray salt
Freshly ground black pepper
Extra-virgin olive oil for drizzling
6 pounds kosher salt
6 cups water, plus more as needed

Preheat the oven to 500°F. Leave the fins on each fish but make a slit from mouth to tail along the bottom. Run your thumb along the slit to open it. With your thumbs, press along the spine to release blood, then rinse the fish in cold running water until clean and pat dry. Leave the scales and the collar on; you want the fish clean inside but intact. Lay the lemon slices inside the fish, overlapping them. Season inside the fish with sea salt and pepper and drizzle with olive oil both inside and out.

Pour the kosher salt into a very large bowl. Add the water, 1 cup at a time, and mix it with your hands, fluffing the salt like snow. In a roasting pan, a 9-by-13-inch baking dish, or any combination of pans that fits your fish, mound up about half the fluffed salt. Lay the fish on the salt. If cooking more than one fish, yin-yang them, so they're laid out in the pan head to tail. If you have an internal thermometer (the kind with a cord that can run outside the oven), make an incision just behind the head of the middle fish where you can insert the thermometer.

Pour on the remaining salt, pressing it in place with your hands so every bit of the fish is covered under a good salt layer. Place the 5 halved lemons in the pan around the fish. Drizzle olive oil over the salt and the lemons.

Roast for about 20 minutes, or until the internal thermometer or an instant-read thermometer inserted in the thickest part of the fish registers 140°F. Remove from the oven and let rest for 10 to 15 minutes: the bigger the fish, the longer the rest. Use this time to gather your friends around the fish, and pour a little more wine for everyone. When you're ready, crack open the salt crust with a big spoon. Use the spoon to move some of the salt from the top of the fish, and transfer the fish to a carving board. With a sharp knife, slit the skin at the top of the fish from head to tail and gently peel away the skin. Maneuver under the fillet to get the spine, gently removing it using two spoons. With a large spoon, transfer the first serving of fish to a plate (it will be juicy). Put a half a roasted lemon on the plate with the fish, and move on to the next serving. Serve with more roasted lemons at the table. Enjoy.

Wood-Grilled Octopus "Under a Brick" with Olive Oil–Braised Potatoes

SERVES 4

This is a dish Bottega has become known for. It's probably a rare night when you say, "I'm in the mood for octopus," but once you get past the learning curve, this dish is worth every bit of effort. Fresh is always better, of course, but if frozen is the only octopus you can find, make sure your fishmonger slacks it properly, letting it thaw a good three days in a refrigerator to make sure the flesh stays firm (see Note, page 123).

You may want to stray beyond your usual grocery stores in the hunt for octopus. If you live near a Japanese or a Mexican neighborhood, my bet is either one will have a market where you can buy fresh octopus.

Wine Pairing: Greco

One 3- to 3½-pound octopus
½ cup Smoky Paprika Oil (page 28),
    or ½ cup olive oil mixed with ½ teaspoon
    pimentón de la Vera (smoked Spanish paprika)
2 tablespoons olive oil (see Chef's Note, page 19)

OLIVE OIL–BRAISED POTATOES
2 unpeeled Idaho potatoes (about 1½ pounds),
    scrubbed and cut on the bias into
    1-inch-thick pieces
½ teaspoon sea salt, preferably gray salt,
    or kosher salt
¼ teaspoon freshly ground black pepper
1 cup extra-virgin olive oil, or as needed
1 teaspoon minced fresh thyme
1 tablespoon minced garlic

PICKLED RED ONION
1 red onion, cut into paper-thin slices
1 tablespoon red wine vinegar

½ tablespoon extra-virgin olive oil,
    plus more for drizzling
1 teaspoon fresh lemon juice
2 cups packed arugula or rucola
    (wild arugula) leaves
½ cup Salsa Verde (page 26), plus more
    for serving (optional)

In a large bowl, combine the octopus and the paprika oil. Marinate for at least 1 hour at room temperature or in the refrigerator for up to 2 days.

Heat a large cast-iron pan or a grill pan over medium-high heat, add the olive oil, then the octopus pieces; weight them down with a smaller pan filled with a few heavy cans inside. Cook for 2 minutes on each side, or until crisp and charred on the outside and hot all the way through. Remove from the heat and set aside.

FOR THE POTATOES: Preheat the oven to 300°F. Arrange the potato slices on one or two rimmed baking sheets in a single layer. Season both sides with the salt and pepper. Pour on enough olive oil to reach about one-third up the sides of the potatoes. Turn the potatoes over to coat with the oil. Scatter the thyme and garlic over the potatoes, sprinkle with a little more salt, if desired, and bake until the potatoes are tender, 20 to 25 minutes. Remove from the oven and let the potatoes cool.

FOR THE ONION: In a medium bowl, toss the onion slices with your fingers to break apart the sections. Add the vinegar, toss again, and let stand for 15 minutes to 1 hour. This is a very quick pickling to just smooth away a little of the onion's sharpness.

Whisk together the ½ tablespoon olive oil and lemon juice and add the arugula. Toss until lightly coated. Spoon the potatoes onto each of 4 warmed plates and top with a small mound of arugula. Place a few of the tentacle pieces on the greens along with one or two thicker slices of octopus. Scatter pickled red onion over the plate and then drizzle the octopus with the salsa verde and a few drops of olive oil. If you like, pass extra salsa verde in small bowls.

Bring a large pot of water to a simmer over medium-high heat. Cut the head off the octopus, leaving enough of the pouch so the tentacles remain attached to each other. Cut open the head and pull out any hard bits, including the beak. Using a knife blade, scrape the inside of all loose matter.

Add the octopus to the pot of simmering water, resting a small colander on top of the octopus if necessary to keep it submerged. Reduce the heat to low and cook for at least 45 minutes. Turn off the heat and let the octopus sit in the poaching water for another 30 minutes, or until tender when pierced with a skewer. If it still feels slightly tough, cook for another 15 minutes and test again. Using tongs, transfer to a baking sheet and let cool to the touch. Rub the reddish-purple skin off with your fingers and discard. If you can't get the skin off around the suction cups, use a small, sharp knife to cut away the suction cups and any remaining skin. Taste the smaller suction cups for sand; if they aren't sandy, leave them on, as they add a nice texture to the dish. Cut the tentacles on the bias, 4 or 5 inches long. Cut the head into thin slices.

How Far Would You Go for Tender Octopus?

I did a good amount of traveling and cooking to promote Mondavi wines in the 1990s. During one memorable trip, I got to take over a kitchen in the Mandarin Oriental Hotel in Bangkok for a two-week promotion. The king of Thailand was expected one night, which meant I was practicing all my tricks, preparing for the dinner and especially focusing on cooking tender octopus.

Now, Italians have all kinds of lore for how to make *polpo* tender: You put a penny in the stock, you put a cork in the pot, you have a Corsican virgin walk around the fire three times clockwise. So there I am with my pennies, my corks, and my Corsican virgin, ready to make the most tender octopus on the block. I cooked my dish, the whole nine-yard, three-hour process, the same way I usually do, and was shocked when my octopus came out overcooked by a mile.

"What's the deal?" I asked the Thai cooks working with me, but they all smiled inscrutably and went back to their own cooking.

Okay. Roll up the sleeves, make it again, cook it half the time I usually do. Again, it's overcooked, and still, mum's the word from the other cooks. So I went to my *comis*, the apprentice assigned to me by the kitchen, and asked him each and every day for two weeks: "How did you get this octopus so tender?" No answer. Finally, on the last day, he beckoned for me to follow him. We went outside and I climbed up behind him on his tuk-tuk (a three-wheeled scooter, about half the height of my ten-speed at home). For the next twenty minutes all I can hear is REEEEEEEEEE. The tuk-tuk made this high-pitched two-stroke whine all the way to the docks, where we jumped onto a dilapidated, thirty-foot-long, super-skinny boat propelled by my *comis* and a very long pole. We pulled away from the dock, and after an hour of winding through the sloughs of Bangkok with my ears still ringing from the tuk-tuk ride, I was starting to think I'd been chef-napped. We docked, and he led me to a ramshackle wooden structure with an orange power cord running out the door and along the ground as far as the eye could see. Inside the shack was a beat-up Maytag washing machine, empty of water but tumbling a load of about three dozen octopi. Trust the Thai to tenderize octopus using modern technology.

I came home and, with the help of my local fishmonger, Mikey, tried to set up my own octo-machine using an old washer and a bunch of training baseballs (because they're heavier than a regular baseball), but the health inspector didn't go for the idea. So we started from scratch and created our own machine, starting with a brand-new cement mixer (never used for its intended purpose), filled with new golf balls. We use our octo-tenderizer every day, maybe one reason our octopus has become one of Bottega's signature dishes.

I've written the preceding recipe assuming that you don't have an octo-machine at your house, but if you come up with a creative way to tenderize you can reduce the cooking time in the recipe. Facebook me and show me your tenderizing technique.

The Fruit of the Vine

Our wine director and assistant G.M., Michael Iglesias, follows two unique ideas with our wine list. The first is pricing. At Bottega, we mark up our wines just twice instead of the normal three to four times. This allows our customers to enjoy wines that they normally could not buy at retail, at an affordable price.

The second idea behind our wine list is to weave together a collection of our favorite Napa Valley and Italian wines, offering vintages across the spectrum that best complement our food and entertaining style. Iglesias offers regular wine classes to every Bottega staff member; he teaches how to taste but also gives the stories behind the wines and the vintners. These stories add such great flavor to the experience.

At Chiarello Family Vineyards, I organically farm 20 acres of Cabernet, Zinfandel, and Petite Syrah. Two of these vineyards are 100 years old and have never been irrigated; these pre-Prohibition vines speak to the history of the Napa Valley with each glass. I've named the vineyards after my wife, daughters, and my son. The idea is simple: when I work in the Eileen vineyard, for example, I spend that time thinking of my wife and what I can do to be a better husband and father.

Larry Turley & wine pro Suzanne Chambers
(Mr. Old vine)   (über-cute wife)

My Latin brother
& wine director
Michael Iglesias

Adriatic Brodetto

SERVES 8 TO 10

This is, without a doubt, one of the best things at Bottega. My wife has had this more than a hundred times. Rich, slow-cooked tomatoes make the sauce so extraordinary, you'll use the technique again and again. This confit method works with peeled fresh tomatoes just as easily as with San Marzano tomatoes from a can. I recommend cooking the confit the day before you make the brodetto.

This stew deserves a beautiful plating, and it gets one: A vibrant gold saffron rouille is ladled right on top of each individual serving, followed by a handful of crunchy, warm croutons. This is everything you want in a seafood stew, times ten.

You don't make this for two people; you make it for ten or twenty, and everything else on the table should be simple: a green salad, really good bread, a magnum of a wine from Southern Italy—stop! Don't even think about dessert.

Wine Pairing: Southern Italian red

TOMATO CONFIT
Two 28-ounce cans whole San Marzano
   tomatoes (juice reserved), or 2 pounds
   fresh tomatoes, peeled
1 teaspoon minced fresh thyme
1 bay leaf
¼ cup extra-virgin olive oil, or as needed
1 teaspoon sea salt, preferably gray salt,
   or kosher salt
¼ teaspoon freshly ground black pepper

SAFFRON ROUILLE
½ cup dry white wine
Large pinch of saffron threads
2 egg yolks at room temperature
1 teaspoon fork-mashed garlic (about 1 large clove)
1 ½ teaspoons Calabrian chile paste (see Resources),
   or ¼ teaspoon red pepper flakes
1 tablespoon pimentón de la Vera
   (smoked Spanish paprika; see Resources)
2 tablespoons fresh lemon juice
2 cups extra-virgin olive oil at room temperature
Sea salt, preferably gray salt
Freshly ground black pepper

BRODETTO SAUCE
¼ cup extra-virgin olive oil
3 yellow onions, cut soup-style (peeled and thinly
   sliced from stem to bottom)
1 tablespoon sliced garlic (about 2 cloves)
¼ cup red wine vinegar
2 teaspoons capers, preferably salt-packed capers
   rinsed and soaked for 30 minutes
3 anchovy fillets, preferably salt-packed anchovies
   rinsed and soaked for 30 minutes
½ cup dry white wine
2 cups Fish Fumet (page 20)
Tomato Confit (at right)

CROUTONS
1 loaf ciabatta bread
1 tablespoon unsalted butter
½ cup extra-virgin olive oil

2 cups extra-virgin olive oil, plus more for drizzling
½ cup sliced garlic
3 dozen mussels, scrubbed and debearded
About 2 pounds monkfish
About 2 pounds rock cod
½ cup chopped fresh basil
¼ cup chopped fresh tarragon
¼ cup chopped fresh flat-leaf parsley,
   plus more for sprinkling
About 1 ½ pounds calamari, cleaned (see page 70)

In a blender, combine the egg yolks, mashed garlic, chile paste, and pimentón; blend until smooth. Add the wine-saffron reduction and lemon juice and blend. With the machine running, gradually add the oil in a thin stream to make an emulsified sauce. Season with salt and pepper. Set aside.

FOR THE BRODETTO SAUCE: Heat a small stockpot over medium heat, add the olive oil, onions, and garlic and sauté for 10 minutes, or until soft. Add the vinegar and cook until the pan is almost dry. Add the capers and anchovies and sauté until the anchovies break up. Add the wine and cook until the liquid has almost evaporated. Add the fumet, bring to a boil, and add the tomato confit. Reduce the heat to a simmer and cook for 20 to 30 minutes. Remove from the heat.

FOR THE CROUTONS: Slice all the crust from the ciabatta loaf. Discard the crusts (or save them for making bread crumbs for another dish), and cut the loaf into 2-inch squares or tear them into uneven pieces. Heat a large sauté pan or skillet over medium-high heat and melt the butter with the olive oil. Add the bread cubes and toast for 30 seconds to 1 minute, tossing until evenly browned. Remove from the heat and set aside.

Heat a very large soup pot or Dutch oven (6 to 8 quarts) over medium-high heat, add the 2 cups olive oil, and sauté the garlic until golden, 2 to 4 minutes. (A shorter, wider pot is better than a tall one, because trying to gently stir all the fish and shellfish in a narrow pot makes your life harder.) Add the mussels, monkfish, and brodetto sauce. (Throughout, treat the stew gently to avoid breaking the fish.) Bring to a gentle boil. Reduce the heat to a simmer and cook for 3 minutes. Add the rock cod and cook for another 2 minutes. Add the basil, tarragon, and the ¼ cup parsley. Finally, add the calamari, submerging it in the sauce. Simmer just until the calamari is cooked through and warm, 1 to 2 minutes.

Ladle the stew into shallow bowls. Top with a few spoonfuls of the saffron rouille. Give it a good sprinkle of chopped fresh parsley and a drizzle of extra-virgin olive oil. Toss on a few croutons (you can rewarm them quickly in a sauté pan if you like), and serve.

FOR THE TOMATO CONFIT: Preheat the oven to 250°F. In a Dutch oven, gently arrange the tomatoes. Add the thyme and with your hands crumble the bay leaf over the tomatoes. Pour in enough olive oil to cover the tomatoes and add the salt and pepper. Bake for about 4 hours, or until tender, then increase the oven temperature to 450°F and bake for 5 to 10 minutes, or just until browned. Remove from the oven and let cool to the touch. In a blender or food processor, blend the tomatoes and their liquid until smooth. Set aside or cover and refrigerate.

FOR THE SAFFRON ROUILLE: In a small sauté pan, mix the wine and saffron. Bring to a boil and cook to reduce by about three-quarters, 3 minutes. Remove from the heat and set aside to cool.

"Angry" Prawns with White Bean Passatina

SERVES 6

In Italy, Tuscans are sometimes called *mangiafagioli*—"bean eaters"—because many Tuscans eat bean soup every day of their life. In other words, they know their way around a white bean. In Tuscany, Toscanelli beans are the lobster, the filet mignon, the highest level of beanmanship. You can use navy beans, great Northern beans, or cannellini in this recipe, but if you find Toscanelli beans, you'll understand why the Tuscans lavish so much affection on these small but mighty legumes.

Seldom will I advise people to go to great lengths for a bean, but these really are unbelievable. Talk to your produce people, or see Resources.

What's a passatina? In simplest terms, it's a purée of beans, but that's like saying a soufflé is just eggs. At Bottega, we serve a passatina to showcase beans with fantastic flavor.

Wine Pairing: Gewürztraminer

WHITE BEAN PASSATINA

1 cup dried Toscanelli beans, rinsed and picked over
½ cup diced yellow onion
½ cup diced peeled carrot
½ cup diced celery
1 bay leaf
Small piece of prosciutto heel
Sea salt, preferably gray salt
Freshly ground black pepper
¾ cup extra-virgin olive oil

"ANGRY" PRAWNS

1 cup all-purpose flour
1½ tablespoons pure California chile powder
1 tablespoon sea salt, preferably gray salt
1 teaspoon freshly ground black pepper
2 pounds extra-large prawns (16 to 20 count), shelled and deveined, tails intact
½ cup extra-virgin olive oil, plus more if needed
4 tablespoons thinly sliced garlic
2 tablespoons seeded and thinly sliced serrano chiles
2 cups packed fresh basil leaves
1 teaspoon Calabrian chile paste (see Resources), or ¼ teaspoon red pepper flakes, plus more for serving
1 tablespoon grated orange zest
Sea salt, preferably gray salt
Freshly ground black pepper

FOR THE PASSATINA: Pour the beans into a large stockpot and add cold water to cover by 2 inches. Turn the heat to high and bring to a boil. Cover, remove from the heat and let stand 1 hour, then drain. Add cold water to cover by 2 inches, and then add the onion, carrot, celery, bay leaf, and prosciutto. Bring to a simmer over medium-low heat and let the beans cook gently, uncovered, for about 20 minutes. Season with salt and pepper, reduce the heat to low, and simmer gently until the beans are tender. The timing will depend on the age and size of the beans you've used; start tasting for tenderness after 60 to 90 minutes. Let the beans cool completely in the cooking liquid. Set the pan aside or refrigerate for up to 3 days, keeping the beans in their cooking liquid.

When ready to purée the beans, discard the prosciutto and drain the beans but reserve 1 cup of the cooking liquid. In a food processor or blender, process 3 cups of the cooked beans (not the liquid) until smooth. Stir in the ¾ cup olive oil. Season with salt and pepper. If the mixture needs to be thinned slightly, add ¼ to ½ cup of the reserved liquid. (Set aside until ready to serve, or cover and refrigerate overnight. Bring the beans to room temperature, then spoon into a saucepan over medium-low heat until the beans are warm, stirring occasionally.)

FOR THE PRAWNS: Before you begin cooking the prawns, have everything you'll need at hand. In a medium bowl, combine the flour, chile powder, salt, and pepper. Stir with a whisk to blend. Dredge the shrimp in the flour mixture and set them aside on a baking sheet. Discard the leftover flour.

Line a baking sheet with paper towels. Heat a large sauté pan or skillet over high heat, add ¼ cup of the oil, and sauté one-half of the prawns (8 to 10 prawns) for 2 minutes, or until evenly pink on both sides but not browned. Using a slotted spoon or wire skimmer, transfer the prawns to the prepared sheet to drain. If needed, add another 2 tablespoons of olive oil to the pan and heat it before adding the next batch of prawns. Repeat until all the prawns are cooked. Remove the paper towels and transfer the sheet of prawns to a 250°F oven to keep warm.

Here's where you shift to high-powered-chef mode: Add the remaining ¼ cup olive oil to the same pan in which you cooked the prawns and heat over high heat; add the garlic and turn your kitchen fan to high. As soon as the garlic begins to turn light brown, add the chiles, shake the pan, and add the basil. The leaves will pop and spurt, so stand back! Cook until the leaves are crispy and translucent, about 2 minutes. Make sure you have at least 2 tablespoons of olive oil in the bottom of the pan. Add more if necessary. Add the chile paste, stir, and remove from the heat. Add the orange zest and season with salt and pepper.

Spoon a mound of the beans on each of 6 warmed plates. Top with 5 or 6 prawns. Drizzle with some of the pan sauce and top with the basil leaves. Serve with small dishes of Calabrian chile paste so guests can add more to suit their tastes.

Seared Day-Boat Scallops, Chickpea Passatina, and Cauliflower Agrodolce

SERVES 6

Day boat means just that: the boats go out in the morning and come back the same day with a fresh catch. Ask for these scallops by name, and take note of one way they differ from scallops that have been frozen. Day-boat scallops show their sex with color; females are more orange or pink than the males. Commercial fishing boats that stay out for weeks at a time are allowed to put a weak chloride solution on seafood. This bleaches any color from scallops, which is why frozen scallops are all a uniform white.

Ask your fishmonger for sushi-quality day-boat scallops; they're worth ordering in advance. If your fishmonger is really good, your day-boat scallops will arrive in a muslin bag that allows air through.

Any rich seafood benefits from this agrodolce, or "sweet-tart" sauce. Try it with salmon or shrimp. Both the passatina and the cauliflower can be made a day ahead if you like. I think the agrodolce actually tastes better the next day. Reheat the cauliflower and the passatina so they're ready to go before you begin cooking the scallops.

Pink chickpeas have a Middle Eastern spiciness that I love. If you can't find them in your specialty market, see Resources.

Ask your butcher for prosciutto hocks or heels—the hard ends too small to be thinly sliced.

Wine Pairing: Italian Riesling

CHICKPEA PASSATINA

1 cup dried pink chickpeas or other chickpeas or white beans, rinsed and picked over
½ cup diced yellow onion
½ cup diced peeled carrot
½ cup diced celery
1 bay leaf
Small piece of prosciutto heel
1 teaspoon sea salt, preferably gray salt, or kosher salt
Freshly ground black pepper
¾ cup extra-virgin olive oil

CAULIFLOWER AGRODOLCE

3 cups white wine vinegar or Champagne vinegar
1 cup sugar
⅓ cup golden raisins
1 sweet white onion, finely diced
½ cup unsalted butter
¼ cup extra-virgin olive oil
1 head of cauliflower (about 2½ pounds), broken into florets
Pinch of sea salt, preferably gray salt
Freshly ground black pepper
2 tablespoons pine nuts, toasted (see Chef's Note, page 27)
¼ cup olio nuovo or finest late-harvest extra-virgin olive oil
2 tablespoons shredded fresh flat-leaf parsley leaves

½ cup extra-virgin olive oil
18 day-boat sea scallops (about 3 pounds), side muscles removed, rinsed, and patted dry
Sea salt, preferably gray salt
Freshly ground black pepper
2 tablespoons unsalted butter
½ tablespoon minced fresh flat-leaf parsley, plus more for garnish
Late-harvest olive oil for drizzling

FOR THE PASSATINA: Pour the beans into a large stockpot and add cold water to cover by 2 inches. Turn the heat to high and bring to a boil. Cover, remove from the heat and let stand 1 hour, then drain. Add cold water to cover by 2 inches, and then add the onion, carrot, celery, bay leaf, and prosciutto. Bring to a simmer over medium heat and let the beans cook gently, uncovered, for about 20 minutes. Add the salt, season with pepper, reduce heat to low, and simmer gently until the beans are tender. The timing will depend on the age and size of the beans you've used; start tasting for tenderness after 60 to 90 minutes. Let the beans cool completely in the cooking liquid. Set the pan aside or refrigerate for up to 3 days, keeping the beans in their cooking liquid.

When ready to purée the beans, discard the prosciutto and drain the beans but reserve 1 cup of the cooking liquid. In a food processor or blender, process 3 cups of the cooked beans (not the liquid) until smooth. Stir in the ¾ cup olive oil. Season with salt and pepper. If the mixture needs to be thinned slightly, add ¼ to ½ cup of the reserved liquid. (Set aside until ready to serve, or cover and refrigerate overnight.)

FOR THE AGRODOLCE: In a large saucepan or sauté pan (at least 10 inches wide), combine the vinegar, sugar, and raisins. Bring to a boil over medium heat and add the onion. Reduce the heat to a simmer and cook until the onion is soft and the liquid is reduced to about 1 cup, 3 to 5 minutes. Remove from the heat and set aside.

Heat a large sauté pan or skillet over medium heat, add the butter with the olive oil, and heat until the butter foams. Add the cauliflower florets and season with salt and pepper. Cook until tender and lightly browned, about 7 minutes.

Using a slotted spoon or wire skimmer, transfer the cauliflower to a sieve or colander to allow excess fat to drip off. Wipe out the sauté pan and return the drained cauliflower to the pan over medium heat. Add the pine nuts and sauté for 30 seconds. Add the vinegar mixture and toss to infuse the flavors. Drizzle with the olio nuovo. Top with the parsley and taste for seasoning. (Use now, or cover and refrigerate for up to 24 hours; reheat in a large sauté pan over medium heat before you begin cooking the scallops.)

To properly brown, the scallops need some room in the sauté pan. If cooking all the scallops at once, use a 14-inch pan. If you don't have one this large, cook the scallops in batches. Heat a large sauté pan over medium-high heat, add the olive oil, and heat until it shimmers. Season the scallops with salt and pepper on both sides and sauté for 2 minutes, or until nicely browned on the bottom. Add the butter to the pan, turn the scallops over, and add the ½ tablespoon parsley. Cook for 1 minute more. Tilt the pan and give each scallop a little basting of butter. Remove from the heat.

Place 3 scallops on each of 6 warmed plates. Spoon a little of the brown butter from the pan over each serving. Add a little cauliflower on top of each scallop with a serving of passatina (seared-side up, if you've seared it; see Chef's Notes, below) on one side of the plate. Drizzle the late-harvest olive oil lightly over each scallop.

CHEF'S NOTES: To dress this up, sear the passatina lightly on one side when you reheat it. In a large sauté pan, heat a little olive oil over medium-high heat and sear the passatina in ½-cup amounts, then gently transfer each seared helping to a warmed plate, seared-side up.

I always buy a sacrificial scallop or two. You get to take it out and taste it during searing to be sure that all the other scallops are perfect.

CHAPTER 7

Meats and Poultry

CARNE E POLLAME

When buying meats and poultry, a restaurateur faces an honest dilemma: buy the very best tasting beef, goat, chicken, and lamb that's available locally, or buy the best-tasting period? In a perfect world, the best lamb, for example, would be sustainably ranched just down the road. I'd send someone over to pick it up fresh every day. In fact, the guy who's raised the best lamb I've tasted *was* just down the road—until he picked up and moved with all his lambs to Colorado. It took me nine years of searching to find lamb with that same flavor closer to home. (The lamb I served at home during those nine years was still good—just not quite the euphoria-inducing lamb that this guy raises.)

So what is my responsibility to my customers? I'm responsible for buying from farmers and ranchers who practice sustainable methods. I'm responsible for buying locally when possible. But the bottom line is, my customers pay me to put the best-tasting food on their plate that I can.

How do I find a way to get lambs just as good as those Colorado lambs? I first widen my circle, checking out local producers that I may not have bought from before. I then put all my powers of persuasion into trying to convince the Colorado rancher into having part of his business here in the wine country. (He's considering this, but it hasn't happened yet.)

How do you buy meats and poultry that taste as good as what we serve at Bottega? That's a tough one. Keep in mind that I've sought out great ranchers for more than twenty years, and I have strong relationships with the people who raise our beef, pork, lamb, and chicken. That's the one word of advice I have for you: relationships. Find a good butcher and talk to him or her every week. Go to farmers' markets and seek out folks who sustainably raise grass-fed meats and poultry. Another good place to start is Heritage Foods (see Resources). You can widen your own circle and improve the flavor of your food while doing the planet a good turn.

Carne e Pollame

Grilled Fennel-Spiced Lamb Chops with Roasted-Cherry Vinaigrette

SERVES 6

Lamb is rich; you don't need a rack per person. I serve three chops per serving and it's the perfect amount, especially with Ancient-Grain Polenta underneath.

I like to clean the lamb bones right to the eye. You can take a paring knife and scrape the bone clean to make it look like the kind in a fancy French restaurant. Wrap some foil around the end of the bone during grilling so it stays bright and beautiful. (Ask your butcher to French the lamb if you'd rather not do it yourself.) When I'm making this at home, I bring the lamb chops to room temperature and grill them rare no more than 1 hour before I plan to serve them, so they need just a little more time on the grill before serving. Then, when guests arrive, I finish grilling them so it takes me half the time and I'm back with my guests sooner.

You can pan-sear the chops in a hot cast-iron grill pan, or grill them. I prefer to use a wood-fired grill.

For the cherry vinaigrette, you don't have to roast all of the cherries. If you roast a portion of them, it flavors the whole batch. If you don't have good cherries, use a pound of pitted and halved fresh apricots in their place.

Wine Pairing: Pinot Noir

ROASTED CHERRY VINAIGRETTE

1 pound fresh sweet cherries such as
    Bing or Rainier, pitted and halved,
    or 1 pound apricots, pitted and halved
8 tablespoons extra-virgin olive oil
Sea salt, preferably gray salt
Freshly ground black pepper
6 scallions, white part only,
    cut on the bias into ¼-inch pieces
1 ½ tablespoons tarragon vinegar
1 tablespoon minced fresh tarragon

18 lamb chops cut from a rack of lamb,
    at room temperature
Sea salt, preferably gray salt
Fennel Spice Blend (page 214)
Extra-virgin olive oil for brushing
Ancient-Grain Polenta (page 68)

FOR THE CHERRY VINAIGRETTE: Preheat the oven to 450°F. In a large bowl, mix the cherries with 7 tablespoons of the oil. Season with salt and pepper. Heat an ovenproof sauté pan or skillet over medium-high heat, add the remaining 1 tablespoon olive oil, and heat until shimmering. Add half of the cherries and toss them once or twice. Transfer the pan to the oven and roast until the cherries around the edges of the pan begin to turn lightly brown, about 2 minutes. Remove from the oven and add to the remaining cherries. Add the scallions, vinegar, and tarragon. Taste and adjust the seasoning. Set aside.

Prepare a hot wood fire in a charcoal grill or have a grill pan ready. Season both sides of each chop with salt and Fennel Spice Blend. Brush lightly with olive oil. If using a grill pan, heat the pan over high heat and oil the pan. Using the cross-hatched grill-mark method on page 159, grill the chops for 3 to 4 minutes on each side. Transfer the chops to a platter and let rest for 5 to 10 minutes.

Place a mound of polenta on each warmed plate. Place 3 chops on top of the polenta with the bones pointing toward the plate's center. Top with a spoonful of the vinaigrette. Ladle any extra vinaigrette into small ramekins to pass at the table.

Note: The Evolution of Grass-Fed Lamb
Grass-fed lamb has come even further in quality in the past ten years than beef. I prefer domestic lamb to the lamb from Australia or New Zealand. Even though I admire how the Aussies and Kiwis have created a great product and generated a lot of new interest in lamb, I buy lamb that tastes like lamb. Lamb from Down Under often has all gaminess bred out of it, so it tastes closer to beef.

For the best flavor, ask your butcher to cut your chops from a rack of lamb while you wait.

Goat's Milk–Braised Lamb Shanks with Carrot, Onion, and Eggplant Caponata

SERVES 6

Every Italian has a recipe for lamb shank, but this goat's milk braise makes my version unique. Most lamb shanks come from the hind shank; we use the foreshank, because it's smaller and more tender, and we cook it bone-in for a little more drama on the table.

The goat's milk braise makes the meat silken, soft, and delicious. You can try this same goat's milk braise with pot roast, veal, and other meats as well. This is a low-barometer recipe, great when the day is stormy and you're happy to be indoors, parked next to a bowl of this lamb.

For me, local fresh goat milk is key. I would never make this with goat's milk from a can. If you don't have local fresh goat's milk, use whole cow's milk.

The goat's milk will curdle as you make the braise, but it will come back together before you're finished; don't worry. You will have some extra sauce, but you'll be glad to have it over pasta with leftover lamb and caponata the next day.

Wine Pairing: Brunello

6 lamb shanks
Sea salt, preferably gray salt, or kosher salt
Freshly ground black pepper
4 tablespoons extra-virgin olive oil, plus ½ cup
4 to 6 garlic cloves, halved
2 cups thinly sliced sweet white onions
6 cups trimmed, cored, and thinly sliced fennel
    (about 4 fennel bulbs)
1 teaspoon fennel seeds, toasted
    (see Chef's Note, page 189)
4 cups fresh goat's milk or whole cow's milk
1 cup heavy cream
1 bay leaf
Carrot, Onion, and Eggplant Caponata (page 171)
Minced fresh flat-leaf parsley for sprinkling

Preheat the oven to 275°F. Remove any dangling silver skin from the lamb shanks but do not expose the meat; leave in place whatever natural cover there is. Season the lamb with salt and pepper and set aside.

Heat a Dutch oven at least 12 inches long over high heat, add 2 tablespoons of the olive oil, and heat until shimmering. Add half the lamb shanks, taking care not to crowd the meat. Brown the meat on all sides. Transfer the lamb to a plate, add the remaining 2 tablespoons olive oil, and brown the remaining shanks on all sides. Transfer to the plate with the other shanks.

Discard the fat in the pan. (It will be too brown to use for the veggies.) Heat the pan over medium-high heat, add the ½ cup olive oil, and then add the garlic, onions, sliced fennel, and fennel seeds. Sauté until lightly browned, about 4 minutes.

Return the browned lamb to the pan and add the goat's milk, cream, and bay leaf. Bring to a simmer over medium heat, cover, and transfer to the oven to braise for about 2 hours, or until the lamb is very tender.

Remove from the oven and let cool to room temperature. Using tongs, carefully remove the lamb pieces from the braising liquid and set aside. Using an immersion blender or regular blender, emulsify the braising liquid. Taste and and adjust the seasoning.

Gently rewarm the sauce over medium-low heat in the same pan and add the lamb to it to reheat for 6 to 8 minutes. (Or, pour about ¼ cup sauce over each lamb shank, cover with foil, and heat in a preheated 350°F oven for about 15 minutes.)

Place about ½ cup of the caponata to one side of a warmed plate. Top with portions of the lamb shank (it will be falling-off-the-bone tender), and finish with a sprinkling of parsley.

Online Commentary— and the Old-Fashioned Kind

I admit to scrolling through the online reviews on Yelp or ChowHound occasionally. On the one hand, I like knowing what kind of experience people have had at Bottega. On the other hand, much of this online discussion feels like a distraction. If I'm a craftsman trying to perfect my craft, reading the reviews on Yelp may take me off point.

As I glance through the comments on these sites, I look for patterns. If a few people talk about a server who isn't attentive, I'll investigate, but honestly, a letter always carries more weight than anything I read online. Recently, we had a couple celebrating a major wedding anniversary, which happened to be the same night that a Hollywood power couple was dining at Bottega. I was concerned that the anniversary couple might feel upstaged, so I stopped by their table a few times to see how their evening was going, and our waitstaff also went out of their way to see that every detail was perfect.

A few days later, I received a beautiful letter thanking all of us (not just me) for making their anniversary dinner so memorable. The online world comes and goes, but if you write me a letter, you have my undivided attention.

Arrosto of Duroc Pork with Roasted Heirloom Apples

SERVES 10 TO 12

There's an old farm phrase that I love: When something is extra-fancy it's called "high cotton." The topmost cotton bolls on the plant produce the finest cotton, woven into what you'd wear to church or a wedding. This dish is high cotton in flavor but low cotton in spirit, because the pork shoulder was traditionally an affordable cut of meat. (I think of this as a *Brady Bunch* classic—pork chops and applesauce—turned on its Italian ear.) You can make the apples up to three days in advance and keep them covered in the fridge.

At our house, this is an overnight dish, because I slide it into the oven just before I go to sleep and I only have to get out of bed once to remove the foil halfway through cooking. When you wake up in the morning, the house smells fantastic. Let the roast cool in its own juices, and serve as a lunch-hour supper or as a long-weekend or holiday brunch. You can also begin cooking at 6 A.M., so the roast comes out just in time for a late-night dinner.

This recipe calls for butterflying the pork, then seasoning and rolling it. Take advantage of your butcher's expertise. Bring along this book and ask for help. This is a dish meant for real meat, not small portions on Styrofoam trays.

If you don't want to deal with the steps involved in butterflying the meat, you can just season the pork shoulder and slide the whole piece of meat into a preheated 275°F oven, slow-cooking for 10 hours or until the meat falls apart at a touch.

It's worth finding Duroc or Berkshire pork for this long-cooked dish. Visit Heritage Foods at www.heritagefoodsusa.com for more options than you might have in your local grocery store.

Wine Pairing: A fruit-forward Napa Valley Cabernet

ROASTED HEIRLOOM APPLES

12 Gravenstein or McIntosh apples

2 tablespoons fresh lemon juice

2 tablespoons unsalted butter

1 tablespoon minced fresh sage

½ teaspoon finely ground sea salt, preferably gray salt, or kosher salt

⅓ cup honey

ZINFANDEL MOSTO COTTO

One 750-ml bottle red wine, preferably a fruity Zinfandel

1 cup plus 2 tablespoons sugar

4 tablespoons high-quality red wine vinegar

1 cinnamon stick

Zest of 1 lemon

8-pound boneless pork butt or pork shoulder, butterflied (see Chef's Note, facing page)

Sea salt, preferably gray salt

Freshly ground black pepper

4 tablespoons Toasted Spice Rub (recipe follows)

FOR THE APPLES: Preheat the oven to 425°F. Peel and core the apples, then cut into 1-inch wedges and toss them in a bowl with the lemon juice to keep them from oxidizing. Heat a medium, ovenproof sauté pan or skillet over medium-high heat, add the butter, and cook until it begins to brown. Add the sage, apples, and ½ teaspoon salt and sauté for 3 to 4 minutes, or until the apple edges just begin to color. Add the honey, transfer the pan to the oven, and roast for about 20 minutes, or until the apples are soft and lightly browned. Mash with a fork for a chunky version or purée in a food processor for a smoother sauce. Set aside.

FOR THE MOSTO COTTO: Pour the wine into a medium saucepan. Add the sugar and 2 tablespoons of the vinegar. Reduce this to a syrup over medium-high heat; don't let it stay at a rolling boil but try to keep it at a strong simmer. The bubbles will grow larger when the liquid reaches a syrupy consistency. At this point, add the cinnamon and lemon zest. Take the pan off the heat and let the mosto come to room temperature, 20 to 30 minutes.

Add the remaining two tablespoons of vinegar and allow the mosto to cool. Strain through a fine-mesh strainer or a chinois. This keeps for up to 3 months refrigerated in an airtight container.

Preheat the oven to 275°F. Unroll the butterflied pork and season the top side with the salt, pepper, and 2 tablespoons of the spice rub. Roll up the meat and secure with kitchen twine every 2 inches, or make a butcher's knot (see Chef's Note, page 33). Don't make the twine too tight, because after 8 hours of cooking, it'll be a challenge to cut it away; just secure it tightly enough so the pork doesn't come unrolled. Season the outside of the meat with salt and the remaining 2 tablespoons spice rub, being sure to season the ends of the roll, too. Using a sheet of aluminum foil, cover the thin end where there is no fat.

Put the pork in a roasting pan and bake for 8 hours, removing the foil after 4 hours of cooking. Remove from the oven and let rest in the pan for 30 minutes.

Cut the pork into slices as best you can. The meat will be so tender it will fall apart, but nobody will mind if slices aren't precise. (If you want real slices, bust out the electric knife.) Make sure to remove the twine before serving. Prop the pork on top of the apples (either rewarmed or served at room temperature) and drizzle the plate with mosto cotto and pan juices if you like.

CHEF'S NOTE: To butterfly a pork shoulder (with some help from your butcher), first, go to a real butcher shop—a place that doesn't sell meat wrapped in plastic. Buy a pork shoulder and ask the butcher to make it a single sheet in thickness. You want a thin sheet of meat about 20 inches long.

When the sheet is open, you'll see a gland that has to be removed. Scrape it off with a small knife and discard the gland. You can remove some fat from the sheet, but leave a good amount because this will baste the pork while it cooks. When you have the sheet thin and fairly even, give it a practice roll to see if it still looks even. If not, unroll the sheet again, and even it out. You can slice off sections of the meat and place them in thin spots. When you're finished, roll it up again until you're happy with the evenness of the roll.

Toasted Spice Rub

MAKES ABOUT 1 CUP

¼ cup fennel seeds
1 tablespoon coriander seeds
1 tablespoon black peppercorns
1½ teaspoons red pepper flakes
¼ cup pure California chile powder
2 tablespoons kosher salt
2 tablespoons ground cinnamon

In a small skillet, toast the fennel seeds, coriander seeds, and peppercorns over medium heat, tossing frequently, until the fennel seeds turn light brown. Don't let them get dark. Turn your exhaust fan to high, add the red pepper flakes, and toss-toss-toss (just three times), then immediately remove from the heat and empty onto a plate to cool completely.

In a blender, combine the cooled spices (don't try to grind the spices before they're at room temperature, or they will gum up your blender's blades), chile powder, salt, and cinnamon. Blend until finely and evenly ground. If you have a small spice mill or a coffee grinder dedicated to spices, grind the fennel, coriander, peppercorns, and red pepper flakes, then empty into a bowl and stir in the chile powder, salt, and cinnamon. Store in an airtight container in a cool, dark place for up to 4 months, or freeze for up to 1 year.

Crispy Pork Shanks with Red Wine Vinegar Agrodolce and Wine-Cooked Apples

SERVES 6

Chef and friend David Burke showed me this crazy method of salt-curing and frying pork. It seems outlandish that you would fry pork after rolling it in sugar, but when you've tried this, you'll be making it more than once. I don't put butter on my bread just to save room for dishes like this one. When you add the agrodolce sauce, this pork is full-on messy, so it might be best to show up for dinner in a toga. If you want to make more of these, go right ahead: I like to pull the pork meat off the bone and add it to salads, fold it into a risotto, or serve it with pasta. You do need two big pots to make this dish, so if you have only one big pot, this might be a reason to invest in a second one.

Along with the agrodolce, which can be made a week in advance, I serve this with simple mustard greens. Whenever you spend more time on a single dish, offer fewer courses and make them simple.

Don't forget to order the pork shanks from your butcher ahead of time.

Wine Pairing: Petite Syrah

Note: Oil Conservation

Many home cooks toss their cooking oil too readily. At restaurants—and I'm talking fine restaurants, here—we can reuse five gallons of oil a hundred times. You can reuse your oil, too. Clean the oil by cutting one large potato into slices and cooking them in your oil at about 375ºF. Remove the potato and let the oil cool. Strain it through a fine-mesh sieve. Store it in a cool, dark place and let it live to see another day.

SALT CURE

8 cups kosher salt

2 cups granulated sugar

2 tablespoons black peppercorns

2 tablespoons juniper berries

6 bay leaves, crumbled

Six 24-ounce pork shanks

RED WINE VINEGAR AGRODOLCE

2 cups red wine vinegar

1 cup granulated sugar

1½ cups finely chopped red onion

2 tablespoons fennel seeds

WINE-COOKED APPLES

4 cups peeled, cored, and diced apples (3 to 4 apples)

¾ cup dry white wine

1 bay leaf

¼ cup dried fruit of your choice

2 teaspoons minced fresh rosemary

2 tablespoons Dijon mustard

1 gallon olive oil

Canola, peanut, or corn oil for frying

1 cup powdered sugar, plus more as needed

FOR THE SALT CURE: In a large bowl, combine the salt, 2 cups granulated sugar, peppercorns, juniper berries, and bay leaves and stir to mix. Pour half of the salt cure into a large roasting pan.

Lay the shanks on top of the salt cure and cover with the remaining cure. All the meat needs to be covered with the mixture, so if you don't have enough salt cure, make another half batch. Place the pan in the refrigerator and let the meat cure for 4 hours.

FOR THE AGRODOLCE: In a medium saucepan, combine the vinegar, 1 cup granulated sugar, red onion, and fennel seeds. Bring to a simmer over medium heat and cook to reduce to a syrup, 15 to 20 minutes (watch to make sure it doesn't burn). Remove from the heat and let cool; it will thicken as it cools.

FOR THE APPLES: In a large saucepan, combine the apples, wine, bay leaf, dried fruit, rosemary, and Dijon mustard. Bring the mixture to a boil over high heat, reduce the heat to medium-low, cover, and let it simmer for about 1 hour. This will have some chunks, but they'll be very tender.

Preheat the oven to 250°F. In a heavy 3-gallon pot or Dutch oven, warm the olive oil over medium heat. Remove the pork shanks from the salt cure, rinse quickly in cold water, and pat dry. Add the pork shanks to the pot and bring to a low simmer over low heat. Transfer the pot to the oven and cook, uncovered, for 3 hours. Remove from the oven and let the pork shanks cool in the olive oil.

In a large, heavy pot or deep fryer, heat 3 inches of canola oil over medium-high heat to 375°F on a deep-fat thermometer.

Give each pork shank a roll in the powdered sugar and carefully drop 3 shanks at a time into the hot oil, cooking until brown, 3 to 4 minutes. Take the pork out of the oil and transfer to a rimmed baking sheet. Do *not* put this on a paper towel, because it'll stick to the paper.

Spoon about ¾ cup of the apples in the center of each of 6 warmed plates. Top with a shank and drizzle with the agrodolce.

Porchetta (Whole Suckling Pig)

SERVES 22 TO 24

We call this "seven o'clock pig," because by 7 P.M. we are out of porchetta every night that it's on the Bottega menu. This is a decadent recipe, pork inside pig, roasted low and slow in a Roman-style marinade.

Certainly you can just roast a whole pig, but there's something about this method that raises the flavor profile to new heights. I love the idea of this same dish, maybe even with polenta, appearing in front of nobles and royalty many centuries ago.

Talk to your butcher (I can't say that enough) and ask him or her to semi-bone the pig for you. Flattery doesn't hurt here. Try handing over a bottle of really good wine while saying something along the lines of, "You're the best butcher I've worked with, and only you are up to a task of this magnitude." Hey, it's worked for me.

This porchetta comes off the heat two hours before the guests arrive. Slice it into pieces with a serrated knife and gently warm it in the oven.

Wine Pairing: Brunello or Syrah

HERB PASTE
1 loosely packed cup fresh sage leaves
½ cup fresh rosemary leaves
½ cup fresh thyme leaves
4 cups fresh flat-leaf parsley leaves
2 cups fresh mint leaves
1½ cups fresh oregano leaves
6 bay leaves
8 garlic cloves
1 tablespoon kosher salt
1 tablespoon butcher's salt (see Resources)
   or coarsely ground black pepper
2 cups olive oil
2 cups dry white wine

One 7-pound boneless pork butt or pork shoulder
One 32-pound suckling pig (see Chef's Note,
   facing page; ask the butcher to semi-bone it)
4 recipes Ancient-Grain Polenta (page 68)
48 fresh figs, or dried figs rehydrated in water
   or a combination of water and wine
Finely shredded fresh basil leaves for garnish

FOR THE HERB PASTE: In a food processor, or in a blender in batches, combine the herbs, garlic, and salts. Process to a coarse purée. With the machine running, add the oil and wine and purée until smooth.

Cut about half of the pork butt into pieces 2 inches square. You'll use these to stuff cavities where the shoulder blade and femur were removed from the suckling pig. Cut the remaining half of the pork butt into strips about 6 inches long and 1½ inches wide. You'll pack these strips where the spine was. The goal is to have boneless meat from neck to tail.

With your fingers or a large spoon, coat the pig with the herb marinade (as shown in the photo at upper left). Place the remaining pork butt on top of the herb-covered pig. Using kitchen twine and a trussing needle, close up the pig in even stitches. Or, if you prefer, just tie the pig closed and forget about the sewing step.

At Bottega, we roast these in restaurant-size ovens. A good option for backyard roasting is La Caja China (see Resources), which is an oversize roasting box ideal for a whole pig. Know the weight of your pig and follow the directions included with the roasting box for the correct cooking time.

Another option is to have your butcher cut the suckling pig in half and place a 3- to 4-pound pork roast inside each half. Your butcher can help you tie the animal so the roast is well wrapped within each half. Preheat two ovens to 250°F. Put each half in a standard roasting pan and cook for 7 to 8 hours or until the pig is completely tender; when done the legs will move freely when tugged on.

Cut off the head and set aside. Slice the center as shown in the top photo at near left, taking care that the pork stuffing stays in place. Spoon polenta to one side of each warmed plate, add a slice of the pig, accompany with a few figs, and top with some shredded basil.

CHEF'S NOTE: You can buy a smaller suckling pig; just reduce the size of the pork butt by the same percentage.

A Meaningful History

Before this valley was a wine destination, the
Chutney Kitchen made jars of chutney to sell
and was a café as well. It was *the* gathering
place in the Napa Valley in the 1980s. If you
had a farming problem, the Chutney Kitchen
was our friendlier version of the Internet;
you could always go there and find farmers
with the answers you needed, along with
some good food.

It is here, where Bottega is today, that the
wine, food, and hospitality for which this
valley is known first came together. Not a day
goes by that I don't think about this building's
past, with much gratitude that I get to work
here and add my own stories to its history.
To occupy this space infuses my food with
meaning and soul.

Smoked and Braised Natural Short Ribs with Roasted Cipollini Onions and Smoky Jus

SERVES 6

Of all the dishes I made on *Top Chef Masters*, this one was by far the most popular. We've been making this dish for twenty years, and I haven't tasted a better short rib anywhere (and I don't say that about many of the dishes I make).

There are three steps: brine, cold-smoke, and braise. You'll brine the ribs for 3 hours, then cold-smoke them for 30 minutes so the smoke flavor gets pulled into the middle of the meat when you braise the ribs—it's not just a smoke jacket. Even in midwinter, it's worth breaking out the grill for a killer cold-smoked and braised short rib. Choose aromatic woods for the wood chips. I use the wood from wine barrels and fruit trees, as well as grapevines. The last step is braising the ribs in red wine for 6 hours, which makes them incredibly tender.

Succulent, bold, tender yet hearty, this beef dish demands a muscular, teeth-staining red wine.

Wine Pairing: Petite Syrah

BRINE
2½ cups water
½ cup kosher salt
½ cup sugar
1½ teaspoons juniper berries
1 bay leaf

6 short ribs, about 1¼ pounds each
A few handfuls of oak, apple wood,
    or other fruit wood chips

ROASTED CIPPOLLINI ONIONS
24 unpeeled cippollini onions (about 2 pounds)
¼ cup extra-virgin olive oil
1 cup balsamic vinegar
Sea salt, preferably gray salt
Freshly ground black pepper

¼ cup extra-virgin olive oil
1 cup diced yellow onion
½ cup diced peeled carrot
½ cup diced celery
2 cups dry red wine
4 cups Roasted Chicken Stock (page 18)
    or store-bought low-salt chicken broth
1 tablespoon juniper berries
1 teaspoon black peppercorns
3 bay leaves
Ancient-Grain Polenta (page 68) for serving

FOR THE BRINE: In a large pot, combine the water, kosher salt, sugar, 1½ teaspoons juniper berries, and bay leaf, and bring to a boil over high heat, stirring to dissolve the sugar. Remove from the heat and let the brine cool completely, then chill it in your refrigerator for at least 1 hour or up to 6 hours.

Arrange the ribs, bone-side up, in a single layer in a nonreactive 9-by-13-inch pan or other pan that fits all the ribs. Pour the brine over the ribs. Cover and refrigerate for 3 hours. Remove the ribs from the brine and discard the liquid.

Soak the wood chips in cold water for at least 30 minutes. While the wood soaks, light an indirect fire in a charcoal grill. Cold-smoking means keeping the temperature at 78ºF. Each time you add damp wood chips to the coal, it will bring down the temperature, so the thermometer will show some movement. Use a charcoal chimney to start a fire in the center of the fuel bed. When the coals are ready, move them carefully to either side and place an aluminum pan in the center. Add at least 2 cups of water to the aluminum pan to keep the meat moist. Allow 30 minutes for the coals to heat up; they should have a light-gray coating of ash.

Drain the wood chips and shake off the excess water. Sprinkle a quarter of the chips over the coals. Put the ribs on the grill, cover the grill, and cook for about 30 minutes, quickly turning the ribs and adding another quarter of the wood chips every 10 minutes before re-covering.

FOR THE ONIONS: Preheat the oven to 375ºF. With a paring knife, trim the top from each cippollini onion and a bare minimum from the root end. In a large pot of salted boiling water, cook the onions for 3 minutes. Drain and let cool to the touch, then peel off their skins.

Heat a large, ovenproof sauté pan or skillet over medium-high heat, add the oil, and sauté the onions for 5 to 6 minutes, until medium-brown on both sides. Add the balsamic vinegar and simmer until slightly reduced, 3 to 4 minutes. Transfer the pan to the oven and cook until the onions are tender, about 12 minutes. Remove from the oven. Season with salt and pepper and set aside.

Reduce the oven temperature to 250ºF. Heat a Dutch oven, a large ovenproof sauté pan, or a heavy roasting pan with a lid over medium-high heat and add the oil. Add the yellow onion, carrot, and celery. Reduce the heat to medium and sauté the vegetables until browned, 10 to 12 minutes. Add the wine and increase the heat to medium-high to burn off the alcohol. Add the short ribs and chicken stock. Bring to a hard boil and add the juniper berries, peppercorns, and bay leaves. Reduce the heat to a gentle simmer, then cover the pan and transfer it to the oven. Braise for 6 hours, or until the short ribs bend and almost break when lifted from the jus. Remove from the oven and let the ribs rest in the pan, covered, for 20 minutes. Turn off the oven.

Using tongs, transfer the ribs to a rimmed baking sheet and place in the oven to keep warm. Pass the broth through a fine-mesh sieve into a wide saucepan. Cook the broth over medium-high heat to reduce until thickened, about 15 minutes.

Spoon polenta onto the center of each of 6 warmed plates, top with 1 rib, and pour on a little of the jus reduction.

Bistecca alla Fiorentina
(Grilled Grass-Fed Porterhouse)
with Grilled Radicchio

SERVES 2

This dish speaks for itself. If you're a beef-lover, you owe it to yourself to try this method of cooking a porterhouse. I treat a steak this big like a roast. Use the coarsest grind on your pepper mill and push the pepper into the meat before grilling. This is a good place to share my three tricks for great beef.

1. Start with good beef.
2. Let the steak come to room temperature before throwing it on the fire.
3. Let it rest for 8 to 10 minutes before you cut into it.

Number 3 bears repeating: Don't cut into the beef until it's had a chance to rest.

Once the beef has rested, I carve it thickly, in good chunks about a finger and a half in width. I don't slice it thin and fan it out on a plate; that's not in keeping with the spirit of this steak.

You can serve this with any *contorno*. I happen to like how the grilled radicchio complements the beef. The trick with that is to soak the radicchio in ice water before grilling so the outside is charred and the inside is still cool, crisp, and fresh—a great contrast to the heartiness of the beef.

Wine Pairing: Cabernet Sauvignon

One 30-ounce Porterhouse steak
Sea salt, preferably gray salt
Coarsely ground black pepper
1 tablespoon extra-virgin olive oil for brushing
1 tablespoon late-harvest olive oil for drizzling
Roasted Lemons (page 34)
Grilled radicchio (see page 78)

Preheat the oven to 400°F. Heat a large cast-iron skillet over high heat for 10 minutes, or until it's so hot it's almost humming. Season the meat liberally with salt and pepper and then brush with the extra-virgin olive oil.

Carefully put the steak in the pan and cook on one side until you see some juices bubbling up on top of the steak, about 8 minutes. Transfer the pan to the oven and cook for about 9 minutes, or until an instant-read thermometer inserted in the center of the steak registers 125°F.

While the steak is in the oven, set a wire rack on a rimmed baking sheet. When the steak is done cooking, transfer it from the pan to the rack and let it rest for 10 minutes. Transfer the steak to a carving board. Cut the meat off the bone and cut it straight down into 1-inch-thick slices. Pour the juices from the baking sheet onto the meat.

Put the bones on a warmed platter and rearrange the meat so it looks as it did before you carved. Drizzle with the late-harvest olive oil and serve with the lemon halves and radicchio.

Note: The Evolution of Grass-Fed Beef

At Bottega, we serve only grass-fed beef, which has come a long way in the past decade. If you take into account the bigger picture, it's odd that corn-fed beef was the norm for so long, when cows are physiologically set up to digest only grasses. Corn isn't optimal feed, although God knows I've had some phenomenal corn-fed beef.

Ten years ago, it was much more of a challenge to beat the flavor and tenderness of corn-fed beef, but these days I'll put the flavor of my grass-fed beef up against corn-fed any day of the week and come out ahead. Ranchers have finally matched the right heirloom breed with the right grasses to get good internal marbling without grain.

When you buy beef, look for marbling—the streaks of fat are the key to flavor.

Grilled Rib-Eye Tagliata
with Grilled Stone Fruit

SERVES 6

To any butcher, the rib-eye is the best piece of meat on a steer. I'm surprised by how many people eat New York steaks when they could be having rib-eye. I love the smoky sweetness of the grilled stone fruit here, and I am definitely not a fruit-with-meat kind of guy. Choose peaches or nectarines that are perfectly ripe but not the least bit soft or mushy. Don't discard the olive oil marinade in which you've placed the peaches, save it to make a good vinaigrette later.

Wine Pairing: Cabernet Sauvignon

GRILLED STONE FRUIT

6 peaches or nectarines, peeled (for peaches),
   pitted, and cut into quarters
½ cup extra-virgin olive oil
¼ cup balsamic vinegar
1 teaspoon sea salt, preferably gray salt
1 teaspoon freshly ground black pepper

6 rib-eye steaks, each about 12 ounces
Extra-virgin olive oil for brushing and drizzling
Sea salt, preferably gray salt
Freshly ground black pepper
2 tablespoons minced fresh flat-leaf parsley

Prepare a hot wood fire in a charcoal grill or have a grill pan ready.

FOR THE FRUIT: Put the fruit quarters in a bowl and add the olive oil, balsamic vinegar, salt, and pepper. Marinate for at least 1 minute or up to 20 minutes.

Heat a grill pan (if using) over medium-high heat. Remove the fruit from the marinade, shaking off any excess liquid. Place the fruit, cut-surface down, on the grill or in the grill pan. On the grill, keep the fruit near the edge of the fire, where the grill is only medium-hot. If the heat is too cold, the fruit will turn mushy before it cooks, and it will burn if too hot. Grill the fruit for 1 minute on each side, or until it shows black grill marks. Using tongs, transfer the fruit to a platter and let it rest while you grill the meat.

Make sure your grill is very hot. Brush each steak lightly with olive oil and season evenly with salt and pepper on both sides. For stellar grill marks, the placement of the steaks on the grill is important: if you imagine your grill as the face of a clock, place the steaks at an angle to the grill grids so the two ends of each steak point to 10 o'clock and 4 o'clock. Forty-five seconds later, turn the steaks on an angle again so the ends point to 2 o'clock and 8 o'clock. Then, after another 45 seconds, revolve the steaks (without turning them over) so the ends point once again to 10 and 4. Turn them over so the ends point at 2 and 8 o'clock. Total grill time is 3 minutes for medium-rare, or until an instant-read thermometer inserted in the center of a steak reaches 125°F.

Transfer the steaks to a carving board and let rest for 1 or 2 minutes. Cut the steak on the bias into slices about two fingers wide. Divide the slices among the plates and serve each plate with 4 quarters of grilled fruit. Drizzle the fruit with olive oil and sprinkle with parsley.

Smoky Paprika Skirt Steak with Salsa Rossa

SERVES 6

Skirt steak is what flank steak would be if it tasted great. This is a funky piece of meat; it has to be pulled and kneaded to be tender, or (as we do here) soaked in olive oil and spices overnight. This meat takes a marinade better than any other piece of beef. Pimentón de la Vera (smoked Spanish paprika) gives it a kick of flavor. Because the spice is so smoky, this lends itself to indoor grilling. It's great grilled outdoors, too, but the spice adds a smoky flavor even when you don't feel like firing up the grill.

The smoky, peppery Salsa Rossa adds its own heat and spice to the dish. I use this on baked halibut, too. You can make it up to five days ahead, if you like.

Wine Pairing: Zinfandel Rosé

About 2 tablespoons pimentón de la Vera
    (smoked Spanish paprika)
3½ pounds skirt steak cut into
    six 6- to 8-inch sections
¾ cup extra-virgin olive oil

SALSA ROSSA
3 large red bell peppers
Extra-virgin olive oil for coating,
    plus 2 tablespoons
1 serrano chile
1 garlic clove, thinly sliced
1 teaspoon chopped fresh oregano
¼ cup fresh tomato purée
Sea salt, preferably gray salt
1 teaspoon red wine vinegar
Freshly ground black pepper

4 cups loosely packed arugula
Whole-Citrus Vinaigrette (see page 76)

Pat the paprika into the steak on each side. Then, using your fingers, lightly coat the steak with olive oil to seal in the spice. Cover and refrigerate overnight.

FOR THE SALSA ROSSA: Preheat the oven to 450°F. Line a baking sheet with aluminum foil. Coat the bell peppers lightly with olive oil and place on the baking sheet. Roast, turning every 10 or 15 minutes, until the peppers are blistered all over, about 30 minutes total. Transfer the peppers to a bowl and cover with plastic wrap so they steam as they cool. Peel the peppers and remove the stems, seeds, and ribs; avoid the temptation to rinse the peppers.

Heat a small sauté pan or skillet over medium-high heat, add the 2 tablespoons olive oil, and heat until it shimmers. Add the chile, reduce the heat to medium, and cook, turning occasionally, until the chile is softened, lightly browned, and blistered on all sides, 3 to 4 minutes. Remove from the heat and let the chile cool in the oil for several minutes, then remove it from the oil. When cool enough to handle, peel the chile and remove the stem and seeds. Finely chop the chile, then use the side of your knife to mash it to a paste.

Add more oil to the skillet if needed to make 2 tablespoons. Reheat the oil over medium heat, add the garlic, and sauté until lightly browned, about 30 seconds. Add the oregano and sauté briefly to release its fragrance. Add the tomato purée and season with salt, bring to a simmer, and cook for about 5 minutes to thicken slightly.

In a blender, combine the red peppers, chile, and tomato mixture and purée until smooth. Add the vinegar, season with black pepper, and purée again. Taste and adjust the seasoning. Cover and refrigerate for up to 5 days or freeze for up to 4 months.

Light a hot fire in a charcoal grill, preheat a gas grill to high, or set a grill pan over high heat. Positioning the steak for diagonal grill marks (see page 159), grill the steak for 2 minutes on each side for medium-rare.

Transfer the steak to a carving board and let rest for 2 minutes. Slice each section of steak on the bias. Pour a spoonful of the salsa rossa in a pool on each plate, and arrange the steak on the salsa. Toss the arugula with the vinaigrette and place a small mound of dressed arugula on each plate before serving.

Grilled Quail with Sausage and Calabrese Romano Bean Ragù

SERVES 6

When I make this dish, I think of my dearest mom and a small kindness she showed me that has carried through all these years. Growing up in the country, quail hunting was a rite of passage, and my friends and I competed (as we did in all things) to see who could bring home the most quail. I set out one morning promising that I wouldn't come home until I had ten quail, but after the first five I couldn't get any more. I came home more quiet than usual. My mom noticed, and she slipped out to the grocery store and came home with five sausages. Instead of two quail on every plate, there was a quail and a sausage for each of us, along with her fantastic Calabrese bean ragù. With a plate this full, nobody in my family thought to ask about the missing five quail.

I cook the sausages just as my mom would, with an initial poach to ensure there are no flare-ups over the fire.

I use boneless quail, but bone-in works too. There's a cool machine that removes the bones from the inside. If your butcher can find a quail producer that does this, you may as well take advantage of it, as it makes the bird much easier to eat.

Wine Pairing: A young Cabernet

6 sausage links, Calabrian pork sausage,
   or your favorite sausage (4 to 5 pounds total)
6 quail, each about 5 ounces, boned
3 tablespoons extra-virgin olive oil for brushing
2 tablespoons Fennel Spice Blend (page 214)
Calabrese Romano Bean Ragù (page 178)

Soak 12 wooden skewers in water for 30 minutes.

In a large pot of salted boiling water, cook the sausages for 4 minutes. Using tongs, transfer the sausages to a platter.

Light a hot charcoal or almond- or oak-wood fire in a charcoal grill. Prepare the birds by removing the wing at the first joint (or have your butcher do this for you). Leave the drumstick portion of the wing. Use the skewers to form a crisscross by skewering from the right wing to the left leg and vice versa. You don't need to pierce the skin of the bird; work so that the skewers are held in place by the legs and wing joints.

Rub each bird with about 1 teaspoon olive oil and season with the spice blend. Place the quail on the hot grill and cook for about 3 minutes on each side, or until the juices run clear when you cut into a thigh (just as you'd check with chicken). While the quail are grilling, add the sausages to the grill. Transfer the quail to a platter. Grill the sausages just until they're heated through and grill marks show clearly, 2 to 3 minutes per side. Allow the quail to cool for a few minutes and then remove the skewers, twisting them slowly so they don't tear the meat.

Spoon the ragù into the center of each of 6 warmed plates. Place a sausage to one side of the beans, and set a quail beside it.

Oven-Roasted Cornish Hens with Panettone Stuffing

SERVES 4

This is one of the best things I've put in my mouth this year. These tender chickens aren't game birds but young chickens— what the French call *poussins*. These birds got a bad rap in the 1970s when frozen-solid freezer bombs came to stand for Cornish hens. These birds are something else entirely. Really, it's not what you call the bird—*poussin* or Cornish—it's where the bird hails from and how it's raised that determines its flavor. (Visit Heritage at www.heritagefoodsusa.com for birds with the right combination of good genes and a healthful lifestyle.)

You can also make this dish using a single 4- to 5-pound chicken: follow the directions, slide it into a 450°F oven for 15 minutes, and then reduce the heat to 375°F and cook for another 30 minutes, or until the chicken is cooked through.

Panettone makes my favorite stuffing, but you can also use brioche or a soft country bread. I generally start with store-bought panettone, usually a loaf that's given to me as a Christmas gift or one bought at an Italian market. If you have a good panettone recipe, make your own, by all means.

This bird is so good you can easily skip the roasted lemon—rosemary jus, but I give you the option in case you want the full monty.

Wine Pairing: Grenache or Zinfandel

BRINE
1 gallon cold water
4 cups packed light brown sugar
1½ cups kosher salt
2 tablespoons black peppercorns
2 tablespoons juniper berries
2 bay leaves

4 Cornish hens or *poussins* (about 18 ounces each)

PANETTONE STUFFING
Half of one 2.2-pound panettone,
    cut into ¾-inch cubes (9 cups)
4 tablespoons unsalted butter
2 tablespoons minced fresh sage
Sea salt, preferably gray salt
Freshly ground black pepper
¼ cup julienned dried apricots
¼ cup dried sour cherries
¼ cup golden raisins
¾ cup finely chopped yellow onion
½ cup finely chopped celery or fennel
½ cup finely chopped peeled carrot
1½ cups Roasted Chicken Stock (page 18)
    or turkey stock, or more as needed
1 large egg, beaten (optional, if you like a
    firmer stuffing)

ROASTED LEMON-ROSEMARY JUS
2 large lemons
Extra-virgin olive oil for brushing, plus ¼ cup
Sea salt, preferably gray salt
Freshly ground black pepper
1 tablespoon minced garlic (about 2 cloves)
1 cup Roasted Chicken Stock (page 18),
    or 2 cups canned low-salt chicken broth,
    boiled until reduced by half
1 teaspoon minced fresh rosemary
1 tablespoon minced fresh flat-leaf parsley
1 tablespoon unsalted butter (optional)

Olive oil for rubbing, plus 2 tablespoons
Sea salt, preferably gray salt
Freshly ground black pepper
1 tablespoon unsalted butter

FOR THE BRINE: Combine the water, brown sugar, kosher salt, peppercorns, juniper berries, and bay leaves in a large pot and bring to a simmer over medium heat. Stir to dissolve the sugar, remove from the heat, let cool, and refrigerate.

Trim the birds by removing the tip of each wing with kitchen shears. Cut away the excess skin above the breast connected to the neck and then cleanly slice off the neck. Add the birds to the brine, cover, and refrigerate for at least 3 hours or overnight. You may need to weight down the birds; if so, place a plate on top and set a few clean heavy cans on the plate so the birds stay submerged.

FOR THE STUFFING: Preheat the oven to 350°F. Spread the panettone cubes out on two rimmed baking sheets. In a small saucepan, melt 2 tablespoons of the butter over medium heat and cook until light brown, about 6 minutes. Remove from the heat and add half the sage. Season with salt and pepper. Pour the sage butter over the bread and toss gently but swiftly. Toast the bread in the oven, turning with a spatula halfway through cooking, until light brown, about 15 minutes. Remove from the oven and pour the croutons into a bowl, leaving the oven on.

Meanwhile, put the dried fruit in a large bowl and add boiling water to cover. Let soak for at least 10 minutes, to make the fruit plump and soft. Drain and set aside.

Increase the oven temperature to 375°F. Heat a large sauté pan or skillet over medium-low heat, add the remaining 2 tablespoons butter, and cook until it foams. Add the onion, celery, and carrot and sauté until soft, 12 to 15 minutes. Stir in the plumped fruit and remaining sage, then add to the cooled croutons and gently toss. Add the 1½ cups stock to moisten. Add more stock if you like a softer stuffing. For a firmer stuffing, stir in the beaten egg now. Taste and adjust the seasoning. Set aside.

FOR THE JUS: Preheat the broiler. Cut a small slice off both ends of each lemon, then cut the lemons in half crosswise. Arrange the lemons, flesh-side up, in a flameproof baking or gratin dish or a nonreactive baking pan, brush with olive oil, and season with salt and pepper. Broil 6 inches or more from the heat source until browned and soft, about 10 minutes. Remove from the broiler and let cool. Squeeze the lemon halves over a fine-mesh sieve suspended over a bowl. Press the pulp through the sieve with a rubber spatula or the back of a large spoon. Discard the lemon shells.

Heat a large sauté pan or skillet over medium-high heat, add the ¼ cup olive oil, and sauté the garlic until light brown. Immediately add the roasted lemon juice (this final flash of heat will cook off any residual acid flavor), 1 cup stock, rosemary, and parsley. Stir to scrape up the browned bits on the bottom of the pan. Taste and adjust the seasoning. If the sauce tastes too lemony, stir in the butter.

Preheat the oven to 375°F. Using 1 cup of stuffing per bird, gently stuff both cavities. With kitchen twine, tie the ends of the legs together, then bring the twine around to secure the neck cavity. Rub each bird with olive oil and season with salt and pepper.

Heat a large roasting pan over high heat and add the 2 tablespoons oil and the butter. When the butter foams, sear the birds, breast-side down, on the stove top, just until slightly caramelized, 3 minutes. Flip and sear the other side for 3 minutes. Transfer to the oven and roast for 20 to 25 minutes, or until an instant-read thermometer inserted at the thigh registers 160°F. Remove from the oven and let rest for 10 minutes. Remove the twine and serve a bird per person.

Conserva di Anitra con Frutta di Mostarda (Whole-Duck Confit with Fruit Mustard)

SERVES 4

If you want a dish that is worth every bit of the time and effort it takes to make it, confit a duck.

Eileen and I recently had some friends over for dinner—the first time we've entertained at home since Bottega opened. I made a duck confit ragù served with simple pasta, a green salad, and that was it. I don't think we even had dessert—we just poured more wine and sat around the table shooting the breeze.

This is a wonderful dish for a party, because the work is done in advance; you just crisp up the duck and serve. Be sure to start at least the day before, so the duck has time to marinate in the spice blend overnight. Duck, like rabbit, is underused by most home cooks, and, like rabbit, it's more widely available now than ever before. I love confitting an entire duck half, but you can confit just the legs if you prefer. Or confit several whole ducks and invite lots of people to dine with you. Once you understand the technique of confit, this method will serve you well.

The *frutta di mostarda* can be made 2 days in advance. It's fruity, sweet, and pungent and sets off the rich duck meat like nothing else I can think of. Again, once you understand the mostarda technique, you can substitute any fruit as long as you start with firm core fruit such as apples or pears. Then you can try adding figs, blueberries, raspberries, any fruit you'd like. Just be sure to learn the technique before you begin experimenting.

Ask your butcher to butterfly the duck for you, or follow the instructions and do it yourself. The duck fat can be ordered from your butcher. If you don't have duck fat, use 6 cups or more of olive oil.

Wine Pairing: Sangiovese

SPICE RUB

2 bay leaves, crumbled

1 teaspoon ground juniper berries

1 teaspoon ground nutmeg

1 tablespoon black peppercorns

1 tablespoon ground coriander

2 teaspoons ground cinnamon

¼ teaspoon ground cloves

¼ teaspoon ground cardamom

¼ cup finely ground sea salt,
preferably gray salt

¼ cup minced garlic

One 5-pound duck
or 4 to 5 pounds duck legs

2 bay leaves

2 fresh thyme sprigs

3 cups duck fat (optional)

3 to 6 cups olive oil (see Chef's Note,
page 19), plus more if needed

FRUTTA DI MOSTARDA

3 cups sugar

½ cup water

2 tablespoons fresh lemon juice

1 shallot, minced

Pinch of red pepper flakes

1 serrano chile, seeded and minced

3 pears, peeled, cored, and diced

4 apples, peeled, cored, and diced

1 cup dried sour cherries

½ cup golden raisins

½ cup dry white wine

2 bay leaves

1 ¾ cups Dijon mustard

Sea salt, preferably gray salt

2 tablespoons extra-virgin olive oil to
crisp duck skin before serving

FOR THE SPICE RUB: Mix together the bay leaves, juniper berries, nutmeg, peppercorns, ground coriander, cinnamon, cloves, and cardamom. Add the finely ground sea salt and garlic. Mix well to make a damp paste. Set aside.

Remove any giblets or neck bone from the duck. Trim the excess fat from the neck. Remove the wing tops (reserve for stock), but leave the drumstick part of the wing on the duck. Cut along either side of the backbone and press the duck flat.

Rub the spice blend inside the body and neck cavities and over the outside of the duck. Wrap tightly with plastic wrap, put in an airtight container, and refrigerate for 24 hours.

Wipe off both sides of the duck, rinse with cold water, and dry with paper towels to remove the spice rub.

Preheat the oven to 250°F. In a large, heavy pot, Dutch oven, or heavy casserole that fits the duck comfortably without too much space around it, place the duck as flat as it will go, breast-side up. Place the bay leaves and thyme on top of the duck and then cover with the duck fat (if using) and 3 cups olive oil (or with 6 cups olive oil). If the duck is not completely submerged, add more olive oil. Bake for 4 ½ hours, or until the meat is so tender it's falling off the bone. Remove from the oven and allow the duck to cool completely in the fat. When cool, put on a rack to drain.

FOR THE FRUTTA DI MOSTARDA: In a large, heavy, nonreactive pot, combine the sugar, water, and lemon juice. Cook over high heat until the sugar turns dark amber. Stir in the shallot, red pepper flakes, and chile, then quickly add all the fruit, the wine, and bay leaves. Reduce the heat to medium-low and cook gently until the fruit is tender, 15 to 20 minutes. Remove from the heat and let cool for at least 10 minutes. Stir in the mustard and season with salt. Let cool to room temperature. Store in a covered container in the refrigerator for up to 3 months, or hot-water process in canning jars to keep longer.

Preheat the oven to 450°F. In a large, ovenproof sauté pan, heat the extra-virgin olive oil until almost smoky. Add the duck, turning it so the skin becomes brown and crispy all the way around, then transfer the pan to the oven until duck is warm and skin is crisp, 6 to 8 minutes. Serve portions of the duck with ramekins of the mostarda. Both of these are great either warm or at room temperature.

CHEF'S NOTE: Save the duck fat by straining it, then set it aside for sautéing potatoes or making frites or the next batch of confit.

CHAPTER 8

Side Dishes

CONTORNI

This chapter reveals the true heart of an Italian meal: the vegetables. Yes, you could always serve the usual starch beside your whole roasted fish or your shanks or your steaks, but this chapter lets you consider a few other options—*cavolo nero*, or black cabbage, in a spectacular five-onion braise, or Brussels sprouts, cooked in such a way that they make an entrance at your table.

Contorni force an Italian to remember that he's Italian. Lamb shanks and duck confit and porterhouse steak— they're all well and good when you're in the money, but vegetables and beans have always been the mainstays in any Italian's diet. One of the things I love most about Italian cooking is the reverence with which vegetables are regarded. From humble corn comes polenta; peasant food, yes, but when treated with the respect it deserves, polenta becomes soulful and memorable as well as one of the most comforting foods on the planet. Or how about the lowly bean? Italians from long ago cooked them *al fiasco*, in a flask in the embers of a fire. If I had to choose one bean dish that had some showmanship, some style, this would be it. And yet this dish dates back to a time when fuel cost more than the beans themselves, and this manner of cooking, like many aspects of Italian cuisine, came about through resourcefulness, the Italian talent of making the best of what you've got on hand.

You'll see these side dishes in surprising places throughout the book—the carrot caponata with the Bruschetta Trio (page 44), or the Calabrese Romano Bean Ragù with grilled quail and sausages (page 161). Leaf through this chapter and widen the scope of your *contorni*. And don't forget what is possibly the most popular contorno at Bottega: our Prosciutto-Wrapped Truffle Fries on page 46.

Contorni

Five Onion-Braised
Cavolo Nero (facing page)

Ancient-Grain
Polenta (page 68)

Zucchini Spaghettini
(page 171)

Five Onion–Braised Cavolo Nero

SERVES 8 TO 10

There's something magical about onions cooked long and slow. Make it five varieties of onions, and you really have a showcase method of preparing kale or black cabbage, the incomparable cavolo nero. Scout out farmers' markets or ask your produce person if they can find cavolo nero for you. Shallots, red and yellow onions, leeks, and scallions all bring subtle flavor notes to this dish, but even if you only have two out of the five onions on hand, you can still make this, and you'll be glad you did.

This is super-slow cooking; the pot stays over the heat for about an hour in all, but since you just stir occasionally, you can attend to other kitchen tasks at the same time.

½ cup extra-virgin olive oil
1 cup finely diced shallots
1 cup finely diced red onion
1 cup finely diced yellow onion
1 cup rinsed and finely diced leeks, white portion only (about 2 leeks)
1 cup finely diced scallions, white portion only (about 16 scallions)
1 cup shredded peeled carrot (about 2 large carrots)
½ cup golden raisins
16 cups finely shredded cavolo nero (black cabbage) or kale (1 to 1½ pounds)
½ cup Vegetable Stock (page 17), plus more if needed
Sea salt, preferably gray salt
Freshly ground black pepper

Heat an 8-quart stockpot over medium-low heat and add the olive oil. Add the shallots, red and yellow onions, leeks, scallions, and carrots and cook for 20 to 25 minutes, or until very soft. Stir occasionally while slowly cooking the vegetables; don't let them get brown.

Add the raisins and the cabbage to the pot. Cook for another 30 minutes, stirring occasionally, until the cabbage is tender and luscious, adding ½ cup stock or water anytime the pot seems dry. Season with salt and pepper. Serve warm, as a side dish for grilled steaks, roasted chicken, or steamed fish.

CHEF'S NOTE: Okay, you read through this recipe, saw the 16 cups of shredded black cabbage, and thought, "No way!" Here's a trick to get around shredding that much cabbage: Beg your produce guy to let the deli cooks in your grocery store thin-slice all the cabbage for you on their meat slicer. Take a bottle of wine for both of them, and beg. It won't take much time on their end, and you'll get to learn the names of these people you see every week behind the counter. It's a win-win-win, because then you get to taste this braise without doing the shredding.

Roasted Branch of Brussels Sprouts with Fennel Spice

SERVES 8 TO 10

A full stalk of Brussels sprouts is a beautiful thing. Try cooking the entire branch with the little heads left on. I'm seeing whole branches of Brussels sprouts in my grocery store these days, so I know you can talk to your produce person, and he or she will find one for you. The only thing you need to watch is that you don't knock off any of the heads or cook them so long that they drop off. The Brussels sprouts can be pulled off with a very light touch, so treat them with care.

You can make the sections longer than 6 inches if you like, but you're limited to the size of your pans and your oven. If you manage to cook a whole branch, e-mail or Facebook me and show me the pic!

1 branch Brussels sprouts, carefully cut into
    6-inch-long sections
3 tablespoons unsalted butter
1 tablespoon Fennel Spice Blend (page 214)

In a pot large enough to hold your branch sections, bring salted water to a boil. Gently lower the sections into the water and cook for 2 to 3 minutes, or just until a Brussels sprout is crisp-tender (drop any heads that have come loose into the water and use those as your test subjects to decide when the branch is ready). Carefully remove the sections from the water and set them aside.

Preheat the oven to 425°F. In a small saucepan, melt the butter over high heat and cook for 1 minute until it just begins to turn brown. Stir in the spice blend and remove from the heat. Put the branch sections in a roasting pan or a rimmed baking sheet and drizzle the butter mixture over them. Slide the pan into the oven and roast until the outer leaves of the heads just begin to show some browning, about 8 minutes. The outer leaves should be brown and crisp. Carefully transfer the sections to a platter. If you like, prop the sections into a tepee for a super-dramatic presentation. Have guests snap the heads off the branch to add to their plates—or just pop in their mouths.

CHEF'S NOTE: This can be flavored with many different spices. Try adding sage leaves to the browned butter instead of fennel spice, or use a blood-orange olive oil instead of butter. The sky's the limit.

Zucchini Spaghettini

SERVES 6

We serve a lot of this. You can cut the zucchini on the bias into shorter lengths, but then you lose the spaghetti-ness of the presentation, which is a big part of its charm. Cutting the zucchini goes by quickly if you use a mandoline and cut each veggie lengthwise. You can do this by hand if you're really, really good with a knife and have some time to kill.

Having a very large sauté pan (14 inches) in your cupboard is a confidence builder. If you don't have a chef-size sauté pan, you can use a big roasting pan (yep, like the one you use to roast a turkey). Set it right on the stove and cook in it. It works great for this dish.

In my book, this is a wonderful way to use a lot of zucchini or any summer squash when you have a bumper crop.

½ cup extra-virgin olive oil
4 garlic cloves, thinly sliced
3 pounds zucchini or other summer squash,
   cut into long, thin spaghetti-like strips
1½ cups Tomato Passata (see Note, page 214)
½ cup loosely packed fresh basil leaves

Heat a 14-inch sauté pan or a roasting pan over medium heat, add the olive oil, and heat until it shimmers. Add the garlic and sauté over medium heat until light golden in color. Add all of the squash and let it cook for 3 to 4 minutes before turning with tongs. Cook another 3 to 4 minutes, or until crisp-tender. Add the passata and basil. Continue cooking until the squash is tender, about 5 minutes.

Pile onto a large serving platter to serve family style or use tongs to serve as a side dish for grilled fish, chicken, or meat.

CHEF'S NOTE: You can also make this into a zucchini gratin. Spoon it into a buttered dish, top it with fresh or dried bread crumbs and grated Parmesan, then bake in a preheated 425°F oven for about 20 minutes, or until lightly browned.

Carrot, Onion, and Eggplant Caponata

SERVES 6

Caponata—eggplant preserved with vinegar and a touch of sugar—is thought to be an old-style fishing-village dish that treats sailors to a few more days of veggies after the boat has sailed away from land. Serve this as a side dish for roast lamb, or spooned onto bruschetta.

7 tablespoons extra-virgin olive oil
1 cup finely diced unpeeled eggplant
½ cup finely diced unpeeled Yukon gold potato
1 cup finely diced peeled carrots
1 cup finely diced red onion
Sea salt, preferably gray salt
Freshly ground black pepper
2 tablespoons golden raisins
2 tablespoons pine nuts, toasted (see page 27)
2 teaspoons grated orange zest
¼ cup white wine vinegar
1 tablespoon sugar
2 tablespoons finely shredded fresh basil

Heat three medium sauté pans or skillets over medium-high heat. Add 3 tablespoons of the olive oil to one pan and 2 tablespoons olive oil to each of the other two pans. Add the eggplant to the first pan (with the 3 tablespoons oil), the potato to another, and the carrots and onion together to the third pan. Season all the vegetables with salt and pepper and sauté until each vegetable is completely soft, 5 to 7 minutes for the egg-plant, 10 to 12 minutes for the potatoes, and 12 to 15 minutes for the carrots and onion. Add the raisins, pine nuts, and orange zest to the pan with the carrots and onion and continue cooking for another 5 minutes, until the flavors are well infused.

Meanwhile, in a small, nonreactive sauté pan or skillet, combine the vinegar and the sugar, bring to a boil over medium-high heat, and cook to reduce until slightly syrupy, 3 to 5 minutes. Combine the hot vegetables in one pan, pour on the vinegar syrup, toss in the basil, taste for salt and pepper, and serve hot or at room temperature.

If a Caponata Could Talk

I think side dishes can sometimes tell the measure of a chef. It's obvious that you go for glory on the big dishes—the short ribs and the stuffed pig—but what do your side dishes say about you? This caponata says a lot about Bottega's chef de cuisine, Nick Ritchie. You don't often see carrots in caponata, and Nick, who created this version, has taken some heat over it. One of the chefs I respect most, Mariano Orlando, once muttered, "This isn't caponata. There are no carrots in caponata." While it's true that Sicilians don't add carrots, northern Italians sometimes do, and since Nick worked for a year at La Campognola di Salò, a restaurant in Salò, Italy, on the shores of Lago di Garda, his instincts in the kitchen

usually serve him well. Like my own, Nick's cooking is a blend of the Napa Valley and Italy, but Nick is a St. Helena baby all the way. He might even be *the* St. Helena baby. At the venerable Ernie's Meats, owned by Ernie Navone, Nick began a tradition when his dad placed him on the meat scale. (Nick weighed in at a whopping 8 pounds, 6 ounces.) Many, many babies graced that meat scale, part of St. Helena's history, and I like knowing that Nick led the way.

It might seem excessive to use three skillets for the vegetables, but I like the end result. When Sicilians cook caponata in one big pot, you get a sort of a ratatouille softness, the vegetables gray and unrecognizable, the eggplant often too oily, and the onions overcooked. With Nick's method, each vegetable is tender but distinct, and the potatoes are golden brown all over and perfect.

Chef Nico —
the pride of
my culinary life

Heirloom Toscanelli Beans al Fiasco

SERVES 6

Watch as I get enthusiastic about a bean. Toscanelli beans are, in the bean world, what lobster is to seafood and *bistecca* is to beef. Toscanelli are the beans that set the bar.

Al fiasco means cooked "in the flask," and this manner of cooking is at once romantic and very practical. During a time when fuel cost more than beans, the last embers of a fire were used to cook beans slowly in a glass bottle until they were perfectly tender. These days, I like this method because it adds a theatrical touch, and beans are way overdue for some time in the spotlight (see page 136 for another way of cooking these beans, and see Resources on where to find them).

Ask your butcher for a prosciutto "heel," the end that is left when the ham is not big enough to get one more slice from the meat. Have him or her cut the heel into two or three pieces.

3 quarts water
2 cups dried Toscanelli beans, cannellini, or
    other dried white bean, rinsed and picked over
2 tablespoons sea salt, preferably gray salt,
    plus ½ teaspoon
2 tablespoons extra-virgin olive oil, plus ¼ cup
2 large garlic cloves, sliced
½ cup diced yellow onion
¼ cup diced carrot
¼ cup diced celery
2 fresh sage sprigs, or 1 chopped fresh sage leaf
Prosciutto heel, cut into 2 or 3 pieces

In a large pot, combine the water and beans. Bring to a boil over high heat, then immediately turn off the heat and let the pot cool on the stove for 1 hour. Add the 2 tablespoons salt. (I like this 1-hour method better than soaking the beans overnight in cold water, but use the method you prefer.)

While the beans are cooling, heat a medium sauté pan or skillet over medium-high heat, add the 2 tablespoons olive oil, and sauté the garlic just until it turns a light golden brown. Add the onion, carrot, and celery and sauté for 3 minutes, or until they release some of their liquid. Add the sage and sauté for 1 minute. Turn off the heat.

Drain the beans and throw away the water (just as you would if the beans had soaked overnight). Add the vegetables and the prosciutto pieces to the beans. Put the pot back on the stove and cook over medium-low heat for 45 minutes, or until the beans are tender and flavorful. Add the ½ teaspoon sea salt halfway through cooking.

Spoon the beans into a 1-quart French canning jar with a glass lid and top with the ¼ cup olive oil. These can be served with seared shellfish, or can dress up grilled meats or roasted chicken.

CHEF'S NOTE: At home, I like to serve these in a special bean-dedicated flask that used to be a wine decanter. You can do the same. Spoon the beans into the vessel. At tableside, pour the beans onto a guest's plate and top with a swirl of some special late-harvest extra-virgin olive oil. You can make a real production out of it. With beans! Who'd have thought?

The Hospitality Irony

The biggest irony in restaurant work is that many of the people who keep the restaurant kitchens running are far from their families, sending money home to their loved ones. As the economy in the United States has gotten rockier, you hear grumbling about immigrants taking jobs, but the fact is, in twenty years I've had only one Anglo ask me for a dishwashing job, and not a single Anglo has ever asked to pick grapes or do the laborious, detailed fieldwork in my vineyards.

Like farmworkers, the folks washing dishes in a restaurant live on the edge. I have two responsibilities to them: keep the restaurant going so they have income, and make sure there's a place in the valley where they can get medical attention and help when needed. This is one reason I donated all my *Top Chef Masters* winnings to Clinic Ole.

Calabrese Romano Bean Ragù

SERVES 6 TO 8

The Romano bean is to Italians what the much-heralded haricot vert is to the French. These are beans you can really cook. These are sandwich beans, hearty enough to spoon between two slices of bread and finish off with a little pecorino. I love that the potatoes are brown and crispy not for their texture but for the way the caramelization crumbles off into the dish. This is one of my favorite uses for potatoes. Look for small Yukon golds, about 2 inches in diameter.

This recipe can be adjusted with vegetables cut even smaller to make a great pasta sauce, or you can make a gratin of it by spooning it into a baking dish and topping with bread crumbs and Parmesan.

1 ½ pounds Romano beans (Italian green beans)
1 pound unpeeled Yukon gold potatoes
⅔ cup extra-virgin olive oil
2 garlic cloves, thinly sliced
Sea salt, preferably gray salt
Freshly ground black pepper
1 teaspoon red pepper flakes
1 tablespoon chopped fresh oregano
1 cup water
1 cup canned whole plum tomatoes, juice reserved

Cut each bean crosswise into three pieces. Cut the potatoes in half lengthwise, then into half-moon slices about ⅓ inch thick.

Add the potatoes to a large pot of salted cold water, bring the water to a boil, and cook the potatoes for 1 minute. Using a slotted spoon or wire skimmer, transfer the potatoes to a colander to drain.

Heat a 12-inch sauté pan or skillet over high heat and add ⅓ cup of the olive oil. Add the potatoes and sauté until light brown, 8 to 10 minutes. Add the garlic, season with salt and pepper, and sauté until the garlic is light brown. Add the red pepper flakes and sauté for 10 seconds, then add the oregano and sauté for 4 minutes. Transfer the contents of the pan to a plate.

Meanwhile, heat a large sauté pan or skillet over medium-high heat and add the remaining ⅓ cup olive oil. Carefully (because it will spatter), add the 1 cup water and 1 teaspoon sea salt. Bring to a boil, add the beans, and cook for 12 to 15 minutes, or until tender. Add more water if the pan looks dry.

Squeeze the tomatoes between your fingers right into the pan with the beans and add the tomato juice. Return to a boil, then reduce the heat to low and simmer for 5 minutes. Add the potatoes and simmer for another 5 minutes. Taste and adjust the seasoning. Serve with any roasted meat, fish, or poultry or as a late-night sandwich—beans spooned between two slices of country bread.

Sautéed Spinach with Preserved Meyer Lemon

SERVES 6

Spinach is good for you, but when's the last time you were excited when someone set a bowl of sautéed greens in front of you? The preserved lemon will change your attitude. It has a bright, wake-you-up lemon flavor that adds just the right contrast, and the tiny squares of lemon pop visually against the dark green of the spinach. This spinach is great beside a rich meat like pork shanks or short ribs. You can use this same method with mustard greens, kale, or any cooking green. There's nothing that can go wrong with this dish as long as it's cooked long enough: keep the heat down and continue to cook until the spinach is dark and tender. Squeeze on fresh lemon juice right before serving.

I never buy prewashed spinach, even to cook at home. People grumble about washing spinach, but I don't mind it. (I know what you're thinking, but at home I am the sous-chef.) Spinach-washing just takes a lot of water and a swift hand.

Spinach takes more salt than other veggies, so taste and don't be afraid to add more. When you blanch the spinach, reserve some of the water to add back at the end if the dish needs a little more moisture.

2 tablespoons kosher salt
6 pounds fresh spinach, stemmed and rinsed
½ cup extra-virgin olive oil
1 tablespoon minced garlic
Sea salt, preferably gray salt
Freshly ground black pepper
1½ tablespoons minced Preserved Meyer Lemons (page 34)
½ teaspoon red pepper flakes
   or ½ teaspoon Calabrian chile paste (optional)
Juice of ½ fresh lemon

Add the kosher salt to a pot with 1½ gallons of water and bring to a boil over high heat. While the water heats, prepare a large ice bath, half ice and half water. Add the spinach to the boiling water and stir to make sure every leaf is submerged. When the water returns to a boil, cook for 4 minutes more. Reserve about 1 cup of the water and then drain in a colander. Press the excess water out with a ladle, and then transfer the spinach to the ice bath, pressing it under to stop the cooking. Remove it from the ice bath and with your hands make a ball of the spinach and *squeeeeeze* until you've made a spinach hardball. Transfer the spinach ball to a cutting board and cut into ½-inch slices. Pull apart with your hands.

Heat a large sauté pan or skillet over high heat, add the olive oil, and sauté the garlic until light brown. Add the drained cooked spinach, taking care to squeeze out the water again before adding it to the pan. Season with salt and pepper.

Reduce the heat to medium-low and cook the spinach for 2 to 3 minutes, or until it's piping hot throughout. Taste for salt and add the preserved lemon and the red pepper flakes, if you want a spicy kick to your greens. Toss. Add a little of the reserved spinach water if you need to. Squeeze the fresh lemon over the spinach, toss, and serve.

CHAPTER 9

Desserts

DOLCI

For me, desserts require a different emotion, a different pace, a different part of my brain. At Bottega, we always clear everything off the table—all the utensils, the salt, even the water glasses—before we bring on dessert. You don't want a water glass that smells like lamb shank when you have in front of you a delicate panna cotta or slice of semolina cake.

I've learned to do the same thing at home. After dinner, we always walk away from the table and take an hour or so before we come back to dessert. We clear the table and replace the silver and glassware. This fresh stage offers an opportunity to fully appreciate the dessert, whether it's a lavish chocolate creation or a simple bowl of fruit.

The desserts at Bottega are beautifully conceived and crafted, true testaments to the pastry chef's art. Working with the person responsible for them, Bottega's pastry chef Michael Glissman, has been a true honor. Michael practically grew up in his grandmother's restaurant in Bancroft, Nebraska, a diner called Mou's Place. "It wasn't fancy," Michael says. "Mou's was a blue-plate-special kind of a place. My grandmother, Marion Redding, was known for her hot beef and her pies." Michael worked there with his aunts, uncles, and cousins and remembers opening the diner at 4 A.M. for hunters' breakfasts, and nights when his family had to sleep on beds in the diner's basement because the snow was too deep for them to drive back to the family farm. He brings this all-hours mind-set to Bottega, along with his extraordinary skill and an infectious sense of humor (every kitchen can use a dose of humor like Michael's).

The desserts I make at home fall more on the rustic side. When my Italian family made desserts, they centered around the fresh fruit. One of my favorite desserts could not be simpler: a bowl of fresh berries (or whichever fruit is at peak), and crisp little crostini that take about 5 minutes to make. Whenever I cook this one, the kids are happy, the grown-ups are happy, and the cook is happy, too.

Siamo alla Frutta (Simple Fruit Bowl with Sweet Crostini)

SERVES 6

Siamo alla frutta means "We are at the fruit." For Italians, this means we've reached the end of the meal, which usually means fruit of some sort. For my money, you can't beat a bowl full of summer fruit that's as close to just-picked as it can be. You can use any fruit you like for this as long as it's soft and ripe. This is the dessert to make when you go berry picking or have a friend drop by with home-grown figs that are still warm from the sun.

Count on a cup to a cup and a half of fruit per person. The surprise with this fruit bowl is the sweet crostini. Made from any artisan or country-style bread that's sliced very thinly, the crostini are covered with softened butter, generously sprinkled with sugar, and broiled. Don't go easy on the sugar. What makes these crostini so good is all the sugar and butter melting into a puddle under the bread slices so they finish with a clear, beautiful sugar coating on both sides. If you're making this for breakfast, a sprinkle of cinnamon would not be out of place.

You can pour on the strawberry syrup or skip this step, depending on your mood. This may be one of the easiest recipes in the book, but I'll bet you come back to it again and again.

Wine Pairing: Moscato di Asti or Birbèt (also known as Brachetto)

SWEET CROSTINI

Six ¼-inch-thick slices country-style bread, sliced in half, or 12 to 18 baguette slices
2 to 3 tablespoons unsalted butter, at room temperature
2 to 3 tablespoons sugar

6 to 9 cups fresh strawberries, raspberries, blueberries, olallieberries, or figs, or 6 to 9 cups peeled, pitted, and sliced peaches or other stone fruit
1½ cups heavy cream, chilled
Strawberry sauce (see page 186)

FOR THE CROSTINI: Position a rack in the center of the oven. Preheat the broiler to 450ºF. Slather each slice of bread with a good amount of butter (1 teaspoon per large slice of bread) and place them on a baking sheet. Sprinkle each bread slice with sugar to cover. Slide the pan into the oven and cook until the bread begins to show some golden color, 3 to 4 minutes. The sugar should be melted so the bread slices rest in a nice puddle of sugar syrup. Remove from the oven and let the crostini cool on the pan.

While the crostini cools, spoon the fruit into bowls. Pour the cream into individual creamers or into one decanter, allowing about ¼ cup cream per serving. Fill a clear glass pitcher with the strawberry sauce.

Heap the crostini into a beautiful bowl. Let everyone choose their crostini and pour the cream or strawberry sauce onto the fruit as they wish.

White Chocolate–Lavender Panna Cotta with Madeira-Rhubarb Pappardelle

SERVES 4

A delicate, creamy panna cotta is always welcome at the end of a meal, and it's not hard to make. The key to this panna cotta is good white chocolate such as Valrhona or Callebaut. Don't skimp; buy the best chocolate you can, always. This pretty dessert is more than welcome on its own (and I encourage you to make just the panna cotta if you need a quick *dolci*), but at Bottega we finish with Madeira rhubarb pappardelle and rhubarb fritti. Once you've tried these crisp, flavor-intense little gems, you'll forget about cooking rhubarb into pies.

Find English lavender buds in specialty stores or baker's supply stores. It may seem as though this recipe calls for very little, but lavender buds add a good amount of flavor. Look for star anise and cardamom pods in high-end grocery stores. Keep the vanilla bean and cardamom pods whole until you're ready to cook with them to retain as much of their flavor and aroma as possible.

I prefer to use gelatin sheets rather than powdered gelatin because I like the softer, creamier texture they give desserts (see Resources for gelatin sheets, or substitute ¾ teaspoon powdered gelatin per sheet). You can make the panna cotta and the rhubarb pappardelle up to 3 days in advance as long as you keep the ramekins plastic-wrapped, the rhubarb covered in its poaching liquid and well sealed, and both refrigerated.

Wine Pairing: Late-harvest Muscat

PANNA COTTA
6 ounces premium white chocolate, chopped
½ cup milk
½ cup heavy cream
1 tablespoon granulated sugar
Pinch of kosher salt
½ teaspoon English lavender buds
2 silver gelatin sheets, or 1 gold gelatin sheet, or ¾ teaspoon powdered gelatin
Ice water
¼ teaspoon vanilla extract

MADEIRA-RHUBARB PAPPARDELLE
6 rhubarb stalks
1 cup Madeira wine
⅔ cup granulated sugar
⅔ cup water
1 cardamom pod
Two 3-inch strips lemon zest
Two 3-inch strips orange zest
2 tablespoons fresh orange juice
2 tablespoons fresh lemon juice
½ vanilla bean, split lengthwise
1 star anise pod
Small pinch of kosher salt
Grind of fresh black pepper

RHUBARB FRITTI
Peanut oil, corn oil, or canola oil for frying
¼ cup cornstarch
¾ cup all-purpose flour
Four 8-inch-long rhubarb stalks
¼ cup powdered sugar

FOR THE PANNA COTTA: Melt the chocolate in a double boiler over barely simmering water or in a microwave in short 10-second bursts. Remove from the heat and set aside. In a medium saucepan, combine the milk, cream, sugar, salt, and lavender buds. Simmer over medium-low heat until bubbles form around the edges of the pan. Remove from the heat and let steep for 10 minutes.

Meanwhile, place the gelatin sheets in a bowl and add ice water just to cover. Let the sheets sit in the water until they feel rubbery to the touch, about 5 minutes. Take out the sheets, squeeze out the excess water, and add them to the warm milk mixture, stirring until dissolved. (If using powdered gelatin, add it to the warm milk now, stirring until dissolved.) Combine the milk mixture with the melted white chocolate. Whisk and then strain through a fine-mesh sieve. Stir in the vanilla.

Spoon the mixture evenly into four 4-ounce ramekins. (You can also spoon it into one large mold or soufflé dish and just scoop out servings for each person.) If you have a torch, you can go over the top of each panna cotta, but it's not necessary. Cover each panna cotta with plastic wrap and refrigerate for at least 3 hours or up to 3 days.

FOR THE PAPPARDELLE: Preheat the oven to 350ºF. Using a mandoline, trim the stalk ends and then evenly slice the rhubarb into thin, horizontal strips about 10 inches long to resemble pappardelle pasta, about four strips per stalk.

Put all the rhubarb strips into a nonreactive 9-by-13-inch baking or roasting pan. Add the Madeira, granulated sugar, water, cardamom pod, zests, and juices. Scrape the seeds from the vanilla bean pod into the liquid. Add the star anise, salt, and pepper. Mix thoroughly. The rhubarb strips should be submerged in the liquid.

Cover the dish with aluminum foil and braise the rhubarb over medium heat just until tender, about 18 minutes. Don't overcook. Remove from the heat and let cool completely.

Store in the dish, covered. The fruit is easily broken, so treat it gently. Pour off 1½ cups of the braising liquid and reserve. Pour the remaining braising liquid over the rhubarb (the container should be small enough so that the rhubarb stays submerged in the liquid).

In a small saucepan, bring the reserved 1½ cups braising liquid to a simmer and cook to reduce to 1 cup, about 2 minutes. Remove from the heat, let cool, cover, and refrigerate for up to 3 days. If you're in a hurry, cool the liquid in an ice bath and then cover and refrigerate.

FOR THE RHUBARB FRITTI: In a deep fryer or a heavy, large pot, heat 3 to 4 inches of oil to 375ºF on a deep-fat thermometer. Reduce the heat to medium-high. Line a sheet pan with paper towels.

While the oil heats, combine the cornstarch and flour in a medium bowl and whisk to blend. Set aside. Using a mandoline or large, sharp knife, julienne each rhubarb stalk into matchsticks about ⅛ inch wide. Toss the matchsticks in the flour mixture to coat.

Shake off any excess flour and carefully add a small handful of the rhubarb to the oil and cook, using tongs to keep the pieces separated, until lightly golden, 2 to 3 minutes. Using a wire skimmer, transfer the rhubarb to the paper-lined sheet pan and dust with the powdered sugar. Repeat to cook the remaining rhubarb.

If you like, you can let the fritti cool and then, an hour before you're ready to serve the dessert, place them in a preheated 150ºF oven for 15 to 30 minutes so it's extra crisp.

Place each panna cotta on a dessert plate and serve with the rhubarb pappardelle and fritti alongside. Drizzle each plate with a little of the braising liquid.

Strawberry Tiramisù Semifreddo ("Half-Frozen")

SERVES 10 TO 12

Tiramisù may be the most common Italian dessert, on the menu in every sort of restaurant. At some point, you need a refresh. Applying strawberries to tiramisù is right up my alley—taking an old standard and giving it some fresh flavor. We sparked it up a little more with a very Italian pistachio genoise, and finally we made it *semifreddo*, "half-frozen." This beautiful dessert needs to freeze for at least 24 hours before serving, so plan accordingly. You can play with the fruit here. Try fresh raspberries, peaches, or any soft fruit. The espresso shot in the cake-soaking syrup is key to the whole "pick-me-up" concept behind tiramisù. If you don't have an espresso machine, you can use instant espresso. What I would do instead is go to my local coffeehouse, have them make three shots (enough for ⅓ cup), and bring it home.

If you'd like to make this dessert but are short on time, go to an Italian bakery and buy a plain sponge cake that measures 12 by 17 inches. This trick will slice a big chunk out of your cooking time. Take the mascarpone out of the fridge about 30 minutes before you start making the filling so it will be at room temperature.

Wine Pairing: Demi-sec Champagne

PISTACHIO GENOISE
½ cup pistachios, toasted
    (see Chef's Note, page 188)
6 eggs at room temperature
1 cup sugar
1⅓ cups cake flour
¼ teaspoon kosher salt
1 teaspoon vanilla extract
4 tablespoons unsalted butter, melted

STRAWBERRY SAUCE
4 cups fresh strawberries, quartered
½ cup corn syrup
½ cup sugar
Pinch of kosher salt
2 teaspoons fresh lemon juice
1 tablespoon Grand Marnier

RUM SABAYON
4 egg yolks
1 tablespoon fresh orange juice
1 tablespoon Kahlúa liqueur
2 tablespoons dark rum
Pinch of kosher salt
¼ cup sugar
1 pound mascarpone at room temperature

CHANTILLY CREAM
2 cups heavy cream
½ teaspoon vanilla extract
¼ cup sugar

CAKE-SOAKING SYRUP
¼ cup Kahlúa liqueur
¼ cup dark rum
⅓ cup brewed espresso (see headnote)
1½ cups Simple Syrup (page 217)

1 cup fresh strawberries, quartered
¼ cup chopped pistachios

In a stainless-steel bowl set over a pan with 2 inches of simmering water, whisk the eggs and sugar until the mixture begins to bubble and has no graininess when you rub a drop between your fingers (careful, it's hot). An instant-read thermometer inserted in the mixture will register 110°F. Remove the bowl from the pan and set aside to cool.

Scrape the sugar-egg mixture into the bowl of a stand mixer. Beat on medium speed until the mixture turns pale yellow and has tripled in volume, 4 to 5 minutes. You'll know it's ready when the mixture forms a slowly dissolving ribbon on the surface when the beaters are lifted.

Sift together the cake flour and salt. Sift about one-fifth of the dry ingredients over the surface of the batter and gently fold them in with a rubber spatula. Repeat, folding gently and carefully, until all the dry ingredients have been added and the mixture is smooth.

Stir the vanilla into the melted butter. In a spiral motion, gradually drizzle the butter into the batter and give it a few last gentle folds to blend.

Pour the batter over the pistachio dust on the prepared pan. Using an offset spatula and starting at one end, spread the batter in one direction so you don't pull any pistachio dust into the batter. Sprinkle the batter with the remaining pistachio dust.

Bake for 20 minutes, or until the cake has pulled away from sides of the pan and springs back when you touch it lightly in the center. Remove from the oven and let cool in the pan on a wire rack.

FOR THE STRAWBERRY SAUCE: In a large sauce pan, combine the berries, corn syrup, sugar, salt, lemon juice, and Grand Marnier. Cook over medium heat until the strawberries shrink and look wilted, about 7 minutes, depending on the berries' ripeness. Remove from the heat and set aside. Strain the berries, reserving the liquid for the sauce.

FOR THE SABAYON: In a stainless-steel bowl set over a saucepan with 2 inches of simmering water, whisk together the egg yolks, orange juice, Kahlúa, rum, salt, and sugar until a slowly dissolving ribbon is formed on the surface when the whisk is lifted, 7 to 10 minutes. Remove from the heat and continue whisking to cool, about 2 minutes.

In a large bowl, whisk the mascarpone just to fluff and lighten it, about 10 seconds. Add the sabayon to the mascarpone and whisk to incorporate, 10 to 20 seconds. Set aside.

FOR THE GENOISE: Preheat the oven to 350°F. Make pistachio "dust" by pulsing the toasted pistachios in a food processor until they're the texture of coarse bread crumbs. Be careful to stop when the nuts are still in chunks—you don't want to make pistachio butter. Using a spoon, put the nuts through a sieve to separate the dust from the chunks and transfer the chunks to a plate. Don't forget to save the pistachio dust inside the processor. You'll use about ¼ cup of pistachio dust for the pan.

Line a 12-by-17-inch sheet pan with parchment paper, give the paper a light coating of vegetable-oil spray, and then sprinkle half the nut dust (about ⅛ cup) onto the oiled paper. Set aside.

CONTINUED

FOR THE CHANTILLY CREAM: In a stand mixer, combine the cream, vanilla, and sugar and beat until soft peaks form. Whisk about one-third of the mixture into the sabayon mixture to lighten it. Fold in the remaining Chantilly cream.

Using a rubber spatula, gently fold the cooked strawberries into the sabayon.

FOR THE CAKE-SOAKING SYRUP: Whisk together the Kahlúa, rum, espresso, and simple syrup. You can put this in a squeeze bottle, if you have one, or a bowl. Set aside.

Using an 8-inch round cake pan as a template, cut a slightly smaller round of cake to fit inside the pan. Cut the round in half horizontally with a long serrated knife so you have two even, round layers of cake. Center a long sheet of plastic wrap inside the cake pan and smooth it along the bottom; it should be long enough to drape over the cake pan's sides and eventually fold over the cake, covering it. Place one of the cake rounds in the pan, cut-side up. Cut the cake that remains in the baking sheet into strips about 12 inches long and 2 ½ inches wide. Place three strips around the circumference of the pan. If you need to patch it so cake surrounds the entire edge of the pan, cut what you need from the cake still in the cake pan.

When the bottom and sides are lined with cake, heavily soak the cake with the cake-soaking syrup. Don't be fainthearted—give it a true soak, either using a squeeze bottle or just spooning on the liquid. Fill the center with the strawberry-mascarpone mixture. (If you have leftover filling, just cover, refrigerate, and serve it later, topped with fruit.) Add the remaining round of cake, cut-side down. Generously douse again with the remaining cake-soaking syrup. Pull up the sides of the plastic wrap to cover the cake. Freeze overnight, or for up to 1 week.

Toss the fresh berries in the strawberry sauce. Spoon the berries and some of the liquid on the cake and scatter the chopped pistachios on top. Have a bowl of hot water nearby for dipping your knife. Cut the cake into 10 or 12 wedges to serve.

CHEF'S NOTE: To toast pistachio nuts, spread the pistachios on a rimmed baking sheet and toast in a preheated 375°F oven for 7 or 8 minutes or until fragrant.

The Sweetest Thing:
A Hot Meal and a Friendly Face

My dearest mother, Antoinette, before she passed, asked me to continue her work for Meals on Wheels. It pained my mom to think of someone not having a warm meal at least a few times a week, and if you were lucky enough to have her deliver your food, then you got the benefit of some great conversation while you ate.

This is another thing that pastry chef Michael Glissman and I have in common. Michael's grandmother, Marion Redding, and his mom, Linda Schwanebeck, delivered hot meals from their diner to Meals on Wheels every single day. I love the idea of the women in Michael's family having the same strong feelings as my mom: the need to make sure that those who most needed a hot meal got one.

I don't deliver meals every single week to shut-ins the way my mom did, but I have kept my promise to her by doing at least two fund-raising events for Meals on Wheels every year, including their gala in San Francisco. The Meals on Wheels near you could always use a helping hand; the benefits of this worthy cause far outweigh the efforts, so please contact them if you have a little time to spare: www.mealsonwheels.org

Biscotti with Pistachios, Dark Chocolate, and Fennel Seeds

MAKES 2 DOZEN BISCOTTI

Biscotti literally means "twice-cooked." To me, biscotti means the perfect end to a lovely supper, whether they're dunked in wine or coffee. During December, we often have biscotti baking parties at our house. Packed in airtight containers, the cookies last through the holidays. When wrapped in colorful cellophane, they make perfect homemade gifts.

Dark chocolate makes these biscotti doubly delicious. Not only is the dark richness of bittersweet chocolate the perfect foil for the nuts and fennel seeds in this biscotti, it also holds up well during baking.

When chopping the pistachio nuts, aim for middle ground. You don't want pistachio dust, but neither do you want pistachios to be so big that they break the biscotti when you're slicing. I use a knife to chop the nuts for this recipe, because it's too easy to overgrind them in a food processor.

Wine Pairing: Vin Santo

2 ½ cups all-purpose flour
1 tablespoon baking powder
½ cup (1 stick) unsalted butter at room temperature
¾ cup sugar
¼ teaspoon kosher salt
2 eggs plus 1 yolk at room temperature
1 teaspoon vanilla extract
¾ teaspoon almond extract
6 ounces bittersweet chocolate
    (62 to 82 percent cacao), coarsely chopped
1 ⅔ cups (7 ounces) unsalted pistachios
    toasted (see Chef's Note, facing page)
¼ teaspoon fennel seeds, toasted and ground
    (see Chef's Note, at right)

Sift together the flour and baking powder and set aside.

In a stand mixer fitted with the paddle attachment, cream together the butter, sugar, and salt until light and fluffy. Beat in the eggs one at a time, then the yolk. Beat for 2 minutes after the yolk is added. Beat in the extracts, then stop to scrape down the sides of the bowl. Beat in the flour mixture just until combined. This is a sticky dough, so it won't pull away from the side of the bowl. Mix in the chocolate chunks, nuts, and fennel seeds just until evenly distributed. If you like you can refrigerate the dough at this point, but it isn't necessary.

Preheat the oven to 350°F. Coat a baking sheet with vegetable-oil spray, line it with parchment paper, and give it another light spritz.

Divide the dough in half. Dust your hands with flour so the dough won't stick to your fingers. Shape each piece of dough into a log about half the length of the baking sheet. Using your hands, lightly flatten the logs so they'll be less likely to break when you cut them.

Bake the logs until golden and puffed, 20 to 25 minutes. Remove from the oven but leave the oven on, reducing the temperature to 300°F. Let the logs cool on the parchment paper on the pan until slightly warm. Using a serrated knife, gently cut the logs on the bias into ½-inch-thick slices. Return the slices to the pan, laying them on their sides. Return the pan to the oven and bake for about 15 minutes, then turn them over and bake for another 5 to 10 minutes until crisp and crunchy. Remove from the oven and transfer the cookies to wire racks to cool. Store in an airtight container for up to 2 weeks.

CHEF'S NOTE: To toast and grind fennel seeds, stir the fennel seeds in a dry skillet over medium heat until fragrant, no more than 3 minutes. Don't let them brown. After toasting, let the fennel seeds cool, then grind them in a clean, dry spice grinder or a coffee grinder that's devoted to spices.

Restaurant Work and Charity

I feel blessed to work in an industry that lets
me lend a hand to those with few advantages.
On occasion, when I get kind of snarky about
how often people ask me to donate (someone
asks me to donate a table for six *every single
day* that I'm in the restaurant), I have my
old friend Sister Katie O'Shea to serve as my
reality check.

Sister Katie is the director of hospitality
for St. Vincent de Paul in San Francisco,
which means that every single day she feeds
the hungry. She used to live and work here
in the Napa Valley, and, like me, she has a
great fondness for causes involving the valley's
farmworkers. Every time I hear Sister Katie
on the other end of the phone saying,
"Michael, me good lad," I know that I will do
my best to get her what she needs, whether
it's warm coats or box lunches or signed
cookbooks. For her, I will drop what I'm
doing, because I know when she asks me that
the cause is urgent and I'm helping meet a
need. I also know that every time I help her,
I get a feeling of euphoria that lasts for the
rest of the day.

Semolina Almond Torte with Limoncello Figs

SERVES 10 TO 12

Cakes like this were classic desserts for Italian families like mine, and they still number among my very favorite *dolci*. This beautiful old-world cake can be adorned any way you like. Here, we poach Mission figs to serve alongside the cake with mascarpone crème and sugared almonds. The mascarpone crème has the flavor of cheesecake without the work. You could also serve this cake with fresh fruit, a spread of great preserves, or a simple dusting of powdered sugar.

This cake works best if you let all the ingredients come to room temperature before you make the batter. For an extra hit of almond, I like to make the batter with almond flour. If you can't locate almond flour, use standard all-purpose flour instead. By all means, purchase limoncello from your local liquor purveyor if you don't have the time to make your own.

Wine Pairing: Late-harvest Sauvignon Blanc or ice-cold limoncello

LIMONCELLO FIGS

18 to 24 Black Mission figs
1 cup Lavender Limoncello
    (page 217 or store-bought)
½ lemon, sliced
¼ cup fresh lemon juice (about 1 lemon)
Fresh ginger, peeled and sliced
    into 10 to 12 dime-size coins
1 empty vanilla bean pod
    (see Chef's Note, page 194)
½ cup filtered water
½ cup sugar
1 cinnamon stick
1 clove
4 juniper berries (optional)
Pinch of sea salt, preferably gray salt

SEMOLINA-ALMOND TORTE

1 ½ cups granulated sugar
8 ounces almond paste, broken into pieces
1 cup (2 sticks) plus 2 tablespoons
    unsalted butter at room temperature
1 teaspoon vanilla or almond extract
6 large eggs at room temperature
¼ cup fine-ground semolina
¼ cup almond flour
⅔ cup all-purpose flour
1 ½ teaspoons baking powder
¼ teaspoon kosher salt

MASCARPONE CRÈME

½ cup mascarpone
½ cup Crème Fraîche (page 35)
½ cup heavy cream
2 tablespoons sugar
1 teaspoon vanilla extract

FROSTED ALMONDS

½ cup sugar
⅓ cup water
1 ½ cups sliced almonds
Pinch of sea salt or kosher salt

FOR THE FIGS: Preheat the oven to 350ºF. Put the figs in a large ovenproof sauté pan or stock-pot. Add the limoncello, lemon slices, lemon juice, ginger, vanilla bean pod, water, sugar, cinnamon, clove, juniper berries (if using), and sea salt. Bring the mixture to a simmer over medium-high heat, then cover the pan with aluminum foil and transfer to the oven. Bake until the figs are tender but not too soft, about 30 minutes. Remove from the oven. Using a slotted spoon, transfer the figs to a bowl and set aside. Strain the liquid through a fine-mesh sieve and return to the pan. Bring to a simmer over medium-high heat and cook to reduce to about 1 cup, about 7 minutes.

FOR THE TORTE: Preheat the oven to 350ºF. Coat a 10-inch cake pan or a 9-by-5-inch loaf pan with vegetable-oil spray, then line with parchment paper. Coat the parchment paper with vegetable-oil spray. Pour ¼ cup of the sugar into the pan and tilt to coat the bottom and sides. Knock out the excess sugar.

In a stand mixer fitted with the paddle attach-ment, combine the almond paste and the remaining 1¼ cups sugar. Beat on medium-low speed until the paste is pulverized and completely mixed with the sugar, about 5 minutes. Don't shortchange this mixing time, or the almond paste will sink to the bottom of the cake during baking.

Add the butter and cream it and the paste mixture until light and fluffy, 2 to 3 minutes, stopping to scrape down the bowl once or twice. Reduce the mixer speed to low and add the vanilla. Add the eggs one at a time, stopping to scrape down the bowl after every addition. Beat for 2 minutes after the last egg has been added.

In a separate bowl, combine the semolina, almond flour, all-purpose flour, baking powder, and salt. Whisk to blend. With the mixer on low speed, add all the dry ingredients at once to the wet ingredients and beat until blended.

Remove the bowl from the stand mixer and with a spatula give it a few turns, scraping the bowl to make sure no dry ingredients are hiding at the bot-tom. Pour the batter into the prepared pan, scraping out the bowl. Spread the batter evenly in the pan and give the pan a light tap on the counter to coax any air bubbles from the batter.

CONTINUED

Bake for about 40 minutes (rotating the pan after 25 minutes), or until the cake is golden brown and has pulled slightly away from the sides of the pan. Remove from the oven and let cool on a wire rack for 1 hour.

FOR THE CRÈME: Because of the high fat content of the mascarpone, this whips up faster than whipped cream, so have the other ingredients measured and ready before you start. In the bowl of a stand mixer fitted with the paddle attachment, beat the mascarpone for 20 to 30 seconds. Remove the paddle, fit the mixer with the whisk attachment, and add the crème fraiche and heavy cream. Continue to whisk while gradually adding the sugar, and then the vanilla. Whisk until the mixture has the texture of whipped cream and soft peaks form. Set aside.

FOR THE ALMONDS: Preheat the oven to 325ºF. In a medium bowl, stir the sugar into the water. Toss the almonds in the sugar water and then spread them on a rimmed baking sheet lined with a silicone baking mat. (Don't use parchment paper, or the nuts will stick.) Bake, turning the nuts with a spatula every 5 to 7 minutes, until shiny with a light golden color, 15 to 20 minutes. Remove from the oven and let cool on the pan. Sprinkle with salt when they are still warm.

Center a slice of cake on each dessert plate. On one side, spoon 1 or 2 poached figs; on the other side dollop some mascarpone crème and top the crème with a sprinkling of frosted almonds. Drizzle the reduced poaching liquid over the figs.

CHEF'S NOTE: Whenever we scrape the seeds from a vanilla bean, we save the empty bean pod. Submerge the pods in your sugar bin to infuse your morning coffee with a hint of vanilla flavor. Then, when you need an empty pod for a recipe like this one, just pull it from the sugar.

Where's That Prize Money Going?

Competing on *Top Chef Masters* was a blast, but an even bigger pleasure is talking to Maria Criscione Stel, Clinic Ole's development director, about how the prize money helps the clinic.

"Because of the recent California budget cuts and the elimination of some health programs, the funds from donations such as your prize money let us continue operating even in this tough economy," Maria says. "Clinic Ole provided nearly 68,000 patient visits last year, and that number keeps growing."

More than 50 percent of the folks who come to Clinic Ole work in wineries, vineyards, and restaurant kitchens, but Maria has seen the demographics change as middle-class families have lost medical insurance coverage and have come to rely on health-care providers at Clinic Ole.

Maria says, "There were 4,100 jobs lost in Napa County last year, and only 100 of those were farming jobs. Because Clinic Ole doesn't turn people away when they have no insurance, we see more people coming to us for affordable health care. In the past six months alone, we've seen 2,500 new patients. Without funds like the *Top Chef* money, grants, and other donations," Maria says, "we'd be in big trouble." From immunizations to diabetes education, the clinic makes a big difference for people sometimes shut out of the traditional health-care system.

Pastry chef Michael Glissman—
a great laugh to go with his great talent

Molten Chocolate Cakes with Hazelnut Crème Anglaise

SERVES 8 TO 12

Just about every single restaurant in the United States had a molten chocolate cake on its dessert menu throughout the 1990s. The last thing I wanted at Bottega was another molten cake. But the first thing most customers want for dessert is warm chocolate, and who am I to say no? So we figured out how to add a little drama to this much-loved classic. We cook these in ring molds lined with parchment and remove the paper at the table. We pour on the anglaise so it looks like lava cascading down a volcano, and then we finish with chunks of hazelnut *croccante* around the plate. At home, you can bake the cakes in ring molds or ovenproof coffee cups. If you want a simpler option to the croccante, try toasting 4 tablespoons of cacao nibs in your oven for a few minutes and use those instead.

I like the double-nut flavor here: almond with the cake and hazelnut with the anglaise. You have two options for making the cake. The first is to use almond flour, which makes a smoother batter and finer cake. If you want to make this the old-school Italian way, in place of the almond flour, toast and grind your own almonds. Either way, this is a great chocolate cake.

The chocolate *tartufi* that are baked into the cake's center can be made ahead and kept frozen for up to 2 months, so molten cake is always just a few steps away. This nut anglaise method works with any nut, so you can infuse the cream with the flavors you like.

Wine Pairing: Marsala

HAZELNUT CRÈME ANGLAISE

1 ½ cups (6 ounces) hazelnuts, toasted, skinned,
   and chopped (see Chef's Note, page 198)
1 ½ cups heavy cream
1 ½ cups whole milk
⅓ cup sugar
6 egg yolks
Pinch of kosher salt

CHOCOLATE TARTUFI

1 ¼ cups heavy cream
7 ounces bittersweet chocolate
   (58 to 66 percent cacao), chopped
Pinch of sea salt or kosher salt
½ teaspoon Frangelico liqueur (optional)

HAZELNUT CROCCANTE

1 cup plus 3 tablespoons water
1 ½ cups sugar
2 ½ cups (10 ounces) hazelnuts, toasted and
   skinned (see Chef's Note, page 198)
2 pinches of sea salt, preferably gray salt

CAKE

12 ounces bittersweet chocolate
   (58 to 66 percent cacao), chopped
⅔ cup (1 ⅓ sticks) unsalted butter
6 large eggs at room temperature, separated
1 teaspoon vanilla extract
¾ cup all-purpose flour, sifted
1 cup plus 2 tablespoons almond flour,
   or 5 ounces sliced almonds, toasted in a
   dry pan over medium heat until fragrant,
   then finely ground with the flour
¼ teaspoon kosher salt
⅔ cup sugar

FOR THE ANGLAISE: Prepare an ice bath. In a
medium saucepan, combine the nuts, cream, and
milk and heat over medium-low heat until bubbles
form around the edges of the pan, about 5 minutes.
Remove from the heat, set in the ice bath, and let
cool. Cover and refrigerate for at least 12 hours
or up to 24 hours to let the nuts infuse the cream
with their flavor.

CONTINUED

Prepare a second ice bath. Remove the infused cream from the refrigerator; strain and discard the nuts. Heat the infused cream over medium-low heat until it scalds and small bubbles show around the edge of the pan, 2 to 3 minutes. In a mixing bowl, whisk the sugar and egg yolks until the mixture forms a ribbon that lasts for 3 seconds on the surface before dissolving when the whisk is lifted. Add the salt. Whisk a few spoonfuls of the hot infused cream into the egg yolks to temper them. Add the yolks to the pan and simmer over medium-low heat, stirring constantly, until the mixture coats the spoon. Strain through a fine-mesh sieve and set the bowl in the ice bath to cool.

FOR THE TARTUFI: In a small saucepan, heat the cream over medium-low heat until bubbles form around the edges of the pan. Pour the hot cream over the chopped chocolate and stir until smooth. Add the salt and the Frangelico (if using) and stir until blended. Pour into a small dish and let cool until set, then refrigerate until firm.

Using a ¾- to 1-ounce ice-cream scoop, teaspoon, or melon baller, scoop up small balls of the chocolate mixture. Set aside. (This makes more than you need, but you can freeze any leftover for the next molten cake or shape into truffles and eat them.)

FOR THE CROCCANTE: Line a baking sheet with a silicone baking mat. Coat the mat with vegetable-oil spray.

In a medium, heavy pot, combine the water and sugar. Bring to a boil over high heat without stirring and cook for 7 to 10 minutes, or until the large bubbles on the surface have given way to small bubbles and a tinge of caramel color forms around the edge of the pan. Stir in the hazelnuts and a pinch of salt and continue stirring constantly while the syrup seizes around the nuts, forming a white coating, then turns liquid again and forms a deep-amber caramel.

Pour the nuts onto the prepared sheet, spread into a single layer with the back of an oiled large spoon, and sprinkle another pinch of salt over the top. Let cool completely. Break into chunks, using a mallet if needed.

FOR THE CAKE: Preheat the oven to 375°F. Place eight to twelve 3-inch ring molds on a baking sheet lined with parchment paper, or use eight to twelve ovenproof coffee cups (not mugs) or custard cups.

Set the ring molds on top of the parchment and make a parchment collar for each mold: Cut a strip of parchment 5 to 6 inches wide and about 14 inches long and stand it up inside each ring mold. When you pour in the cake batter it will hold the collar in place. If baking in coffee or custard cups, you don't need the parchment paper.

In a double boiler over simmering water, melt the chocolate and the butter together. Remove from the heat and set aside to cool for about 20 minutes, or until just warm.

In a mixing bowl, whisk the egg yolks to blend. Whisk in a few spoonfuls of the warm chocolate mixture to temper the eggs. Gradually whisk in the remaining chocolate mixture. Add the vanilla and stir until smooth.

In a medium bowl, combine the flours (or the ground almonds with flour) and salt. Stir with a whisk to blend. Stir the dry ingredients into the chocolate mixture. Set aside.

In a large bowl, beat the egg whites until frothy and then gradually beat in the sugar until soft peaks form. Using a rubber spatula, gently fold one-third of the beaten whites at a time into the chocolate mixture.

Fill the prepared ring molds, coffee cups, or custard cups one-third full with batter. Place a chocolate tartufi into each mold or cup and spoon the remaining batter to fill the container two-thirds full. (Bake now, or refrigerate for up to 3 days.)

Bake for 13 to 15 minutes (18 to 28 minutes if the batter was refrigerated), or until the center of the cake is puffed and risen but not completely set. These are meant to be slightly soft and molten, so don't overcook.

Pour the anglaise into a pitcher and set it on the table. If the cakes are in ring molds, remove the metal ring, serve each one with the paper collar still in place, and then "unveil" them at the table, removing the paper and pouring on the anglaise. If baked in coffee cups or custard cups, just pour on the anglaise. Add a few chunks of the croccante to serve.

CHEF'S NOTE: To toast and skin hazelnuts, spread the nuts on a rimmed baking sheet and toast in a preheated 375°F oven until lightly browned and fragrant, 10 to 12 minutes. Remove from the oven and bundle in a clean dish towel, rubbing the nuts together to remove the skins. Discard the skins.

Three Tartufi (Chocolate Truffles)

I want the last bite that a guest has before leaving Bottega to be sensual and unusual, and these truffles are both. I generally steer away from odd flavor combinations, but while in Parma visiting a cheese producer, I first tasted dark chocolate with Parmesan. They brought out trays holding truffles like these, and I was stunned by how much I liked the two flavors together.

I worked with Bottega's pastry chef, Michael Glissman, to come up with two other truffles that worked well with the first as a trio. This is a small but intense finale, served on antique bone china.

Wine Pairing: A Napa Valley Cabernet Sauvignon or whatever red wine you had with your meal

Balsamico Tartufi (Basil Truffles)

MAKES 2 DOZEN 1½-INCH TRUFFLES

1 cup heavy cream
1 cup loosely packed fresh basil leaves, chopped
8 ounces bittersweet chocolate, coarsely chopped
6 tablespoons unsalted butter
Pinch of kosher salt
⅓ cup granulated sugar
1½ tablespoons balsamic vinegar
Grind of black pepper
3 egg yolks
¼ cup sifted powdered sugar for coating
¾ cup unsweetened cocoa powder for coating

In a medium saucepan, combine the cream and chopped basil. Simmer over medium-low heat for 5 to 7 minutes to reduce the cream while infusing it with basil flavor. (The reduction should measure 5 to 6 ounces when it's finished.) Remove from the heat, cover, and let stand for at least 1 hour. Strain the cream through a fine-mesh sieve and set aside. Discard the basil.

In a double boiler over barely simmering water, melt the chocolate and butter. Immediately add the salt and granulated sugar. Whisk the reduced infused cream into the chocolate, then whisk in the balsamic vinegar and pepper.

In a medium bowl, whisk the egg yolks until blended. Gradually whisk in just a few spoonfuls of the warm chocolate mixture. Gradually whisk in the remaining chocolate mixture until smooth. Cover and refrigerate for at least 3 hours or overnight.

Using a ¾- to 1-ounce ice-cream scoop, a melon baller, or a teaspoon, scoop out the chocolate mixture and roll between your palms into balls about 1½ inches in diameter. Place on a rimmed baking sheet and refrigerate again for 1 to 2 hours, until set and no longer tacky. Combine the powdered sugar and cocoa in a small bowl and stir with a whisk to blend. Line a baking sheet with parchment paper. Roll each truffle in the powdered sugar mixture so it's thoroughly coated and then set it on the prepared pan. Slide the pan into the fridge and chill for at least 1 hour. Remove from the refrigerator at least 30 minutes before serving.

Parmesan Tartufi (Parmesan Truffles)

MAKES 2 DOZEN 1½-INCH TRUFFLES

1 cup heavy cream
6 ounces Parmesan rinds, plus ¾ cup
　freshly grated Parmesan cheese
8 ounces bittersweet chocolate, coarsely chopped
6 tablespoons unsalted butter
Pinch of kosher salt
⅓ cup granulated sugar
1 teaspoon Frangelico liqueur
3 egg yolks
¾ cup unsweetened cocoa powder for coating
¼ cup sifted powdered sugar for coating

In a medium saucepan, combine the cream and Parmesan rinds. Simmer over medium-low heat for 5 to 7 minutes to reduce the cream while infusing it with Parmesan flavor. (The reduction should measure 5 to 6 ounces when it's finished.) Remove from the heat, cover, and let stand for at least 1 hour. Strain the cream through a fine-mesh sieve and set aside. Discard the rinds.

In a double boiler over barely simmering water, melt the chocolate and butter. Immediately add the salt and granulated sugar. Whisk the reduced infused cream into the chocolate, then whisk in the Frangelico.

In a medium bowl, whisk the egg yolks until blended. Gradually whisk in just a few spoonfuls of the warm chocolate mixture. Gradually whisk in the remaining chocolate mixture until smooth. Stir in the grated Parmesan until blended. Cover and refrigerate for at least 3 hours or overnight.

Using a ¾- to 1-ounce ice-cream scoop, a melon baller, or a teaspoon, scoop out the chocolate mixture and roll between your palms into balls about 1½ inches in diameter. Place on a rimmed baking sheet and refrigerate again for 1 to 2 hours, until set and no longer tacky. Combine the powdered sugar and cocoa in a small bowl and stir with a whisk to blend. Line a baking sheet with parchment paper. Roll each truffle in the powdered sugar mixture so it's thoroughly coated and then set it on the prepared pan. Slide the pan into the fridge and chill for at least 1 hour. Remove from the refrigerator at least 30 minutes before serving.

Sage-Pancetta-Brandy Tartufi

MAKES 2 DOZEN 1½-INCH TRUFFLES

1 cup heavy cream
½ cup loosely packed fresh sage leaves, chopped
2 ounces pancetta, finely chopped
8 ounces bittersweet chocolate, coarsely chopped
6 tablespoons unsalted butter
Pinch of kosher salt
⅓ cup granulated sugar
1 teaspoon brandy
3 egg yolks
¾ cup unsweetened cocoa powder for coating
¼ cup sifted powdered sugar for coating

In a medium saucepan, combine the cream and sage. Simmer over medium-low heat for 5 to 7 minutes to reduce the cream while infusing it with sage flavor. (The reduction should measure 5 to 6 ounces.) Remove from the heat, cover, and let stand for at least 1 hour. Strain the cream through a fine-mesh sieve and set aside. Discard the sage.

Heat a small sauté pan over medium heat and sauté the pancetta until it renders its fat. Set aside and let cool.

In a double boiler over barely simmering water, melt the chocolate and butter. Immediately add the salt and granulated sugar. Whisk the reduced infused cream into the chocolate, then whisk in the brandy.

In a medium bowl, whisk the egg yolks until blended. Gradually whisk in just a few spoonfuls of the warm chocolate mixture. Gradually whisk in the remaining chocolate mixture until smooth. Stir in the pancetta. Cover and refrigerate for at least 3 hours or overnight.

Using a ¾- to 1-ounce ice-cream scoop, a melon baller, or a teaspoon, scoop out the chocolate mixture and roll between your palms into balls about 1½ inches in diameter. Place on a rimmed baking sheet and refrigerate again for 1 to 2 hours, until set and no longer tacky. Combine the powdered sugar and cocoa in a small bowl and stir with a whisk to blend. Line a baking sheet with parchment paper. Roll each truffle in the powdered sugar mixture so it's thoroughly coated and then set it on the prepared pan. Slide the pan into the fridge and chill for at least 1 hour. Remove from the refrigerator at least 30 minutes before serving.

Truffle hunting (indoors)

The ABC's of Truffle Making

Making chocolate truffles is much easier than you'd expect. It's all a matter of buying great chocolate and then infusing cream with the flavors you want. Here are some thoughts to speed along your truffle making.

You could use the microwave to melt chocolate, but in these cases the double-boiler method gives a slightly smoother consistency to the finished truffles.

At the restaurant, we use ¾- to 1-ounce ice-cream scoops to shape the truffles. You can also use a melon baller or shape the balls with your hands. If you find the chocolate sticks to your palms, try dipping your hands in ice water, drying them well, and then rolling the truffles. You can use food-grade gloves, too, if you like.

Use great ingredients—fine fresh herbs, the best Parmesan you can find, great cocoa powder. There aren't many ingredients in these truffles, so each one counts.

CHAPTER 10

Libations

LIBAGIONI

The cocktails you serve should be a sensation. Forget about having an open bar—you'll spend half your paycheck stocking it and the whole evening bartending. At home, I serve just one well-considered cocktail and have ready two wines (one red, one white) and two beers (one pilsner, one ale). And don't be afraid to allow your guests to supply some of these. If a friend calls to say, "What can I bring?" they're asking because they don't want to arrive at the party empty-handed. My response falls along the lines of "Thanks, a Pinot Noir from the Sonoma Coast would be fantastic," or "A twelve-pack of ale would be great."

The cocktail should begin to tell the story of your meal. A thoughtful, well-made cocktail offers you an opportunity to enhance a gathering. At Bottega, the same words that describe our food—seasonal, creative, classically inspired—apply to our drinks as well. The libations in this chapter aren't about just starting with fresh ingredients, but how the flavors complement or anticipate the flavors of your meal. Drinks should show the same layering of flavors that happens in the kitchen. While a rim is a chance to add something to the drink, the garnish should be integral to the cocktail's flavors and not an afterthought.

We've written each recipe in this chapter to make one cocktail (except for the limoncello and the limoncello spritzers). If you're making these drinks for a party, multiply the recipe ingredients by the number of guests expected and then double that—making two cocktails for each guest is a good rule of thumb. If I'm expecting more than six people, I like to have the drinks made and waiting in pitchers in the refrigerator so that I can begin pouring as soon as guests arrive.

Libagioni

Tips from the Bottega Bar

When I'm putting together a restaurant staff, the two hardest roles to fill are the sommelier/bar chef and the pastry chef, because I look for talented people who see their work as complementing my work. I always feel a disconnect when a bartender is out there mixing up drinks that have nothing to do with the food I'm serving.

I was lucky to find wine director Michael Iglesias. Because he is aware of what our diners are eating, his seasonal drinks and wine choices reflect and complement the flavors on Bottega's plates.

Michael has his bar staff pay close attention to *mise en place*. Just as with cooking, having a few tools and house-made bar ingredients at hand makes your bartending faster, smoother, and more competent.

Bar Tools

Fine-mesh cocktail strainer or sieve

One-ounce and half-ounce measures

Cocktail shaker, preferably stainless steel

Long-handled spoon

Demitasse spoon for measuring (or ½ teaspoon)

Wooden muddler

Zest knife, preferably with a wooden handle

Chilling the Barware

I'm strict about plate temperature. This is a small thing that makes a big impact—serving hot foods on warmed plates, and cold foods on chilled plates. This holds even more true for cocktails. A drink tastes better from an icy-cold glass, end of story. Don't forget to chill the glasses when making cocktails at home.

Spanking the Basil

After you've poured the cocktail into a chilled glass, spank the basil by laying one leaf on your palm and slapping it hard with your other hand. The goal isn't to bruise the leaf but rather to bring up all the oils. (Be careful not to put too much hip into it, or you'll have a palm full of pesto.) When spanked and then floated in the drink, the leaf gives you a hit of basil aroma when you lift the glass to your face and adds a little basil oil for extra flavor.

Garnishes

When I sit at the bar, the garnishes have to look fresh and interesting, and I also want them to reflect the seasons. At Bottega, you'll see earthenware bowls full of clean, bright basil leaves sitting on the bar, ready to be spanked. You'll see slices of blood orange when it's in season, house-cured olives in the autumn for our martinis, and, in summer, lavender that Michael Iglesias brings from his garden. To me, this inspires confidence in a bar chef, and it's something to consider when setting up cocktail garnishes at home. When the ingredients for the bar are fresh, beautiful, and homegrown, you know the drinks will exceed your expectations.

Floated, Not Hung

We like to float a garnish in the drink or—in the case of the amarena cherry in our Manhattan—let it sink to the bottom. When citrus fruit is hung from the glass rim, most folks can't resist giving it a squeeze before dropping it into the cocktail. A good cocktail is already well balanced and doesn't benefit from that extra citrus.

Stir It, Don't Shake It

Here's the deal with shaken versus stirred: When you shake a liquor, especially gin, you will cloud the liquid. If you stir it instead, after you strain the drink it's still crystal clear. Some people believe that only shaking can make a cocktail ultra-cold, but stirring vigorously with an up-and-down motion—until the outside of the glass feels ice-cold to your fingers—is how it's done at Bottega.

Negroni

MAKES 1 COCKTAIL

If I were James Bond (an Italian Bond, of course), a Negroni would be my drink. It's a masculine drink, not sweet but with huge flavors. It commands the question, "What's that *you're* drinking?" One reason I love this drink so much is that the bitter tinge gets your palate ready for a meal.

We have to admit a small bias for 209 gin, because Distillery No. 209 began here in St. Helena. (Why should *local* be reserved for vegetables?) Leslie Rudd, owner of Distillery No. 209, makes an artisan gin that is crisp with bright notes of citrus and spice. Punt e Mes adds floral botanical notes to the drink. This Negroni is simple, classic—perfect.

1 ounce dry gin, preferably No. 209
1 ounce sweet vermouth, preferably Punt e Mes
1 ounce Campari
Ice cubes
1 orange slice for garnish
  (blood orange, when in season)

Pour the gin, vermouth, and Campari into a heavy tumbler half-filled with ice. Stir vigorously until the outside of the glass feels ice-cold to the touch. Strain into a martini glass, and gently drop the orange slice into the drink.

St. Helena Dirty Martini

MAKES 1 COCKTAIL

Any drink worth having is worth having dirty. If it's not a veteran chef's proverb, it should be. If I'm at a cocktail party, and there's no dinner planned for afterward, this is my drink of choice (even if it's tough to get a crispy olive at other folks' bars). Marko Karakasevic and his father, Miles, make exquisite vodkas right here in the Napa Valley. Marko is one of the local artisans who makes me happy to call St. Helena home. He is the thirteenth-generation spirits-maker in his family, and the vodkas, tequilas, and wines made by Charbay Distillery all find their way to Bottega.

When my wife and I married, Marko made the drinks for our wedding. He came with big plastic containers filled with drinks that were ready to be poured into pitchers. It was an eye-opener for me that drinks made ahead of time could taste so perfect. (Yes, the fact that it was our wedding made everything taste better, but I've had his drinks since, and they still rank high in my esteem.) The moral of the story: Don't be afraid to make your drinks before the party begins.

2 ounces vodka, preferably
    St. Helena Domaine Charbay
Ice cubes
½ to 1 ounce olive brine
2 crispy blue cheese–stuffed olives (facing page)

Pour the vodka into a heavy tumbler half-filled with ice. Stir vigorously with an up-and-down motion until the outside of the glass feels ice-cold to the touch. Add the brine and stir. Strain into a martini glass.

Serve with the olives skewered while still warm from the pan or placed beside the drink in a small ramekin—don't drop the crispy olive into the martini.

Crispy Blue Cheese–Stuffed Olives

MAKES 12 OLIVES

Slightly crispy outside, rich and savory inside, these blue cheese–stuffed bites are the ideal accompaniment to an ice-cold martini. At Bottega, we deep fry these olives in peanut oil, but at home I generally sauté them in olive oil. If you don't have time to fry the olives, then just serve regular green Sicilian olives into which you've piped some good blue cheese. Let them firm up in the fridge for 30 minutes before serving.

Don't drop these olives into the cocktail; either skewer and place them across the glass or serve on a small warmed plate or ramekin next to the glass.

12 Sicilian pitted green olives,
    preferably unstuffed, or any large,
    perfect martini olive
½ cup (5 ounces) blue cheese, preferably
    Point Reyes Original Blue
½ cup all-purpose flour
½ cup buttermilk
½ cup Fritti Flour (page 71)
Peanut oil (for deep fryer) or
    olive oil (for sauté pan)

Unstuffed giant bar olives are best, but if all you find is stuffed olives, use a cocktail fork or kitchen tweezers to pull out the pimiento. Break up the blue cheese and spoon it into a pastry bag or a squeeze bottle. Rest the bottle (but not the bag) for 1 to 2 minutes in a bowl filled with hot water to warm the cheese slightly. We keep the pastry bag near the stove to warm but don't put it against direct heat. Pipe the softened cheese into each olive and refrigerate for 30 minutes to let the cheese firm up.

While the olives chill, set up a dredging station with flour in one shallow bowl, buttermilk in another, and the fritti flour in a third.

Dip a cold olive into the flour, rolling to coat; dip it in the buttermilk, and then the fritti flour. Repeat with the remaining olives.

If deep-frying, in a Dutch oven or heavy pot, heat 2 inches of peanut oil to 375ºF on a deep-fat thermometer. Cook 6 olives at a time just until golden brown and crisp, 30 seconds. If using a sauté pan, heat 2 tablespoons of olive oil over medium heat, add all the olives, and stir them gently until browned, about 1 to 2 minutes.

Using a slotted spoon, transfer the olives to paper towels to drain. Serve warm, alongside drinks.

The Iglesias School of Muddling

Knowing how to muddle leaves of mint or basil means your drinks taste better. Iglesias does it perfectly. He treats the herbs with care, not crushing or bruising the leaves but instead coaxing out the oil for maximum flavor.

He starts with his trusted muddler, which shows the signs of years of cocktail making. He strips the leaves of any stems, tosses the leaves into a heavy glass tumbler, and pours on the citrus juice and the simple syrup. Then he rubs the muddle against the sides of the glass, circling while massaging the leaves around and around until the smell of mint or basil rises up to his nose. He doesn't slam the muddler into the bottom of the glass as if he's churning butter. (In fact, I've seen Michael cringe when he's caught sight of other bartenders crunching the leaves this way.) Arm yourself with the knowledge of how to bring each ingredient to its peak and your cocktails will inspire and delight.

Spanked-Basil Gimlet

MAKES 1 COCKTAIL

This drink is refined, clean, and elegant. The blend of flavors is finely tuned: you begin with the eye-opening aroma of basil, shift to the freshest-tasting wave of viognier-based vodka, and end on a soft note with the taste of elderflower. I like to strain out the basil leaves and serve a clean, clear cocktail in a martini glass. Michael Iglesias sometimes leaves in the muddled basil and pours the drink into a tumbler for a Gimlet Rustico. Either way, be sure your glass is icy cold before you pour this.

12 big fresh basil leaves, plus 1 extra leaf
    for spanking (see page 205)
1 ounce fresh lime juice
½ ounce Simple Syrup (page 217)
1½ ounces House-Infused Cucumber Vodka
    (at right) or Hangar One vodka
½ ounce St.-Germain elderflower liqueur

In a cocktail shaker or a sturdy bar glass, muddle the 12 basil leaves with the lime juice and the simple syrup (see muddling tips, page 210). When the basil's aroma becomes more pronounced, pour in the vodka and the liqueur. Strain and pour into a chilled martini glass, or pour the drink, leaves and all, into a chilled tumbler. Top with a fresh-spanked basil leaf.

House-Infused Cucumber Vodka

MAKES ABOUT 10 CUPS,
ENOUGH FOR 4 DOZEN COCKTAILS

Infusing vodka with fresh cucumbers creates a cocktail ingredient that is so vibrant and refreshing, you'll turn to it often for summer-time drinks. Michael Iglesias makes our house-infused vodka and keeps it in a large container in our walk-in refrigerator. Whenever he takes down the container to fill the bar bottles, people drift over and get close so they can get a good sniff. The smell is so enticing, it's like aromatherapy—you almost want to put your face in it.

Infuse vodka in any large nonreactive container such as a gallon-size clean glass jar with a tight lid. Make sure the container you choose fits in your refrigerator.

8 cups vodka (two and a half 750-ml bottles)
1½ cups gin (half a 750-ml bottle)
Long strips of zest from ½ lemon, ½ lime,
    and ½ orange
2½ cucumbers, peeled, seeded,
    and chopped into 1-inch chunks

Combine all the ingredients in the desired container. Seal tightly and refrigerate for at least 2 days or up to 3 days. (After 3 days, the cucumber slices can turn slightly bitter.) Strain and discard the cucumber and zests. This blend will keep its garden-fresh flavor for up to 2 weeks in the fridge.

BARTENDER'S NOTE: The great thing about this house-made vodka is you can refresh its flavor. Just peel, seed, and slice another 2 cucumbers and add them to the vodka. Let them infuse the vodka for 24 to 48 hours. Remove and discard the cucumbers. You'll find your vodka has a fresh cucumber flavor once again.

Heirloom-Tomato Bloody Maria

MAKES 1 COCKTAIL

Yes, you can use canned tomato juice with this recipe in the winter, but I firmly believe in savoring Bloody Marys only when summer-kissed tomatoes are available. When the weather turns chilly, I shift to a Manhattan or a Negroni and enjoy summer drinks all the more when they're in season. For those people who must have their Bloody Marys in midwinter, we buy an Italian passata that is as close as you can come to juicing fresh tomatoes. You can make your own fennel spice blend or buy it. (See Resources for the Calabrian chile paste, imported passata, and the spice blend.)

Ice cubes

1 ½ ounces House-Infused Cucumber Vodka
(page 213)

5 ounces heirloom tomato purée or Tomato Passata
(see Note, at right, or store-bought), chilled

1 demitasse spoon Calabrian chile paste or a few
drops of Tabasco or your favorite hot sauce

1 demitasse spoon sea salt, preferably gray salt

Lime wedge and Fennel Spice Blend
(at right) for the glass rim

1 cucumber slice for garnish

1 fennel frond for garnish

In a heavy tumbler filled with ice, mix the cucumber vodka, tomato purée, chile paste, and salt; stir vigorously. Moisten the rim of a chilled glass with the lime wedge and dip in it in a saucer of the spice blend. Carefully add fresh ice to the rimmed glass and then strain the drink into it. (This makes the drink colder without diluting it.) Float the cucumber slice and the fennel frond on top of the drink.

Fennel Spice Blend

MAKES ABOUT 1 ½ CUPS

1 cup fennel seeds

2 tablespoons coriander seeds

2 tablespoons white peppercorns

3 tablespoons kosher salt

In a small skillet, toast the fennel seeds, coriander seeds, and peppercorns over medium heat, stirring constantly, just until light brown and fragrant, 1 to 2 minutes. Don't let it get too brown. Remove from the heat and pour onto a plate to cool completely.

In a blender, combine the seed mixture and salt. (Don't try to grind before they're cool or the spices will gum up your blender's blades.) Whir until the mixture is a powder, lifting the blender and shaking to redistribute the spices. Stored in an airtight container in a cool, dark place, this blend will stay lively for up to 4 months or in the freezer for 1 year.

Note: Tomato Passata

Passata means "to pass" in Italian—in this case to pass tomatoes through a sieve or a press. At Bottega, we use an imported tomato passata (see Resources) because the taste and texture is consistent, season after season. You can also make your own passata by puréeing one 28-ounce can of whole organic peeled tomatoes with their juice in a blender or a food processor. Measure just what you need for this recipe and refrigerate the rest.

Manhattan

MAKES 1 COCKTAIL

It's a blustery day in NYC. There's a gal on your arm walking way too many blocks. Not a cab in sight. You burst through the doors of an Upper East Side bar, pour yourselves into a couple of cush chairs, and beckon for two Manhattans. This is a classic cocktail that I love to sip and savor.

Though the Manhattan was originally made with rye, sweet vermouth, and bitters, my favorite version these days is made using a wheated Kentucky bourbon such as Buffalo Trace or Maker's Mark. I like a very botanical vermouth, such as Antica Formula or Punt e Mes. You don't want to add tired bitters to exceptional liquors. Michael Iglesias found an amazing organic bitters blend at a farmers' market in Vermont. Called Urban Moonshine, it's the freshest-tasting bitters we've tried (see Resources). If you can't get your hands on some, Frei Brothers or Reagan's Bitters are reliably good.

2 ounces wheated bourbon
    such as Buffalo Trace
1 ounce sweet vermouth
    such as Antica Formula
2 dashes orange bitters
Ice cubes
1 amarena cherry (see Resources)
    or orange slice for garnish

Pour the bourbon, vermouth, and bitters into a heavy tumbler half-filled with ice. Stir vigorously with an up-and-down motion until the outside of the glass feels ice-cold to the touch. Strain into a martini glass. Drop in the cherry or an orange slice.

Cory—bar chef extraordinaire

Strawberry Pazzo

Our wine director, Michael Iglesias, created this drink after trying my Strawberries Pazzo and Torte Sabiosa. (Since I first tasted the combination of strawberries and black pepper with Lorenza De'Medici decades ago, this flavor combo has been a part of my cooking repertoire, so I like seeing it represented in a cocktail.) Iglesias created the pepper-infused gin so the flavors would be distinct. First you taste the sweet strawberries and then you get a sophisticated, peppery gin finish.

Don't pass over this recipe just because we ask you to infuse gin with peppercorns. This infusion only takes 24 hours, and it's as easy as pouring peppercorns and liquid into a bottle.

1½ ounces black pepper-infused gin
  (at right)
¾ ounce fresh lime juice, chilled
3 ounces strawberry purée, chilled
½ ounce Simple Syrup (facing page),
  plus more to taste
Ice cubes
1 large, perfect fresh basil leaf for spanking
  (see page 205)

Mix the pepper gin, lime juice, strawberry purée, and simple syrup in a cocktail shaker with ice and strain through a fine-mesh sieve. Taste and add more simple syrup if you like a sweeter drink. The character of strawberries changes from month to month, so add more syrup or lime to adjust the flavor. Spank the basil leaf and float it on the drink.

Black Pepper-Infused Gin
MAKES 2 CUPS

Michael Iglesias recycles spirit bottles explicitly for infusing spirits with spices and herbs, so a clean, empty wine or vodka bottle is ideal here, or use any clean glass container. Michael doesn't measure his black peppercorns; he just pours them into a standard-size wine bottle until the peppercorns are about 1 inch deep.

After 24 hours, the pepper gin should be the color of good old Scotch. If you let it sit longer than 24 hours it will become much darker, and the pepper flavor will be overwhelming. Don't toss it if it's gotten too dark; just add more gin to temper the spiciness.

2 cups gin, preferably Tanqueray 10
½ cup (4 ounces) black peppercorns

Pour the gin over the peppercorns in a clean glass container. Store in a cool, dark place for 24 hours. Strain, and put the peppercorns aside for another use. Cover the container and refrigerate for up to 2 weeks.

CHEF'S NOTE: You bet you can reuse those peppercorns. Spread them on a few layers of paper towels to dry. When completely dry you can crush them and press them into steaks or venison.

Lavender Limoncello

MAKES ABOUT 9 CUPS

Once you blend it, this liqueur has to sit for
4 weeks, but it's worth the wait.

1 dozen Meyer lemons, or a mix of lemons and limes
3 fresh lavender sprigs
2 liters vodka or white rum
6 cups sugar
1 cup water

Using a bar zester or a vegetable peeler, cut the zest
from the lemons, making sure you don't get any of
the white pith. In a large, clean glass container with
a tight-fitting lid, combine the citrus zest, lavender
sprigs, and vodka. Let stand undisturbed in a cool,
dark place for 4 weeks, then strain.

In a large saucepan, combine the sugar and water.
Bring to a boil, then reduce the heat and simmer,
stirring occasionally, until the sugar is completely
dissolved. Remove from the heat and let cool completely. Stir the sugar mixture into the lemon mixture.

Store in an airtight container in the refrigerator
for up to 6 months or in the freezer for up to 1 year.
(Although Iglesias says this keeps "forever," make
a new batch every year when your lemons are
fantastic.)

Serve in small aperitif glasses or make a spritzer
(recipe follows).

Spritzer Variation

MAKES 8 DRINKS

Make a pitcher's worth of spritzers for a light,
summery way to enjoy your limoncello.

30 ice cubes
6 cups seltzer water
6 cups limoncello
1 sliced lemon, preferably Meyer

Add the ice to a large pitcher or drink dispenser.
Pour in the seltzer and limoncello and stir. Pour
into chilled tall glasses and float a lemon slice in
each glass.

Simple Syrup

MAKES 1⅓ CUPS

This is a bar basic that you can keep at the
ready in your refrigerator for up to 6 months.

1 cup sugar
1 cup water

In a small saucepan, bring the sugar and water
to a boil over medium heat. Simmer until the
sugar is completely dissolved, about 3 minutes.
Remove from the heat and let cool completely.
For bartending purposes, we store this in squeeze
bottles kept in the bar fridge. Or, refrigerate in a
covered container.

Resources

A.G. Ferrari Foods
www.agferrari.com
Amarena cherries, pasta flour.

Anson Mills
www.ansonmills.com
Fine-ground polenta.

Bruno's Marketplace
www.brunosmarketplace.com
Wax peppers.

Catalina Offshore Products
www.catalinaop.com
Live sea urchins.

Chef Rubber
www.shopchefrubber.com
Gelatin sheets (gelatin leaves),
caviar-making trays.

Chefs' Warehouse
www.chefswarehouse.com
Spices.

Chiarello Family Vineyards
www.chiarellovineyards.com
707-256-0750
The 95-year-old vines around my
home are sustainably farmed;
making these wines has been the
most satisfying of all my personal
endeavors. Cabernet, Old Vine
Zinfandel, Old Vine Petite Syrah.

D'Artagnan
www.dartagnan.com
800-327-8246
Duck, rabbit, foie gras.

Giusto's Vita-Grain
www.giustos.com
650-873-6566, or
866-972-6879
Organic flour and fine-ground
polenta.

Heritage Foods
www.heritagefoodsusa.com
718-389-0985
Heritage Foods was started in
2001 to save a turkey. The
Bourbon Red was listed as "rare"
until Heritage helped connect
home cooks with the farmers
trying to keep this breed in
existence. These days, Heritage
offers you links to small-scale
farmers and ranchers with every
kind of livestock, from Duroc
pork to young chickens and Dark
Cornish chicken. Heritage offers
a way to support farmers outside
of the mega-industrial meat
complex, but it's not just about
conservation; anything you order
from Heritage will have flavors
that you won't find in your local
supermarket's meat and poultry.
Chicken, lamb, pork, tuna, turkey.

Katz & Company
www.katzandco.com
Artisan oils, vinegars, and honey.

Krieger Limited
Florence, Italy
fax: 390550935520
Pink chickpeas.

La Caja China
www.lacajachina.com
Oversized outdoor roasting box.

La Tourangelle
www.latourangelle.com
Pistachio oil, truffle oil.

NapaStyle
www.napastyle.com
866-776-1600
I founded NapaStyle in 1999 to
offer home cooks the ingredients
and equipment that I use in my
kitchens. Butcher's salt (fleur de
sel and Provençal herbs), ceramic
salt grinder, Calabrian chile paste
(also called Silafunghi hot chili
sauce), fennel spice blend, salt
slab, tomato passata.

Navarro Wine Grape Juices
www.navarrowine.com
Pinot Noir grape juice and other
unfermented wine grape juices.

Rancho Gordo
www.ranchogordo.com
Heirloom beans (varieties vary
by season), Toscanelli beans.

Sausalito Springs Watercress
www.sausalitosprings.com
Watercress.

The Spanish Table
www.spanishtable.com
206-682-2827
Pimentón de la Vera (smoked
Spanish paprika).

Sur La Table
www.surlatable.com
Bar tools.

Urban Moonshine
www.urbanmoonshine.com
Organic orange bitters.

Whole Foods Markets
www.wholefoodsmarket.com
Ascorbic acid (also called
vitamin C powder), squid ink
or cuttlefish ink.

Index

Table of Equivalents

The exact equivalents in the following tables have been rounded for convenience.

Liquid/Dry Measurements

U.S.		METRIC	
¼	teaspoon	1.25	milliliters
½	teaspoon	2.5	milliliters
1	teaspoon	5	milliliters
1	tablespoon (3 teaspoons)	15	milliliters
1	fluid ounce (2 tablespoons)	30	milliliters
¼	cup	60	milliliters
⅓	cup	80	milliliters
½	cup	120	milliliters
1	cup	240	milliliters
1	pint (2 cups)	480	milliliters
1	quart (4 cups, 32 ounces)	960	milliliters
1	gallon (4 quarts)	3.84	liters
1	ounce (by weight)	28	grams
1	pound	448	grams
2.2	pounds	1	kilogram

Lengths

U.S.		METRIC	
⅛	inch	3	millimeters
¼	inch	6	millimeters
½	inch	12	millimeters
1	inch	2.5	centimeters

Oven Temperature

FAHRENHEIT	CELSIUS	GAS
250	120	½
275	140	1
300	150	2
325	160	3
350	180	4
375	190	5
400	200	6
425	220	7
450	230	8
475	240	9
500	260	10